THE LEADERSHIP GENIUS OF ELON MUSK

THE LEADERSHIP GENIUS OF
ELON MUSK

DENNIS KNEALE

BROADSIDE BOOKS

HarperCollins books may be purchased for educational, business, or sales promotional use. For information, please email the Special Markets Department at SPsales@ harpercollins.com.

Broadside Books™ and the Broadside logo are trademarks of HarperCollins Publishers.

FIRST EDITION

Library of Congress Cataloging-in-Publication Data

Names: Kneale, Dennis, author.
Title: The leadership genius of Elon Musk / Dennis Kneale.
Description: First edition. | New York, NY: Broadside, [2025] | Identifiers: LCCN 2024042580 (print) | LCCN 2024042581 (ebook) | ISBN 9780063381261 (hardcover) | ISBN 9780063381278 (ebook)
Subjects: LCSH: Musk, Elon. | Businesspeople—United States—Biography. | Businessmen—United States—Biography. | Leadership.
Classification: LCC HC102.5.M88 K54 2025 (print) | LCC HC102.5.M88 (ebook) | DDC 658.4/092—dc23/eng/20241118
LC record available at https://lccn.loc.gov/2024042580
LC ebook record available at https://lccn.loc.gov/2024042581

---

24 25 26 27 28 LBC 5 4 3 2 1

For Doreen, Sophia, and my daughter,
Jing Jing, most of all

I'd rather be optimistic and wrong than pessimistic and right.

—*Elon Musk on* The Joe Rogan Experience, *September 7, 2018*

CONTENTS

INTRODUCTION

As an anchor at CNBC, I once interviewed Silicon Valley veteran Carol Bartz, who had been the CEO of Yahoo for fourteen months at the time. Yahoo still was the number one website in the world, but it was losing business to Google and Facebook, and she had been brought in to fix it.

Bartz had the hallmarks of a successful CEO: strong leadership skills, decisiveness, strategic insight, deep experience, a certain boldness. She had spent fourteen years running the graphics-software firm Autodesk, building annual sales fivefold to $1.5 billion. Upon arrival at Yahoo, she wiped out management layers, killed dormant services, and axed 5 percent of the staff.

Our interview ended without incident, which is what you want if you are the CEO of a public company. Yet Carol Bartz seemed less than urgent in her comments. Maybe she wasn't scared enough. She had earned almost $50 million in salary, bonus, and stock options for her first year, 2009, even as Yahoo's annual sales had fallen 10 percent from the year before. She had exercised options on $2 million in stock after just nine months at Yahoo, an impolite move: Why cash in so soon if you are there to make the stock double or triple in price?

Two months after our chat on CNBC, Bartz, in May 2010, got tagged as the most overpaid CEO in the S&P 500. In September 2011, the Yahoo board of directors fired her in a phone call. "They fucked me over," she told a *Fortune* reporter at the time.

By year-end, Yahoo's annual revenues had fallen below $5 billion, down 30 percent from when Bartz joined. The stock had barely budged, while the S&P 500 was up 45 percent in the same period.

Yahoo ultimately disappeared into Verizon, which merged it with another has-been brand, AOL, and later gave up on the business and sold it to a private equity firm, taking a $4.6 billion loss. How could such a high-flying company fall so far, so fast, in spite of the best efforts of a world-class chief executive?

You can make all the right moves, follow all the right rules, say all the right things, and still flop. Yet Elon Musk, one of the world's richest men, makes a lot of wrong moves. He breaks a lot of rules and he says a lot of "wrong" things that spark controversy around the world. In November 2023, one year after buying the Twitter platform, Musk took the stage at a *New York Times* DealBook conference and said of advertisers that want censorship, "Go. Fuck. Yourself." He said it twice. CNBC and the rest of the media covered it like a scandal. How dare he!

Somehow, despite breaking every rule for what a CEO should be, he is one of the best CEOs in the history of business. The main pursuit of this book is to explore how he does it, and why it works, and why one of the most important, enormously successful innovators and business creators in American history also is one of the most controversial and criticized figures of our time. Hounded by the government, attacked by politicians, derided by short sellers, and denounced by the media.

This is an odd combination: to be so accomplished yet reviled by so many political leaders, media figures, regulators, activists, and Big Tech rivals. This is in part due to Musk's $44 billion purchase of Twitter. This allowed Musk to expose the Twitter Files scandal, which revealed the most massive, widespread government violation of our First Amendment rights in U.S. history. Most of the silenced voices were those of conservatives.

The antipathy toward Elon Musk also owes to his own sizable ego and his continual willingness to take on critics and provoke and antagonize his enemies. What other CEO of a publicly held company has ever challenged a rival CEO to a cage fight? Elon has done this to Meta chief Mark Zuckerberg. This raises a two-part question: Does greatness require being a world-class asshole, and if not, does it end up producing one?

Musk's bluntness and his irrepressible style have won him a following of 195 million accounts on Twitter, now known as X, including millions of admirers and legions of detractors. People search his name on Google more than ten million times every month, more than for any other CEO in the world.

His continual stream-of-consciousness posts draw hundreds of headlines and stir debate among millions of fans who wish they had even half this man's gumption and gall, whether he discusses politics and media or business, astrophysics, and the latest new feature on X.

Elon Musk has dreamed the impossible, defied the odds, and bet it all so many times that this has morphed into his modus operandi. He thrives on turmoil and turns crisis into opportunity, diving in where most other leaders, executives, and thinkers fear to tread. To do this, he relies on a magical alchemy that combines Einstein's otherworldly intellect, the innate and intuitive vision of Steve Jobs, and P. T. Barnum's shameless promotional swagger.

Every entrepreneur recommends you take risks and go where others won't, but Musk seeks out goals that almost all other experts think are undoable, implausible, and impossibly futuristic. Perhaps he does this *because* everyone else feels this way.

Electric cars that are better than gas-powered vehicles? We thought it would never happen. Likewise, the doubters said that only NASA and the governments of China and Russia could pursue the notion of space travel. And internet coverage across the backwaters of the poorest nations: thirty years after the advent of the World Wide Web, only Musk's Starlink network has made advances on this front.

In addition to chasing impossible dreams, he ignores what is in vogue. Government entities, including NASA and the military, and corporate behemoths such as Boeing, focus fiendishly on following fads and extolling DEI—diversity, equity, and inclusion—policies that can often lead to less diversity, less fairness, and the exclusion of white people. Meanwhile, Elon skips this as off-point, freeing himself to pursue the important stuff.

Along the road less traveled, Musk has created some of the most important companies of the twenty-first-century economy: Tesla, with a world-beating 60 percent share of the market for electric cars; SpaceX, for private satellite launches; the Starlink satellite constellation; as well as cutting-edge companies Neuralink (which develops microchip-in-brain technology), the Boring Company (which builds subterranean high-speed traffic tunnels), and, most recently, xAI, which aims to provide a safer counterbalance to the two dominant players in artificial intelligence, Microsoft and Google.

Now Elon Musk is the star of two bestselling nonfiction books: *Elon Musk* by Walter Isaacson, the former *Time* magazine editor and the biographer, fittingly, of Einstein and Steve Jobs; and *Breaking Twitter*, by Ben Mezrich, the author of *The Accidental Billionaires*, the story of Mark Zuckerberg and Facebook.

Isaacson's tome offers 688 pages of meticulously reported details on Musk's origins in Pretoria, South Africa, and how his wayward and difficult father motivated young Elon and his many business triumphs and travails. At times, it borders on hagiography, holding up Elon Musk as almost superhuman, a superhero. And rightly so, speaking frankly.

In a darker light, Mezrich's 336-page *Breaking Twitter* accuses Elon Musk of myriad misdeeds. He fired most of the staff at Twitter and let banned conservative accounts back on the platform. Horrors. Two reporters for the *New York Times*, Kate Conger and Ryan Mac, take an even harsher view of Musk in their book published in September 2024, *Character Limit: How Elon Musk Destroyed Twitter*. Destroyed?

None of these books, however, offers readers insights from his many melodramas and come-from-behind victories, lessons that might help the rest of us—in business, and in life and how to live it. Perhaps without intending to do so, Musk has built an Ethos of Elon that imbues everything he believes, says, and does. We can benefit from it.

Until Elon Musk writes a book of his own, we must divine the lessons ourselves. This is why I have written *The Leadership Genius of Elon Musk*. Alternate title, with apologies to *This Is Spinal Tap*: *This One Goes to Eleven: The Eleven Lessons of Elon*. One per chapter.

In pursuing this book, I took a deep dive into Elon's history, examining and curating thousands of his posts and public comments. In divining the lessons lurking in Elon's thinking, business strategies, and tactics, I also rely on my thirty-plus years as a business journalist. Previously, I was a senior editor at the *Wall Street Journal* in New York, then the managing editor of *Forbes*, and then an anchor at CNBC and Fox Business Network. Now I am a media strategist, writer, contributor to Newsmax TV, and host of the podcast *What's Bugging Me* on Ricochet.

In my career, I have covered and interviewed hundreds of high-performing CEOs and entrepreneurs, including some of the best-known billionaires in the world. Name-drop alert: Jeff Bezos of Amazon once crashed a dinner party I hosted. I once had dinner-for-four with Bill Gates at the old Windows on the World atop the World Trade Center. I chatted with Facebook founder Mark Zuckerberg at the World Economic Forum in Davos, Switzerland, two years in a row. Mark Cuban joined me on-air for half an hour and still returns my emails.

I have had private lunches with Rupert Murdoch, Barry Diller, Larry Ellison, and Sir Martin Sorrell, and dinner with Donald Trump. And I have danced with the then wife of Google founder Sergey Brin. Even in this pantheon, Elon Musk stands out for his intellect, inspiration, and creativity—and for his brazen, balls-out approach to life and business. No other modern-day entrepreneur comes close to the flurry of innovation and disruption he has thrust upon the world.

His mere espousal of a bold idea is enough to inspire hundreds of millions of dollars in investment. In 2013, he published a white paper describing plans for a newfangled "hyperloop" that would let people and packages travel inside a miles-long underground vacuum tube at speeds of a few hundred miles per hour.

This led an associate to form Hyperloop One, which went on to raise half a billion dollars in venture funding in the next five years or so; a second company, Hyperloop Transportation Technologies, recently landed an $875 million contract with the French government.

Success builds on itself and feeds the confidence to keep reaching for greater things. Elon's extraordinary run began more than twenty-five years ago with Zip2, a city-mapping guide for newspapers. He bet his life's savings—all of $28,000—on Zip2. This was in 1995, with his brother, Kimbal, and in 1999, near the high point of the internet bubble, Compaq bought Zip2 for $305 million, netting Musk $22 million.

Months later, Musk formed X.com, pursuing the "everything app" and funding it with almost half of his Zip2 windfall. This turned logic on its head in Silicon Valley. Usually, a startup runner provides the sweat equity, and venture capital firms provide the funding.

X.com merged into another shop to form PayPal, but Musk soon bailed in a conflict over direction, and Peter Thiel later took over as CEO. Thiel and the board wanted to focus solely on PayPal as an online payment infrastructure, while Musk wanted to build an app that offered all manner of services—not just online payments but also banking, investing in stocks and bonds, collecting receivables, and other elements of an "everything app."

In February 2002, PayPal went public on the stock market, and the value of Musk's 11 percent stake doubled to $60 million on the first day. A month later, he founded SpaceX and started pouring his own money into it.

When PayPal was acquired by eBay in October 2002, Musk's $60 million stake suddenly soared to $175 million, up almost threefold in just eight months. Rather than sit on his winnings, and never have to work another day of his life, Elon doubled down again: he pumped $100 million, half his total net worth, into SpaceX in the next few years. His 45.2 percent stake in the rocket launcher is now worth $95 billion.

In early 2004, Musk put $6.5 million into a struggling startup called Tesla, becoming its chairman. In the next four years, he would put up a total of $70 million in personal funds and take control of Tesla to save it, again making an unlikely and bold bet. On himself. When Tesla stock is at $180 a share, his 13 percent stake is worth upwards of $75 billion.

Musk's acquisition of Twitter in October 2022, for $44 billion, exposed him to a new and higher level of fame—and infamy. The mainstream media said Musk would destroy the platform, but rather than breaking Twitter, Musk is transforming X into the premiere media platform of our age. It is incredibly robust and powerful, continually adaptive, and far more influential and far freer than the *New York Times*, or CNN, or Fox News, or any of the other media platforms that rely on it.

At the same time, Musk is building X into something much bigger than just a media platform. He wants it to be the central touchstone for hundreds of millions of people, where everything begins and where a lot of their lives will be spent planning, arranging, acquiring, and doing. A kind of metaverse without virtual reality goggles.

He signaled this on July 23, 2023, when he dropped the Twitter brand—arguably one of the more recognizable brands in the world—in favor of X, the brand name he has dreamed of building for more than twenty years. X will be a massive marketplace for instantaneous, information-based commerce, from banking and bill paying to stock investing and online shopping, dating, video calls, entertainment, podcasts, TV shows, and much, much more.

Here we get to another lesson that will come up again and again in this book. Musk rarely compromises on his values, his methods, or his vision. He is capable of changing his mind, but he rarely changes what he thinks matters the most.

Thus, we see Elon Musk and his lessons at work writ large as he develops X and once again imagines a future most other people—especially his critics in Washington and in the media—fail to see. Even among hypercritical competitors in Silicon Valley, a growing respect and awe are emerging for the what and the how of all the things that Elon is doing at X. How he could cut 80 percent of staff at Old Twitter—yet, just weeks later, host 147 billion impressions in the men's World Cup. And grow the user base up past half a billion people worldwide. How X iterates furiously and continuously, spinning out dozens of features every week to test them in a food-fight strategy to see what sticks, and fixing it on the fly when something fails.

Media companies rely on X to vastly expand their reach. It is how the *New York Times* can get seen by thousands of media outlets and millions of readers in an instant, even though its weekday print circulation is down to just three hundred thousand. This is one reason why the media commonly trash Elon Musk: How dare he acquire their private playground, where conservative voices were censored and the media were happy to let it happen, uncontested?

This offers another Elon lesson—let free speech reign and ring out, the consequences be damned. It is regrettable that a South African–born, naturalized U.S. citizen and innovator has to school reporters in how to protect and advocate for the First Amendment protection of unfettered free speech—even hate speech.

All of this innovation, adaptation, and attitude from Elon Musk can hold lessons for the rest of us, which you will find in this book. Please read it and reap, and enjoy the hell out of it. Regardless of whether you like him, this man is so much fun to watch.

THE LEADERSHIP GENIUS OF ELON MUSK

THIS ALL MAY BE FAKE, SO JUST GO FOR IT.

Elon's belief in the matrix enables and empowers all else that follows.

A sizable portion of the large brain and expansive mind of Elon Musk truly believes we are living inside a superreal virtual simulation, mere characters in someone else's videogame. In fact, he says the chances are billions to one *against* the case that we are living in "base reality."

Most of us in this world are entirely sure we live in base reality. This is because, um, we are *here* and *alive*, and we have loved ones and pets, and we drive cars and go to jobs, and raise children and have personal triumphs and traumas. We feel pleasure, and we bleed and feel pain. Pain, in fact, may be the realest reality of all: almost impossible to escape.

How can all of this be a game? This is us; this is life. This *is* reality.

Wrong, and Elon Musk will be delighted to show you why. For a decade or more, he has pondered the argument that all of this is a simulation. It may have started as an intellectual exercise, a thought experiment, yet this has taken hold in him, and it now is his heartfelt belief, one that may guide everything he does. It also may be the core secret to his success, and one that you can incorporate without having to believe it literally.

This incredibly realistic virtual-reality game might be run by some unseen, unknown being in another solar system, galaxy, or universe. Or in some other hidden dimension. Perhaps this game is controlled by one user—or, more likely in Elon's vision, there may be millions or even billions of users, playing their own game about their own lives, each person controlling their own program in a far-off future right here on Earth.

We just don't know it because we live inside our games (or inside someone else's). The technology is so advanced, the images and feelings are so real, that the game is utterly indistinguishable from reality.

How could this possibly be true—and how can Musk, one of the most brilliant innovators we have ever seen, begin to believe it? Especially when he works so hard on tackling some of the most daunting problems on Earth: the climate change "crisis" we have heard about for forty or fifty years, the grave threat to free speech, the very real risk that AI will run out of control and menace mankind.

If everything is an illusion, why bother?

We will let Elon Musk present his argument in a moment, but first, let's ponder the possibilities if he were right, and how this might free you. Free you to live your life in a fuller, bigger, and richer way, more emphatically and dramatically. To dare to be great and just go for it. Because what is the worst that could happen? This is all just one big simulation, anyway.

On the inside of our own simulation, we are unable to suddenly jump from the rooftop of one skyscraper to another, because the laws of physics and gravity inside this bubble are every bit as reigning and irrefutable as in base reality. Any attempt at skyscraper-jumping will end the simulated life of your character.

But once we are aware that we might be living like Jim Carrey in *The Truman Show* (1998), we can make other changes in attitude. We can savor life and enjoy it more, take more risks and make more leaps. We can open our hearts more to tell people how much we love them, and summon more courage to speak out against a wrong, and open our minds more to listen to dissenting views—because this is all fantasy and entertainment; all of this is unreal.

Similarly, maybe we could get less upset about so many things that upset so many of us so terribly these days, because . . . they aren't really *real*.

President Trump and MAGA extremists, or President Biden and corruption allegations; radical Democrats and the border crisis, antifa rioters, and Black Lives Matter protesters; political scandals, political prisoners, and questioned elections; urban crime, chronic homelessness, the fentanyl death epidemic, and the Covid crisis.

If we came to believe this is all one big game, even wrenching personal matters—from arguments with our romantic partners and workmates to divorce and loss and life-and-death health crises—might be more manageable, viewed in a more detached and insulated way.

In fact, you could make these changes in your life just by *believing* in the simulation—even if it turns out our base reality lies here, and there is nothing else. Placebo effect.

Keeping Musk's belief in the simulation theory in mind could give us a way of dissociating ourselves from all the Sturm und Drang, a way to step outside the picture and look at it in a new and brighter way. A more positive and playful way, because what the fuck—this is just pretend. And if it were true that our "reality" is a simulated one that is entertaining someone else, somewhere else, then couldn't we jack up the love, pleasure, joy, kindness, generosity, tolerance, and openness toward our fellow performers?

As long as this is entertainment, we should have as much fun as possible.

This certainly is what Elon Musk appears to be doing, every day of his life. The man has a zest and zeal for living that go far beyond what is normal for most of us. His appetite for action and impact is prodigious.

Elon plies an uninhibited lust for life with unending gusto. This guy runs multiple companies at once and creates new ones. He takes risk after unlikely risk, building wealth and betting large portions of it on his next idea. He gives the middle finger to government bullies and grandstanding politicians, and he trolls the rich and famous on X.

Musk is a paragon of what fainthearted liberals call "toxic masculinity." And proudly so: he shoots from the hip and wears his testosterone like a bulletproof vest. He has fathered twelve children with three different women.

His simulation infatuation frees him to think up impossible ideas and create companies to pursue them. It unshackles him to live as freely and uninhibitedly as possible, and this is where the rest of us can learn a lesson. It all might be a game, so just go for it.

This also may help him ease the way by hewing to the very real possibility that all of his hardships and triumphs, and his loves and losses, are storylines. Plots in an optical and sensual illusion that surrounds him. Maybe we have more control over this all-enveloping videogame than we realize, as Neo (Keanu Reeves) learns at the end of the first of the four films in the Matrix series. By the second film, Neo knows how to fly. So does Elon Musk.

On various public occasions, Musk, who turned fifty-three years old on June 28, 2024, has discussed his simulation inclination earnestly and in detail. He has talked about this topic hundreds of times in private conversations with his friends and his year-younger brother, Kimbal. So much so that the two of them made a pact to put aside the topic of virtual simulation whenever they were in a hot tub.

Musk's belief in the simulation may be reinforced by his admitted use of ketamine to fight off bouts of depression. The drug can have trippy, psychedelic effects. In high enough doses, it can have a dissociative visual impact that makes everything look like props on a movie set. Fans say the chemical can create a sharp,

Potemkin-village-style visage and spark the feeling that everything may be an illusion.

When Elon talks about reality and the chances of an all-immersive, virtual simulation, here is the weirdest thing about it all: the more you listen to it, the more convincing he is. One of the earliest entries in Musk's simulation explanation came in October 2014 at a *Vanity Fair* gig called the New Establishment Summit. Musk was onstage with Walter Isaacson, who would circle around years later to become Elon's authorized biographer.

They were at the Yerba Buena Center for the Arts in San Francisco. In the Q and A at the end, Elon started talking about the simulation theory, and this opened up an outpouring of futuristic observations that would presage new businesses in the next few years: Musk's Boring Company for the creation of underground high-speed traffic tunnels; the development of a hyperloop vacuum tube for high-speed travel (with other investors adopting Musk's concept); and X née Twitter, reviving Musk's broken dream of the X everything app.

It is as if his simulation soliloquy opened the pathways in Musk's brain to contemplate the impossible as achievable. In reading the transcript of Elon's session with Isaacson, you can almost see the mind of Elon Musk in action, jumping from one thought to the next, which leads to the next, like falling dominoes.

In the Q and A, a young Indian male student cheekily asks Musk why, if virtual reality will be every bit as good as being there, Elon focuses on making electric cars and rockets for transportation. Elon fires right back: "Well, maybe we're in a simulation right now. Yeah. Seriously, sometimes it feels like that."

He then lays out a very logical case: given technology today, "if you extrapolate into the future," videogames a hundred years or two hundred years from now will be "indistinguishable from reality." And there may be "millions, maybe billions of such simulations.

So, then, what are the odds that we're actually in base reality? Isn't it one in billions?"

"Obviously, this feels real," Elon adds. "But it, I mean, it seems unlikely to be real." His audience titters nervously, wondering, is this man serious? He is.

In 2016, Musk again addressed the verisimilitude of simulation, this time at the Code Conference in Rancho Palos Verdes at the posh Terranea Resort on the lush California coastline. In the Q and A, a black-clad, goateed techie named Josh asks Musk about the simulation theory, and Elon responds: "I've had so many simulation discussions it's crazy. In fact, it got to the point where basically every conversation" was about this topic.

Think of the first commercially successful videogame fifty years ago: Pong, "like, two rectangles and a dot. That was what games were," Musk says. Now we have 3D reality in games, and "given that we're on clearly a trajectory to have games that are indistinguishable from reality," and that billions of people will be playing these futuristic games, "it would seem to follow that the odds that we're in base reality are one in billions. So, tell me what's wrong with that argument."

"I believe we should hope that that's true," Musk tells his questioner. "Because, otherwise, if civilization stops advancing, then that may be due to some calamitous event that erases civilization. So, maybe, we should be hopeful that this is a simulation because otherwise, either we're going to create simulations that are indistinguishable from reality, or civilization will cease to exist. Those are the two options." A rather stark binary choice.

Elon touched on this theme again in February 2018 in an on-stage interview with Mohammad Al Gergawi, a UAE cabinet minister, at the World Government Summit in Dubai. The opening question was a softball: "So, what is life for you? Is it a dream? Is it real?"

Musk: "As I get older, I find that question to be more and more confusing or troubling or uncertain. Particularly when you see the advancement of something like videogames." He runs through a similar explanation on this, and concludes: "And then it seems like, well, how do we know that that didn't happen in the past, and that we're not in one of those games ourselves?"

Al Gergawi, not getting it, responds: "Interesting, interesting."

By September 2018, Musk was ready to bring his simulation beliefs to a much larger audience. He appeared on episode number 1169 of the *Joe Rogan Experience* podcast on September 7, a meandering, two-and-a-half-hour conversation that remains the most downloaded Rogan podcast ever: sixty-nine million downloads by summer 2024.

It almost broke the brain of Joe Rogan, who usually keeps up with his guests at their pace. In schooling Rogan, Elon added the simple math of passage of time. Let us say you find it ridiculous and impossible that the tech of today could create a simulation so real you are unaware that this is fake. Would you believe this is possible, say, ten thousand years from now? Of course. Now consider the next thought in Elon's process:

The universe is 13.8 billion years old. Earth is 4.54 billion years old, and civilization on Earth—at least, the latest one—is perhaps 7,000 years old, less than an eyeblink in time. If you believe undetectable simulation is doable in 10,000 years, you have 1.38 million possible time spans in which this technology could have advanced this far, somewhere in the universe.

So, the chances we now live in base reality become one in 1.38 million, by this ten-thousand-year measure. Think of how arrogant is the idea that we live in the one true reality: that in almost fourteen billion years, we humans here on Earth are the only inhabitants capable of creating this "simulaverse"—and only thousands of years from now.

And then, given the extremely likely odds that, yes, this super-reality envelops us now, *even as you read these words*, certainly billions of people (or beings) could be playing their own separate games, and we get back up to a one-in-billions chance that this life we live is the real one. Rogan and Musk's conversation, lubricated by whiskey and other libations, is fascinating. And philosophical.

At one point, Elon explains, "I always felt like things are too dark, because I think that you kind of have to be optimistic about the future. There's no point in being pessimistic. Society turned negative." He adds: "I'd rather be optimistic and wrong than pessimistic and right."

Then Elon talks about the end of the world. "It's just a question of when, right? So, it really is all about the journey." Because "the universe as we know it will dissipate into a fine mist of cold nothingness eventually." This will take a "very long time. I think it's really just about how can we make it last longer?"

This, in essence, may be Elon Musk's raison d'être.

At one point he asks Joe Rogan, "Why do you think you're where you are right now? You might not be," and Joe responds: "I'm gonna spark up a joint if you're gonna keep talking, the manager's gonna come in here. I'm gonna have to lock the door." Elon cracks up.

Later, Musk declares: "Love is the answer." This back-and-forth took up ten minutes just before the first-hour mark of their interview, and an hour and ten minutes later, Joe Rogan does indeed "spark up a joint." The two men have been drinking whiskey throughout their chat, and now Rogan takes out a blunt—a stubby cigar with part of its tobacco dug out and replaced with pot—and lights it up.

"So, is that a joint or is that a cigar?" Elon asks.

"No, it's marijuana inside tobacco," Rogan answers. "You probably can't [smoke] because of shareholders, right?"

Elon: "It's legal, right?" Yes, so Rogan hands him the spliff, and Elon takes one puff and hands it back.

Minutes later, Rogan tells Elon, "You essentially have a gift, right? . . . There's not a million Elon Musks, there's one, mother-fucker! Do you think about that when you strike out?"

Elon muses for a few seconds and says: "I don't think, I don't think you'd necessarily want to be me. I don't think people would like it very much. It's very hard to turn it off." The continuous stream of ideas and questions and visions and ambitions, he means. Moments later, Musk's phone pings with new messages.

"Gettin' texts from chicks?" Rogan asks him.

"No," Elon answers. "I'm getting texts from friends saying what the hell are you doing smoking weed." Then he tells Joe Rogan, "I am not a regular smoker of weed . . . almost never." And then: "Yeah. I don't actually notice any effect." So, maybe it was the whiskey.

This was during the day on a Friday, and the one-toke-over-the-line mushroomed into a multibillion-dollar doobie. Musk's single puff was enough to rattle Tesla fans (or short sellers betting against the stock). Shares of TSLA fell as much as 11.4 percent in a day, a $5.7 billion decline on hemp headlines. They soon recovered and grew twentyfold in the next three years.

...

The notion that all of life is an illusion goes back thousands of years. One of the earliest references dates to 1500 BC and the concept of *Maya*, a Sanskrit word for "illusion" (or "delusion," as it happens), found in Buddhism and Hinduism. The word appears in the Rig Veda, a sacred text in Hinduism that dwells on the nature of reality and the origins of the universe.

In the late twentieth century, one early advocate of this-all-must-be-a-dream was an Austrian computer scientist named Hans Moravec, who is a robotics professor at Carnegie Mellon to this day. In his 1988 book *Mind Children: The Future of Robot and Human Intelligence*, he predicted that computer intelligence would outpace that of humans in forty years (2028: a bit early). He posited that simulation and replication will become so powerful and immersive that we will be unable to separate the fake from the real—and, who knows? Maybe we are already there.

The simulation idea went wide with the 1999 premiere of the hit sci-fi film *The Matrix*. Keanu Reeves plays a mild-mannered office worker in the future who begins to suspect that all he sees is unreal. He wakes up to realize he was right: he has been living inside a simulation wasteland, while his physical form lies dormant inside a pod in linked-up suspended animation, used as one of millions of human batteries to power the robots that are in control.

When *The Matrix* came out, I was awestruck by the special effects and the simulation theory's possibilities. The film went on to gross almost half a billion dollars on a $63 million production budget, and the four-film franchise hauled in almost $1.8 billion.

The simulation theory drew new scientific heft from a seminal paper published in *Philosophical Quarterly* by an Oxford University philosophy professor in 2003. Nick Bostrom's article, packed with algebraic equations that look like hieroglyphics, would inspire a passel of papers over the next twenty years from philosophers and scientists. Some have embarked on physical experiments, intent on proving whether we are living inside a VR game right now.

The one problem being that the creators of this simulation might make an adjustment to render it impossible for the researchers to find proof that this is a simulation, after all. Right?

Bostrom starts his paper by arguing that *"at least one"* (italics his) of these three prospects must be true:

1. that humans will go extinct before reaching a posthuman stage of advancement;
2. that any posthuman civilization is "extremely *unlikely* [italics mine] to run a significant number of simulations of their evolutionary history";
3. that "we are almost certainly living in a computer simulation" right now.

"It follows that the belief that there is a significant chance that we will one day become posthumans who run ancestor-simulations is false, *unless we are currently living in a simulation.*" (Italics mine.)

In other words, to believe in simulation theory is to be inside the simulation. You are believing in something in which you already are involved.

It is, in a way, a digital equivalent to believing in God: some supreme being somewhere else is all-seeing and in control of all that we witness. It all will be okay if we believe. And behave. This supreme being, perhaps one of billions running their own separate simulations, is not in control of all outcomes; it is running this simulation because it wants to learn what happens, and what happens is up to us, individually.

A corollary: characters inside each simulation may possess the compute power to run simulations of their own, to be digital demigods; and the characters inside those sub-simulations, in turn, may be able to run their own mini-simulations, too. So, if we are living inside a simulation, how do we know we are at the highest level of this scenario, rather than a few levels down inside a Russian-doll-like assemblage of simulations? Bostrom writes:

> It is possible to draw some loose analogies with religious conceptions of the world. In some ways, the posthumans running a simulation are like gods in relation to the people inhabiting the simulation: the posthumans created the world we see; they

are of superior intelligence; they are "omnipotent" in the sense that they can interfere in the workings of our world even in ways that violate its physical laws; and they are "omniscient" in the sense that they can monitor everything that happens. However, all the demigods except those at the fundamental level of reality are subject to sanctions by the more powerful gods living at lower levels.

Bostrom says that because no one can be sure they are at the "basement level" in the first simulation, everyone would have to be aware "that their actions will be rewarded or punished, based perhaps on moral criteria, by their simulators." He therefore concludes: "An afterlife would be a real possibility." This is deep stuff.

The limiting factor undercutting this ethereal thesis is technology's as yet unrealized ability to pull it off. Bostrom estimates that getting a computer to emulate the human mind would require crunching processing operations per second totaling 10 to the 14th power (a 1 followed by 14 zeroes) or up to 10 to the 17th power. This may be doable today, if on a tiny scale: the world's fastest supercomputer, Frontier at the Oak Ridge National Laboratory in Tennessee, operates at 10 to the 18th power. Exascale computing.

The maximum human bandwidth for taking in information is about 10 to the 8th power bits per second, so the cost of replicating or imitating sensory effects would be "negligible." Bostrom figures producing a realistic simulation of all human history would require per-second processing operations of 10 to the 33rd to 36th power "as a rough estimate." A computer capable of running operations at 10 to the 42nd power per second could run a full simulation in a short span of time.

Eventually, the Oxford philosopher takes it full circle: he says option 3 (that we are inside a simulation now) "is the conceptually most intriguing one."

"If we are living in a simulation, then the cosmos that we are observing is just a tiny piece of the totality of physical existence. The physics in the universe where the computer is situated that is running the simulation may or may not resemble the physics of the world that we observe. While the world we see is in some sense 'real,' it is not located at the fundamental level of reality."

In his conclusion, Nick Bostrom suggests, "In the dark forest of our current ignorance, it seems sensible to apportion one's credence roughly evenly between (1), (2), and (3). Unless we are now living in a simulation, our descendants will almost certainly never run an ancestor-simulation."

The Bostrom paper spawned a spate of studies seeking to confirm it. Or debunk it as scientific silliness. Bostrom himself published a correction to his main formula in 2011. In August 2021, Viking Nilsson of Uppsala University published "An In-Depth Look at Bostrom's Simulation Argument." He packs it with new mathematical equations and lends further support to the whole idea: if it is plausible that technology can advance, one day, to be able to stage perfect simulations, then it is likely we already exist inside one.

Nilsson tracks the advances since the first supercomputer, the ENIAC, in 1945: it ran five hundred floating-point operations per second and cost almost half a million dollars. Adjusted for inflation, this translates into a cost of $1.9 trillion per gigaflop, he points out. Today, one gigaflop costs 4¢! A Sony PlayStation 5 can crunch out 10.3 *teraflops* and costs $399, the philosopher says. So, $1 today will get you fifty *quadrillion* times more compute power than an inflation-adjusted dollar could buy seventy-five years ago.

Viking Nilsson also says these all-enveloping environments, if they exist, most likely are running Monte Carlo simulations like those we use today for financial modeling and weather forecasting. The simulation thesis, he writes, also could explain the Fermi paradox—why we here on Earth have never found incontrovertible evidence of alien life, though we are but one small planet among billions and billions in existence for 13.8 billion years, three times as long as Earth itself. Answer: because the simulation creators hide this from us.

He adds that it is doubtful a futuristic society would deprive anyone of access to the compute power for running these "ancestor simulations, given how many eccentric billionaires there are in our present-day society." Good one: Elon, are you out there?

Nilsson says the Bostrom argument "at the very least is compelling," but it relies on the "principle of indifference" and "this is a step that can be disputed, and if so the entire argument falls." Until these issues are settled, "the argument cannot be considered water-proof."

A less polite review of the Bostrom simulation argument, "The Fiction of Simulation: A Critique of Bostrom's Simulation Argument," was published in November 2021 by Miloš Agatonović of the University of Belgrade in *AI & Society*. Agatonović writes that the idea is "unsound since it relies on the indistinguishability assumption that even in principle cannot be tested." That is, how can scientists test that this might-be simulation is real if it is so great that it cannot be distinguished from base reality? How are they supposed to even spot it?

Agatonović finds "structural similarities between general fiction and the simulation argument" and says the unsound theory "seems persuasive, because the argument immerses the reader in a fictive world with the help of tacit assumptions, leveraging just enough common sense to remain compelling while covering over an untestable premise."

Elsewhere, an enthusiastic endorsement of Bostrom's theory appeared in a paper published in the *AIP Advances* journal of the American Institute of Physics on October 6, 2023. Melvin M. Vopson of the School of Mathematics and Physics at the University of Portsmouth in the UK offers "scientific evidence that appears to underpin the simulated universe hypothesis."

In 2022, Vopson invented the second law of infodynamics, which states that while entropy—that is, complexity, waste, decay—in the universe is constantly on the rise, this must be offset by something else: a *decrease* in "information entropy." He found this decreasing entropy to be inherent in digital storage, in DNA sequencing that sheds information in each new generation, and in nature that prefers order and symmetry.

One key clue: if this all were a simulation, it would require massive, planet-wide compute power to do it well, and this would require the universe to reduce, as much as possible, the burden of information storage and processing power.

As Vopson writes: "This remarkable result demonstrates that the symmetries manifesting everywhere in nature, and in the entire universe, are a consequence of the second law of information dynamics, which requires the minimization of the information entropy in any system or process in the universe."

Vopson waits until the penultimate paragraph of his thirteen-page paper to slip in the biggest assertion: "Since the second law of infodynamics appears to be manifesting universally and is, in fact, a cosmological necessity, we could conclude that this points to the fact that the entire universe appears to be a simulated construct."

Did you get that? He called it a "fact" *that the entire universe appears to be a simulated construct.* Maybe Elon Musk is right after all.

In the piles of research and dozens of video clips that I gathered for this book, a revealing thirty-four-second clip shows up. Lex Fridman, a Russian-American computer scientist and podcast host, asks his pal Elon: If he or someone else were to invent the ultimate AGI (artificial general intelligence), an all-knowing digital god, what would be the one question he would ask "her"?

Elon stares off into space for thirteen full seconds of deep thought before answering, then looks up and asks: "What's outside the simulation?"

REDUCE, REDUCE, REDUCE.

In a world of incredible, increasing complexity, simplify.

For a man with a net worth spanning twelve digits, Elon Musk lives a Spartan life. This is another thing that separates him from the Establishment billionaires whom we came to know before he joined the ranks of the gaudy *riche*.

Bill Gates, now worth almost $140 billion, earned his first $1 billion in net worth at age thirty-one in 1987. A year later, he paid $2 million for a lakefront lot in Medina, Washington. He spent seven years building his version of Charles Foster Kane's Xanadu. It is composed of the timber of five hundred Douglas firs and seven different varieties of stone, encompassing sixty-six thousand square feet, seven bedrooms, and twenty-four bathrooms (ten with bathtubs).

The lodge-style mansion alone is valued at more than $130 million, plus $14 million in purchases of adjacent properties. The house has a twenty-seat movie theater, a twenty-one-hundred-square-foot library with a hidden bar and two secret bookcases, a trampoline room with a twenty-foot-high ceiling, six kitchens, a garage for two dozen cars, and a gym that occupies twenty-five thousand square feet.

Jeff Bezos hit his first billion-dollar mark a decade after Gates, in 1998 when Amazon went public. He was thirty-four years old. Today his wealth is more than $200 billion. In early 2020, he paid $165 million for the Warner Estate in Beverly Hills, a 13,600-square-foot mansion on 9 acres; a year later, he put up

$78 million for a 140-acre estate in Maui. He also owns a few properties in Washington State, apartments in New York, estates in California, and a ranch in Texas.

Lately, Bezos is said to be renting a home in Malibu from Kenny G, the jazz soprano saxophone soloist, for $600,000 a month, even as Bezos in 2023 spent another $147 million on two mansions on Indian Creek Island, off the coast of North Miami in Florida.

The Amazon founder also owns the largest sailing yacht in the world, the *Koru*, which spans three masts and 417 feet in length, with nine staterooms to accommodate eighteen guests (and space for a full-time staff of thirty-six). The ship cost a reported half a billion dollars. Its sheer girth and height required the partial dismantling of the 145-year-old Koningshaven Bridge in Rotterdam, in the Netherlands, for the gargantuan craft to be able to make it out to sea.

Mark Zuckerberg of Facebook fame became the youngest newly minted billionaire, hitting that milestone at age twenty-three in 2007, a few years before the company went public. Now with a net worth of almost $200 billion, he holds $320 million in property, much of it in Hawaii.

He lives with his wife and three young daughters in a five-bedroom mansion in Palo Alto, California, that he bought for $7 million in 2011 after which he invested another $50 million sprucing it up and buying four homes surrounding it. It features a saltwater pool, a sprawling garden, a barbecue pit, and a robot butler equipped with the booming voice of Morgan Freeman.

Zuckerberg also owns two waterfront homes on 10 acres on Lake Tahoe, bought for almost $60 million; 707 acres on Kauai island that cost him $116 million and 600 acres more on the North Shore of Kauai ($53 million); plus 110 acres of farmland ($17 million).

Wired magazine reports that he is building a compound on Kauai's North Shore that, all together, will cost $270 million. It will include an underground shelter covering five thousand square feet, with its own energy and food supplies and a blast-proof door; a dozen buildings with thirty bedrooms and thirty bathrooms, and two adjacent mansions that together occupy fifty-seven thousand square feet. (A football field, from goal line to goal line and sideline to sideline, covers only forty-five thousand square feet.)

The Facebook founder, who still runs the company he renamed Meta, also owns the *Ulysses*, a 350-foot-long yacht that he bought from another billionaire (Graeme Hart of New Zealand) for $150 million in 2015. It was a bargain off the $195 million original price, albeit it costs $2 million *per month* to operate. It includes a 240-foot-long tender boat, plus a motorcycle and a 4x4 truck.

Elon Musk, by contrast? While he started off following the same path of accumulation and ostentation, Musk has reduced his home surroundings to one of the cheaper, more minimalist options you could find. He resides in a prefab, modular home that he rents from SpaceX in Boca Chica, Texas. The Boxabl Casita, a foldable home just nineteen feet by nineteen feet, costs $60,000, less than most Tesla models. "It's kinda awesome, though," as Elon tweeted in June 2021.

Other times, he would rather crash on the couch at a friend's place than hole up in a five-star hotel. Yachts, vacation homes, and a fleet of fancy cars are easily within Elon's reach, yet this billionaire avoids owning them.

Musk didn't earn his first billion dollars until age forty-one in 2012, largely via Tesla and SpaceX. In May 2020, he announced that he would sell "almost all physical possessions" and stop owning any home, once he had fled California and moved to Texas. As he put it on another Joe Rogan podcast in May 2020:

"I think possessions really weigh you down, and they're kind of an attack vector. [Critics] will say, 'Hey, billionaire, you've got all this stuff.' Well, now I don't have stuff, now what are you going to do?"

The next year, he sold off seven homes he had accumulated in the Los Angeles area for more than $100 million. One Bel Air colonial mansion, which he had rented for two years before buying it for $17 million in 2012, consumed twenty thousand square feet for seven bedrooms, thirteen bathrooms, a library with two levels, and a wine cellar, pool, and tennis court. All of this, packed into seven-tenths of an acre right across from the Bel-Air Country Club. He sold it for almost $30 million.

Musk also got rid of a house nearby, a five-bed, four-bath ranch-style home on a quarter of an acre in Bel Air, which he bought for $6.75 million in 2013 and sold for a tiny profit in 2020. The lofty price tag owed to its previous owner, the late actor Gene Wilder, who had lived in the house for thirty years. The old structure was set for demolition when Musk bought it to rescue it and "preserve its soul," as he said at the time.

To help the sale go through, Elon even loaned the buyers—Wilder's nephew, Jordan Walker-Pearlman, and his wife, Hollywood producer Elizabeth Hunter—$6.7 million.

Further, four mansions in Bel Air, bought for almost $75 million from 2015 to 2017, sold to a real estate developer for $84 million in 2020. And Elon sold a historic mansion in Hillsborough, California, in 2021. It had thirteen bedrooms and ten bathrooms, a ballroom, and Chinese wallpaper dating back to the 1700s.

The mansion, built in 1912 on forty-seven precious acres and with more than sixteen thousand square feet of floor space, was known as Guignécourt, named for its original owner, Christian de Guigné, a French count who immigrated to America in the late nineteenth century. He married the daughter of a mining tycoon and built a booming chemicals business. The property was in family hands for four generations, until Christian de Guigné IV listed it for sale in 2013. Asking price: $100 million. Musk, ever shrewd, paid less than $32 million to buy the mansion in 2017, selling it four years later for $40.8 million.

Elon eliminated these assets from his life, even though it made him sad to do this. He saw these trappings of wealth as an unnecessary distraction and obligation. Reduce, simplify, shed the unnecessary. This minimalist, trimming-back regimen shows up in many aspects of how Musk builds his businesses, leads his workers, and manages his career. It shows up in the way he lives his life.

The rest of us really ought to cut back on our possessions and the unnecessary complexities in our lives. Elon Musk offers a how-to guide to doing more with less. Everything you see offers an opportunity for reducing some of what is there.

Too many of us have too much stuff; we are burdened by owning too many things. Life is an accumulation of possessions, a steadily rising pile of increasing complexity, progressing entropy, and expanding waistlines. We add and add and add things and purchases and accessories, without ever throwing things out and reverting to bare necessities.

Chasing after more of the things that we think we want adds to this burden of having too much. And, so, we end up struggling to accommodate the expanding mountain of owned objects and obligations, rather than seeking to whittle it all back.

This has spawned the storage industry, which rakes in $40 billion a year from people who are unable to part with possessions they no longer need or utilize. More than thirty million people in the United States, including half of renters, lease space in fifty-two thousand facilities across the country, covering 2.5 billion square feet of space. That is seventy-eight square miles of stuff that, if we really needed it, would be in our homes instead of in a storage unit miles away.

In the land of plenty, we have become a nation of hoarders. In surveys, some 54 percent of Americans say they feel overwhelmed by the clutter in their lives. We need an intervention. This is why the decluttering business, or "home organizing industry," takes in more than $11 billion a year. Thousands of blogs and YouTube videos preach the organizing gospel. Clutter consultants charge

$55 an hour to help clients cut through the morass of too many things.

The Japanese simplicity sermonizer Marie Kondo built a multimillion-dollar business advising people on how to cut back. Her first book, *The Life-Changing Magic of Tidying Up: The Japanese Art of Decluttering and Organizing*, sold eleven million copies in forty countries after its release in 2011. It inspired a TV movie of the same name, a journal, an illustrated guide, and a graphic novel. And a Netflix series released in 2019: *Tidying Up with Marie Kondo.*

Yet Marie Kondo has nothing on Elon Musk in decluttering and cutting back. His entire being seems anchored by a devotion to minimalism and doing more with less: producing more Teslas with fewer people, building cars and spaceships powered by as few moving parts as possible, streamlining factory processes to reduce steps and stations.

Musk is a big believer in first principles and breaking down any problem to its barest essence and core challenges. This demands an obsession with reducing and discarding distractions and unnecessary details. This lets him stop worrying about things that don't matter by removing them from his field of vision.

As he told one interviewer in December 2013: "First principles is kind of a physics way of looking at the world. And what that really means is you kind of boil things down to the most fundamental truths and say, okay, what are we sure is true or as sure as possible is true. And then reason up from there. That takes a lot more mental energy."

He explains an effort to develop an EV battery pack that will be far cheaper than the $700-per-kilowatt cost of current technology. "So, first principles, we say, okay, what are the material constituents of the batteries? What is the market value of the material constituents? So, you can say, okay, it's got cobalt, nickel, aluminum, carbon, and some polymers for separation, and a steel can. So, break that down on a material basis and say, okay, what if we bought that in the London Metal Exchange? What would each of those things cost?

"Like, oh, jeez, it's like $80 per kilowatt hour. So, clearly, you just need to figure out clever ways to take those materials and combine them into the shape of a battery cell, and you can have batteries that are much, much cheaper than anyone realizes."

Musk's obsessive focus on reducing parts grants a competitive edge to Tesla. The Tesla Model 3 holds some ten thousand unique parts, while the gasoline-powered autos made by Detroit contain more than thirty thousand pieces: three times as many chances for something to go wrong.

The focus on cutting back is unrelenting: in the total number of parts, in assembly-line steps and floor space, in overall costs. A Tesla engineer making a presentation in one video talks about how they redesigned the assembly line to reduce it by 10 percent: "We made these huge Giga castings, and we deleted hundreds of parts, and we thought maybe we could do this in other places. Yeah, I mean, in a way, the constraints become part of the solution rather than a problem."

Tesla engineers worked to reduce the footprint of the assembly operation so that more people and robots spent more time working on the car rather than standing idle or walking back and forth from workstation to line. "That means we have better operator density, less time doing nothing. I call that space-time efficiency. It has nothing to do with quantum mechanics," the engineer explains. "But we get 44 percent more operator density, which means more work, less time walking back to the station, 30 percent improvement in space-time efficiency."

The engineer adds: "In the end, what does that mean? To increase the scale and adoption of electric vehicles on the orders of magnitude that we just showed you? We have to make constraints part of the solution. It leads us to greater than 40 percent reduction in footprint, which means we can build factories faster with less cap-ex and more output per unit. . . . We'll reduce costs as much as 50 percent."

We have to make constraints part of the solution.

This point is a critical insight for all Earthlings, and it was inspired by Elon himself. An assemblage of Musk sound bites by Leaders.com includes this one: "I think frugality drives innovation, just like other constraints do. One of the only ways to get out of a tight box is to invent your way out."

The constraints, which most of us view as the problem, actually are part of the solution. This is a useful construct for any business looking to expand while facing financial constraints, and for any team working on a new product but with limited resources. It can inspire any small business starting from nothing: the lack of ample funding will force better, sleeker solutions.

Abundance becomes an obstacle, an invitation to inefficiency. Less is not just "more"; less is better.

Forty years ago, when the Commodore home computer held only sixty-four kilobytes of memory, software programmers had to write tight, sparse code that could cram huge functionality into very few algorithms. The Commodore operating system measured twenty thousand lines of code.

Today an Apple MacBook laptop computer starts at sixteen giga-bytes of memory—250,000 times as much memory as the C64. This lets the Apple OS gobble up more than a hundred million lines of code: 5,000 times as much programming to run the ma-chine. This is flabby and slack, at best. If memory were scarce and expensive, programmers would write tighter.

Musk's emphasis on minimalism applies to the workers of his companies. Tesla, even as it has grown prodigiously and profited hugely in recent years, has consistently cut back on workers at var-ious points. It laid off 9 percent of staff, or thirty-six hundred people, in 2018; 10 percent of all white-collar employees in 2022 (ten thousand jobs cut); and another 10 percent of its global staff in 2024, axing another fourteen thousand jobs.

Elon keeps the executive suite to a minimum, as well. Tesla lists only three executives at the top of the company, while Ford Motor Company lists eight.

Under Elon's leadership, Tesla imposed these cuts even as the number of cars it produces each year rose strongly. In 2017, Tesla's 37,543 workers assembled 50,067 electric vehicles, and by 2023 its payroll was up to 140,473 to produce 670,000 units that year. This means Tesla increased staff by 275 percent . . . so it could produce 1,200 percent more output.

Or looked at another way, Tesla produced 1.33 cars per worker in 2017—and almost 5 cars per worker (4.77) in 2023. That is a 260 percent increase in output per worker in six years. Tesla has been able to reduce parts, processes, and costs enough to make two cars at the old cost of making just one. The giant automakers in Detroit have almost no chance of reducing to this degree.

Ford has almost 40,000 more workers than does Tesla: 177,000 people, 25 percent more staff, to hammer out 183 percent more cars than Tesla, topping 1.9 million units per year. The problem for Ford is the bottom line: it had net earnings of $4.3 billion in 2023, compared with $15 billion at Tesla, more than triple Ford profits.

Overall, Ford's revenue per employee is 44 percent higher than Tesla's, at $995,000 vs. $690,000 at Tesla at year-end 2023. But Tesla posted bottom-line earnings per employee of $102,000 in 2023, four times as much as Ford, at $24,292. This is one reason why, by June 2024, Ford's total market value was shy of $50 billion, while Tesla's was at $567 billion, almost twelve times as much— and more than the next four largest carmakers (Toyota, BYD of China, Mercedes-Benz, and Ferrari) combined. At some points, Tesla has been valued at more than $1 trillion.

The same spare approach is standard operating procedure at SpaceX, as well. The company's workhorse, the Falcon 9 rocket, consists of fewer than four thousand components, compared with tens of thousands of parts for the rockets flown by NASA, Boeing, the China space agency, and Russia. The cost of launches is further reduced by reusing each Falcon 9 in future flights, rather than building a new rocket from scratch each time.

And like Tesla, SpaceX trims the workforce even as its business grows like crazy. The rocket launcher laid off 10 percent of staff in 2019. In 2021, the company employed ninety-five hundred people, and they pulled off twenty-nine launches. By 2023, SpaceX's staff totaled thirteen thousand, and launches surged to ninety-six in a single year. Meaning the company expanded its workforce by 27 percent so it could increase launches per year by 230 percent.

Always shoot to do more with less.

At SpaceX, Elon has distilled his minimalist approach to manufacturing and design down to just five key steps. He explained them impromptu to YouTube host Tim Dodd as they toured the SpaceX base in Boca Chica, Texas, in August 2021.

On Dodd's *Everyday Astronaut* show, Musk said he urges engineers to question every requirement (step 1), because most requirements in any established process are dumb and inefficient. He tells them to eliminate any part or process that they can get away with cutting (step 2)—to cut so much that they have to add back in 10 percent of what they took out.

As Elon tells the YouTuber: "If you are not occasionally adding things back in, then you are not deleting enough."

Then comes step 3: simplify and optimize, only after they have ejected the unnecessary parts. Otherwise, you end up wasting time on improving a part that gets excised later. Thereafter he exhorts staff to accelerate the cycle time of product development (step 4), and to automate the resulting streamlined, fewest-parts-possible process (step 5).

When Elon first conceived of building his own rocket, he broke it down to its essence: steel and fuel. He developed an "idiot index" comparing the price tag of something with the actual cost of the components, as Walter Isaacson reports in the book *Elon Musk*. Musk found that a finished rocket costs fifty times the actual cost of the basic parts required to build it.

His bent for reducing complexity, and simplifying the complicated, led to a dramatic reversal of course in the development of Starship, the largest, heaviest, tallest rocket ever to climb into the skies. While the Falcon 9 is composed of an aluminum-lithium alloy, Starship had to be bigger, sturdier, and able to withstand an interplanetary trip to Mars someday. So, SpaceX engineers conceived and created a costly, fancier fabrication: a carbon-fiber composite for the hull of the giant spacecraft.

It was to be the very latest in state-of-the-art technology. Estimates are that SpaceX spent upwards of $24 million for the materials, plus $20 million or more on production gear, and the company's engineers spent tens of thousands of hours on this project.

The composite was sophisticated, complicated, and expensive, requiring the creation of 60 to 120 layers, laced with high-strength resins for reinforcement, at a stiff cost of $135 per kilogram. Worse yet, some 35 percent of the output of this composite was rendered useless in production and cutting, lifting the real cost to $200 per kilogram. Plus, the fiber composite could withstand temperatures of only 300 degrees Fahrenheit, so a rocket hull would require extra heat shielding: more parts.

So, Elon scrapped the whole thing. After he talked to SpaceX engineers and pressed them into agreeing, they ended up building the massive, four-hundred-foot-tall rocket ship out of cheap, shiny, good old-fashioned stainless steel. It could withstand temperatures of 1,500 degrees, so no extra heat shielding would be required on the windward side that is exposed to superhot temperatures upon reentry. This simplified the hull's design.

And while the fiber composite costed out to $200 a kilogram, stainless steel cost just $3 per kilogram, a massive reduction in materials costs. An astonishing cost advantage.

Still, sometimes Elon cuts back too much. Before the first full launch of the two-stage Starship, engineers warned Musk that the launchpad would require a top layer of reinforced steel. Otherwise, it might get blown to bits by the power of Starship's thirty-three massive Raptor rocket engines raining fire down upon the concrete surface.

Elon rejected their advice and told them to leave it out. Big mistake. When Starship launched for the first time in April 2023, the thrust of the rocket engines devastated the launchpad and blew it apart, sending concrete chunks flying for half a mile before they landed in the sea.

It is one of those instances where the engineers took out so much that they had to put some of it back in. Afterward, as biographer Walter Isaacson relates, Musk was newly enlightened and unapologetic about it. He simply instructed his team to make sure the pad for the next launch would carry the protective steel shield that he had initially told them to do without.

Do more with less. Elon's reduction ethos may be best illustrated by the massive payroll cuts he imposed immediately upon acquiring Twitter in October 2022. All told, Twitter had run up almost $4 billion in net losses in eight of the previous ten years (from 2012 to 2021). This, despite logging more than $20 billion in sales in that period. It had two profitable years (2018 and 2019) but was back in the red the next three years in a row. In 2022, it was on track to lose another $1 billion as Musk stepped in.

Musk's first move was to fire a phalanx of senior officers that included CEO Parag Agrawal, CFO Ned Segal, legal and policy chief Vijaya Gadde, and general counsel Sean Edgett.

A week later, on Thursday, November 3, a company-wide email went out to Twitter staff, telling them that by nine o'clock the next morning, they would receive an email with the subject line "Your Role at Twitter."

The next day, in a single, instant 50 percent whack, half the people on the payroll got emails telling them, "Today is your last working day at the company." Ultimately, 6,000 would get the gate, an 80 percent cut, as well as 4,400 of the 5,500 contractors Old Twitter had employed, another 80 percent cutback.

There it is, ladies and gentlemen: the 80/20 rule writ large. Anyone who has managed workers knows that 80 percent of the work is done by the best 20 percent of your staff. And those 20 percent are the ones you keep tapping for still more work, because they get it done. Instead of creating complexity, obstacles, and problems.

No wonder Musk wanted to cut deep and fast, shedding 50 percent of Twitter staff in one first swipe. When Musk hosted his first company meeting at Twitter, during the first week of the takeover, he took questions from shell-shocked staff. One worker asked him what the "big vision" was, and Musk said: "Well, I mean, I don't know. I don't have a great answer to that. But I can tell you, philosophically, what works at SpaceX and Tesla is people being in the office and being hardcore, and a small number of people can get a tremendous amount done in that situation."

He told the employees that at Tesla, the Autopilot system, one of the most advanced AI-aided driving programs in the world, is the work of just 150 engineers, besting rival teams of three thousand people. He added: "I'm a big believer that a small number of exceptional people can be highly motivated and do better than a large number of people who are pretty good and moderately motivated. That's my philosophy."

Reduce, reduce, reduce. In fact, Musk fired so many people at Twitter, so quickly, that he overdid it. He had to put out a call to engineers to come back to the company so he could rehire them. Which is akin to his telling Tesla engineers to take out so many parts that they have to add back in 10 percent of what they had removed, because they had reduced a little too much.

Four weeks after the drastic cuts slashed Twitter's staff to one-fifth of its former size, the World Cup football soccer tournament began. The newly trimmed Twitter was able to host 147 billion impressions on the World Cup in a two-week period. What were all those excess workers doing all day long, before they got Elon's axe? Clearly, they were unnecessary—and no business can afford to employ unnecessary staff for long.

The reductions, done swiftly and without remorse, riveted Silicon Valley: How could Musk axe 80 percent of staff and keep the platform running unhindered? In the next year, Twitter's monthly users would double to 550 million worldwide, served by only a fraction of the old staff.

This set a new standard for sleek operations in a company and underscored that the best businesses are constantly growing staff and cutting back, and growing and cutting back, reducing staff even in the most buoyant times. Trim your sails and reduce ballast and inefficiency, continuously.

This streamlining, always-reducing approach shows up in Elon's style of interaction and communication. He dispenses with unnecessary and time-consuming pleasantries and long, throat-clearing preambles. Musk prefers to cut to the chase and just say the blunt thing he wants to say, sparing little time for small talk and convention. As when he said on CNBC to any advertiser that would try to muzzle free speech on X: Go. Fuck. Yourself. (See lesson 6.)

Elon seems unable, or unwilling, to deploy his approach of continual reduction in one particular realm: women and children. He never deigns to cut back on either—and, in fact, he urges more population growth for global well-being and productivity.

As the synth-pop singer Grimes was giving him a son, Musk also was having twins (a boy and a girl) with Shivon Zilis, a senior executive at his brain-tech startup, Neuralink. It is reported that the two women were friends, and Grimes was unaware of the other liaison. Zilis and Musk had a third child in 2024.

Keeping just one woman happy can be impossibly challenging; to add a second one, or even a third, exponentially increases this burden, a result of hubris or insanity. It may be that only a billionaire can pull off a stunt of this magnitude, and only by buying peace. But even most billionaires choose against trying something like this.

Otherwise, Elon errs on the side of less consumption, and so should we all. Something elemental is at work in this Muskian desire to lead by cutting back and contracting. Doing without, and making do with less, permeates more aspects of our lives than we realize, from the diets we pursue and the New Year's resolutions we make to the few close friendships we keep.

And even in the sentences you are reading on these pages: my writing process is a constant search-and-destroy mission to excise superfluous words and phrases. Write shorter.

This applies even to the food Elon Musk eats. Grimes famously recalls spending a six-day stint with Musk, subsisting on peanut butter sandwiches, as he put in huge hours at Tesla. No one ever asks her why she never ordered in some takeout of her own. Step up, lady.

Musk himself has talked about struggling to keep his weight down and finding some success with intermittent fasting. Today 10 percent of us, more than thirty million people (including this author), practice intermittent fasting, confining eating to, say, only eight hours a day and fasting for the other sixteen hours (including eight hours of sleep). Most people do the reverse, eating sixteen hours a day.

The human body, in fact, thrives and operates at peak efficiency when it is deprived of just enough intake to survive comfortably. Hunger is good. A stripped-down diet awakens the system and sets our cells alive. Fasting as a medical remedy dates to Hippocrates four hundred years before the birth of Jesus Christ.

In March 2020, a paper published in the journal *Aging* ("Fasting for Stem Cell Rejuvenation") studied planarian flatworms, which can go three months without any food at all. Authors Cristina González-Estévez and Ignacio Flores reported:

"Throughout the centuries, humankind has relentlessly searched for ways to live longer and healthier lives. . . . Among all anti-aging interventions, calorie restricted diets and periods of fasting stand out as the most compelling and robust methods to prolong life and health span and to reduce the risk of diabetes, neurodegeneration, autoimmune disorders, spontaneous tumors and cardiovascular disease."

The flatworms they studied showed that those that starved the most had the most robust stem cells, allowing them "to quickly respond to any injury even while fasting." The researchers adding: "Therefore, natural cycles of fasting and feeding promote the maintenance of a healthy and always cycling stem-cell population, thus making planarians immortal." Immortal!

A lot of us could benefit from consuming less. Thirty-one percent of American adults are overweight, and another 42 percent are obese. Among children ages two to nineteen, 16 percent are overweight and almost 20 percent are obese; 6 percent are morbidly obese.

These are the consequences of abundance: the U.S. obesity rate is double the average of that in the other member countries of the Organisation for Economic Co-operation and Development. Among OECD nations, the United States has the second-highest death rate from heart disease, a higher mortality from lung disease than the UK or European nations, higher incidences of severe arthritis, and the highest diabetes rate. So, when in doubt, cut back; consume less.

Even Elon's wardrobe is a matter of reduction: just a bunch of black T-shirts, some with logos; black jeans; and a few scarves.

His primordial need to cut back on almost everything, to reduce, reduce, reduce and simplify to the utmost, may run deeper than just his own desires. His reduction maxim, in fact, may be integral to the most basic laws of the universe and how it functions. It may be a way to counterbalance and offset the tendency of the universe to produce more entropy, complexity, waste, and inefficiency as time moves forward. And Elon gets this.

The universe is governed by four basic laws of thermodynamics, and the first two apply well here. The first law of thermodynamics, established in 1824, states that the universe, because it envelops everything, cannot create new energy or destroy it and get rid of it; instead, energy is transformed from one form to another—from, say, heat to motion.

Stick with me here: the second law of thermodynamics, set down in 1850, says that in every transformation of energy from one state to another, a lot of the energy is lost, wasted. This is known as entropy. Decay, complexity, rising inefficiency, waste: entropy.

See also: government, big business, organizations, systems. The second law says that the entire universe tends toward producing more entropy rather than less of it.

But the strange thing is, despite this ever-increasing volume of entropy and complexity, the overall total mass of the entire universe stays constant and doesn't ever increase. How can this be so if the decay and complexity of entropy are constantly on the rise? Something else must be on the decline to offset this.

Melvin Vopson, of the University of Portsmouth, who also is a solid-state storage engineer, talked to me about this for more than an hour one evening, on a Zoom call from his home. As he explains it:

"This is the fact: that the universe cannot be allowed to exchange heat with anything. Or energy, okay? So, mass is energy, so you can't add more mass to the universe. You can't take mass from the universe. You can't add energy of any kind to the universe. You can't expel energy from the universe in any way."

And why can't you? Because the universe is everything, it is already in there, he says. "If you can [expel energy], it means the universe is inside something else. So, all our physical models are out the window. Okay?"

He adds: "So, now the question is, if everything in the universe, including the entire universe, evolves to a high entropy state, how can you explain that the change in entropy has to be zero?" With the second law of thermodynamics, which states that although everything in the universe increases in entropy over time, this doesn't increase the mass of the universe overall, because it's already in there.

And then Vopson had a Eureka moment a few years ago: it may be that "information entropy" was always reducing itself, cutting back on lines of code that represent information inside a system, organism, or structure. Maybe this cutback was the offset for keeping balance in our entropy-prone universe.

To test this idea, Vopson started by looking at the DNA sequencing of the SARS-CoV-2 virus that causes Covid-19. Each new variant could be calculated for how much information it held, stored in the binary form of base pairs of the four nucleotides that are the building blocks of DNA: adenine paired with thymine, or cytosine paired with guanine. AT or CG in various orders and strings and combinations. He started with the first version in December 2019 and compared that with the next variant, and the next, and the next, and so on.

Vopson was surprised to discover that the SARS virus, from one variant to the next, was constantly reducing the information inside itself. It was diligently discarding some of the base pairs of AT and CG, yet the virus was still able to function and multiply and perpetuate itself. Making itself more efficient with each successive iteration. As he tells me:

"And I found something very interesting. I found that the number of mutations, they scale inverse proportionally to the information entropy of the genome itself. In other words, the more mutations you have, the lower the information entropy of your RNA genome is."

This could mean the data reduction inherent in these mutations is intentional and by design, rather than by random mathematical chance, as the conventional view of mutations holds. An embedded, preternatural tendency toward cutting back on information entropy: to run more efficiently by deleting instructions and stored information that turn out to be unnecessary.

The same thing, basically, that Elon Musk asks his engineers to do at Tesla and SpaceX.

Fascinated, Vopson began to look for this entropy-reduction bent elsewhere. As he puts it: "The range of applicability is just insane on this. I said, wait a second, if this is happening in the genomes, could it be a more universal law? Could it be . . . something underlying everything in nature, maybe, this reduction of information entropy, a reduction of information content?"

He went on to find this data-reduction bias in the behavior of disk drives, which never act on their own to add or "write" new data, yet will delete data over time. And in Spiegelman's Monster, the result of a 1965 experiment involving a bacteria RNA strand that underwent seventy-four generations, reducing its base pairs of DNA from 4,500 to just 218, a reduction of more than 90 percent in stored information.

Thus, as I outlined in the previous chapter, Vopson devised the second law of infodynamics, as the counterbalance to the second law of thermodynamics. His new law "requires the information entropy to remain constant or to *decrease* over time" (italics added), as he put it in a paper published in *AIP Advances* on July 11, 2022. He wrote:

"This is exactly the opposite to the evolution of the physical entropy, as dictated by the second law of thermodynamics. The surprising result obtained here has massive implications for future developments in genomic research, evolutionary biology, computing, big data, physics, and cosmology."

He went on to uncover similar data-cutting bias in genetics and mutations; in Euclidian geometry, mirroring, and mathematics; and even in the symmetry found everywhere in nature, and in the basic rules of molecular structure for how electrons arrange themselves. He says:

"These are real things. This is real physics; this is happening. This is how the world functions. If the electrons would not occupy those states the way they occupy them, there will be no chemical stability. There will be no solids. There will be no matter. Nothing will look the way it looks. So, these rules are paramount to actually everything in the universe. Now I have found a governing rule that dictates they take the lowest information entropy."

But where does this self-imposed efficiency originate, and who put it in place, whether by God or the universe or some other force? This is where it gets a little weird.

Let us circle back to Elon Musk's firm belief that we may be living inside a massive virtual simulation. One controlled by someone else, somewhere else, in another time. If this were true, it would require massive compute power to run this gigantic videogame— say, almost fifty planets' worth of computers all working on this one thing. So, this fake universe would need to reduce, everywhere possible, the information required to run our simulation.

It is all about preserving bandwidth. And storing less information.

Tantalized by this possibility, Melvin Vopson published a follow-up paper, "The Second Law of Infodynamics and Its Implications for the Simulated Universe Hypothesis," on October 6, 2023, in the *AIP Advances* journal of the American Institute of Physics. As he explained it to me in our Zoom call:

"I am not by any means saying that I found the proof that we live in a simulation. I'm just saying I found what I call a fingerprint, if that makes sense . . . that points to this possible conclusion that our reality is not what it seems. And we might be living in a simulated world, but it's not nailed down. We need additional work, maybe experimentation, empirical observations, but it does, indeed, point to that direction. Yes."

He elaborates in the second paper, writing that his second law "essentially minimizes the information content associated with any event or process in the universe. . . . This behavior is fully reminiscent of the rules deployed in programming languages and computer coding. Since the second law of infodynamics appears to be manifesting universally and is, in fact, a cosmological necessity, we could conclude that this points to the fact that the entire universe appears to be a simulated construct.

"A super complex universe like ours, if it were a simulation, would require a built-in data optimization and compression mechanism in order to reduce the computational power and the data storage requirements. This is exactly what we are observing via empirical evidence all around us, including digital data, biological systems, atomistic systems, symmetries, and the entire universe."

Reduce, reduce, reduce: Elon's way is the way of the universe, whether it is a simulation or base reality. He gets this in a deeper way than the rest of us. Cutting back, seeking to simplify, pushing for spare, seamless design, shedding waste, and eliminating unnecessary steps: this is a better way to live. The universe demands it— or maybe the simulation does.

THE HIGHEST NAIL GETS POUNDED DOWN FIRST. STRAP ON A HELMET.

When the Establishment attacks

The Establishment comes down hard on Elon Musk. He wants to save the world, while his many detractors—so many of them!—want to make him bow down to his superiors. Politicians, regulators, nongovernmental organizations (NGOs), tort lawyers, and shareholder activists are all avowed Enemies of Elon.

What's not to like? Yet the Establishment has made a blood sport of investigating him, attacking him, suing him, filing charges against him and his companies, and trying to damage the businesses he is relentlessly building. They demonize him so that anything and everything he does is seen through the darkest lens. Instead of a visionary, they see a liar and charlatan. Instead of indefatigable enthusiasm and optimism, they see bragging from a rip-off artist akin to Harold Hill in *The Music Man*.

And once you have demonized and villainized Elon Musk, each new thing he does is suspect in some way. Take shots at him first, find out the facts later. He is guilty and unworthy of a chance to prove himself innocent. Trifling things can become international incidents.

The powers that be want this man handcuffed and muzzled like a dangerous suspect, figuratively or otherwise. Why do they fear Elon Musk, and what are they so afraid of?

One answer is that they fear him for buying Twitter—and exposing one of the most rampant, roughshod, unconstitutional government violations of the First Amendment in American history. The #TwitterFiles exposé, authorized by Musk and reported by independent journalists led by Matt Taibbi, showed that the FBI, CIA, Department of Homeland Security, CDC, and dozens of other government agencies and NGOs had pressured Twitter to silence thousands of accounts of conservative Americans.

Elon Musk has become "Progressive Enemy No. 1," as the *Wall Street Journal* editorial board put it on September 23, 2023, in "The Harassment of Elon Musk: The Tesla CEO Faces a Remarkable Number of Government Probes." No Musk misdeed is too minor to draw the attention of government bureaucrats or preachy politicians.

Cut to San Francisco, two months earlier: July 24, 2023 (my birthday, as it happens). Musk has just renamed Twitter as X, and a cherry picker lift is in place at its headquarters on Market Street in downtown San Francisco. Workmen are beginning to remove the vertical Twitter sign topped by its "iconic" symbol, as the local press later would call it, the eyeless bluebird logo. They manage to remove "@tw" and "tt" before city police intervene and order them to cease and desist, leaving the "i" and "er" in place.

For lack of a permit. A few days later, on a Friday, Musk had workers erect a giant, illuminated X logo on the rooftop of the building. By Monday morning, the city had ordered the company to take it down, after twenty-five callers complained about its unstable structure and how brightly it was lighting up the nighttime.

So, San Francisco government officials and police made time to crack down on the Twitter sign changes—in a city that allows homeless encampments to set up on public streets, where open use of illegal narcotics is routine, severely mentally ill patients roam untreated, and foul acts are committed with impunity. Priorities.

This anti-Musk enmity starts at the top. Musk acquired Twitter in late October 2022. The midterm elections occurred on November 8, 2022, and the day after, President Biden held a rare press conference on the surprisingly good results (for Democrats).

Reporter: "Mr. President, do you think Elon Musk is a threat to U.S. national security? And should the U.S., and with the tools you have, investigate his joint acquisition of Twitter with foreign governments which include the Saudis?" Biden grins wryly as if to say, *You rascal, you*, pauses, and then he carefully. Chooses. His. Precise. Words. As if he were listening to someone recite them to him via an invisible earpiece.

President Biden: "Heh heh. I think that Elon Musk's cooperation and/or technical relationships with other countries, uh, is worthy of being looked at. Whether or not he is doing anything inappropriate, I'm not suggesting that. I'm suggesting that it's worth, worth being looked at. Uh, and, uh, um, and uh, that's all I'll say."

"How?" a reporter shouts back.

President Biden: "There's a lotta ways."

Right: so, Elon Musk *might* be doing something inappropriate. We don't know what, but let's have a look-see! A cagey old politician: by "not suggesting" that Musk was doing anything inappropriate, President Biden was bringing up precisely that possibility—so much so that it should be "looked at."

Mark this spot: Twitter had a Saudi wealth fund as an investor long before Musk came along, and the fund stayed on after the acquisition. The Saudis also own stock in myriad large U.S. companies, so this is small beer. When the feds do target Twitter for its foreign investors—and I betcha a signed dollar they will—the media will leave out Biden's tacit request in 2022.

In the summer of 2023, Musk came under so many assaults from so many directions that the whole thing began to look like a political persecution. Or a comedy of errors. In a matter of weeks starting on August 24, he drew fire from the government on seven different fronts.

1. The National Highway Traffic Safety Administration (NHTSA) was ready to unveil its ruling in a two-year-long investigation of Tesla's Autopilot driving system. This was prompted by three dozen crashes involving the self-driving software, resulting in twenty-three deaths since 2016. In April 2024, NHTSA completed the investigation and issued no fines or penalties—and launched a new probe into two dozen new deaths. Never mind that more than forty thousand people die in two million car accidents every year.

2. The U.S. Justice Department charged SpaceX with discriminating against refugees in hiring. A strange case given conflicting laws and rules that forbid employers from hiring undocumented migrants, especially in sensitive high-tech fields.

3. Justice launched a criminal investigation, and the Securities and Exchange Commission initiated a separate civil probe, of reports that Tesla had ordered millions of dollars of specialized glass to build a home for Elon Musk. A glass house: it sounds like a joke. By late summer of 2024, no charges were filed, but both agencies had broadened their reviews to scrutinize other possible misspending.

4. Federal prosecutors, in a new effort, were investigating Tesla's mileage claims about how far its EVs can drive on a single charge.

5. The Justice Department filed an argument in support of the Federal Trade Commission regarding an old Twitter privacy settlement dating back to 2011. This, despite zero evidence of any new consumer harm. As Musk took over and fired several thousand workers, a few complained that he was ignoring old FTC-enforced provisions dating back a decade.

6. The Equal Employment Opportunity Commission (EEOC), on September 29, 2023, filed a lawsuit against Tesla in federal court in Northern California, alleging harassment of minority workers. The EEOC was copycatting a California State complaint, which itself followed the path of a lawsuit filed by Owen

Diaz, a Black worker at the factory in Fremont, California, who won a $3.2 million judgment against Tesla in a jury trial. The case remained unresolved a year later.

7. Senator Elizabeth Warren called for the Department of Defense and Congress to investigate Musk for his role in a recent controversy regarding the Ukrainian military, SpaceX's Starlink satellite network, and a botched mission to blow up Russian ships off the coast of Crimea.

Seven separate battlegrounds in two months. That is a lot of government warfare directed at a single target. And it is only a portion of all the efforts underway even now to hinder, hamper, and trash Elon Musk. Two more fronts of attack opened up in the next few months.

In December 2023, the Federal Communications Commission rescinded an $885 million contract that had been awarded to Musk's Starlink network to provide internet service to 640,000 homes and businesses in rural areas across thirty-five states. This brought a bitter dissent from Republican FCC member Brendan Carr, who accused the Biden administration of targeting Musk repeatedly. Opening line:

"Last year, after Elon Musk acquired Twitter and used it to voice his own political and ideological views without a filter, President Biden gave federal agencies a green light to go after him." He quotes President Biden's saying there were "a lotta ways" to do this and adds:

"There certainly are. The Department of Justice, the Federal Aviation Administration, the Federal Trade Commission, the National Labor Relations Board, the U.S. Attorney for the Southern District of New York, and the U.S. Fish and Wildlife Service have all initiated investigations into Elon Musk or his businesses.

"Today, the Federal Communications Commission adds itself to the growing list of administrative agencies that are taking action against Elon Musk's businesses. . . . Today's decision certainly fits the Biden administration's pattern of regulatory harassment." The ruling "cannot be explained by any objective application of law, facts or policy."

A month later, Elon Musk came under assault in another venue, this time the Delaware Chancery Court. A local chancellor, Kathaleen St. Jude McCormick, threw out the compensation package awarded to Elon Musk in 2018 by the Tesla board, which had the approval of 73 percent of Tesla shareholders (before counting the shares owned by Elon and his brother, Kimbal).

Elon's pay package was pegged at $2.28 billion when Tesla put it into effect, but by 2023, it was valued at a stunning $56 billion. This is because Tesla stock, in the meantime, rose more than tenfold from $17 a share to $185 a share in early 2024, and this was down from a high of $370 in October 2021. Elon's compensation was made up solely of Tesla stock, and this used to be considered a good thing: tie the CEO's pay to the performance of the stock so he benefits only if shareholders benefit, too.

So, while his golden handcuffs were now said to be worth $56 billion, he created more than half a trillion dollars in extra wealth for the shareholders of Tesla in those five years.

The chancellor ran wild in her ruling, opening with a line that seemed designed as clickbait: "Was the richest person in the world overpaid?" She cited the "deeply flawed" process by which a cozy board had approved the terms and argued the price was "unfair" and "an unfathomable sum." She invoked *Star Trek* ("To boldly go where no man has gone before") and Shakespeare's *Henry V* ("Once more unto the breach, dear friends, once more").

Clearly enjoying herself. Chancellor McCormick had tangled before with Elon Musk: she issued the ruling that forced him to proceed with his takeover bid for Twitter in late 2022.

Hours after her ruling on his pay package on Tuesday, January 30, 2024, Elon posted a new poll on X, asking whether Tesla should move its corporate headquarters to Texas and out of Delaware, the base for most major business incorporations. Of 1.1 million voters, 87 percent voted yes; 13 percent voted no. Two days later, on February 1, Musk announced plans to propose moving the company's incorporation to the Lone Star State at the next Tesla shareholder meeting.

On June 13, 2024, Tesla staged its annual shareholder meeting. Seventy-two percent of shares were voted for Elon's compensation contract, under the same terms as before and now down to $48 billion in value. This was on par with the original vote taken before shareholders knew how much it really would cost them. It was a major show of appreciation. Likewise, Tesla investors also approved moving the company's incorporation to Texas.

Elon always refuses to bow; he refuses to slink away. Instead, he chooses to stand and fight. He takes to X to rally public opinion. And files lawsuits to strike back against his attackers. And takes new actions that clearly defy his detractors. There it is: backbone. An abundance of it. When even the most powerful forces try to come down on Elon Musk, he rises up to put them back in their proper place. Elon is the highest nail that gets pounded down first. Instead of whining about it, he straps on a helmet. Bring it.

This can set a guiding example for the rest of us. Standing up to superior forces and speaking out is something we all should do when we have done our homework and we are in the right factually and morally. If only we had the means and the moxie. Musk possesses both. Like some reverse-energy superhero, he thrives on the attacks and draws strength from them. Instead of letting these jerks beat him down. He has the contrarian Christopher Columbus syndrome: the more they insist you are wrong, the more in the right you feel. Musk trusts his instincts.

These traits were redolent as Musk navigated the seven separate government crackdown efforts that made news in just three weeks from August to September of 2023. Let us do a LIFO (last-in first-out) accounting and start with the last entry first: the Ukraine/Starlink flap, and the sanctimonious senator from Massachusetts.

In her hectoring of Musk, Senator Warren was surfing the headlines regarding the release the same week of *Elon Musk*, the biographer Walter Isaacson's eponymous tome spanning ninety-five chapters across 688 pages. At the bottom of page 430, Isaacson reports that Musk, in April 2022, had spurned the pleas of the Ukrainian military to let his privately owned Starlink satellite network be used to guide a surprise, first-ever drone attack on Russian ships near Crimea.

Isaacson writes that the Ukraine military had sent six submarine drones, armed with explosives, traveling beneath the Black Sea toward the harbor at Sevastopol on the Crimean Peninsula. In the middle of the night, Ukrainian military and government officials, including a deputy prime minister, called Musk and SpaceX executives to urge them to turn on Starlink coverage so their surprise attack could proceed.

Musk rejected their pleas. He discussed the matter with Isaacson during this tense time—incredible access for an author or journalist. Musk told him that the attack, if successful, would have been "bad for the world." He worried that it could escalate U.S. involvement in the Russia-Ukraine war or even led to World War III.

Here is how Walter Isaacson ends up describing the confrontation in *Elon Musk*:

> Allowing the use of Starlink for the attack, he concluded, could be a disaster for the world. So, he secretly told his engineers to turn off coverage within a hundred kilometers of the Crimean coast. As a result, when the Ukrainian drone subs got near the Russian fleet in Sevastopol, they lost connectivity and washed ashore harmlessly.

Isaacson had intended to portray his subject as courageous and heroic in this account; biographers tend to do this—why spend all that effort profiling a lout? Instead, he ended up making Elon Musk look arrogant and power hungry, and Democrat supporters of Ukraine, government officials, and the media went on the attack.

Headline in the *New Republic*: "Putin Suck-up Elon Musk Shut Off Starlink to Stop a Ukrainian Attack." Suck-up?

> The *Independent*: "Elon Musk Sparks Fury by Admitting He Thwarted Ukrainian Drone Attack on Putin's Naval Fleet." Thwarted?

> *Vanity Fair*: "Elon Musk Did Major Damage to a Ukrainian War Offensive Last Year: Report." Deck: "The mercurial billionaire turned off Starlink communications."

> Yahoo News: "Musk Denies Treason Allegations over Restricting Ukraine's Access to Starlink." Treason? Treason!

> *Business Insider*: "Zelenskyy advisor slams Elon Musk . . . 'Why do some people so desperately want to defend war criminals?'"

> The *New York Times*: "Elon Musk Refused to Enable Ukraine Drone Attack on Russian Fleet." Deck: "News that Mr. Musk did not allow the use of his Starlink satellite network highlights concerns in Kyiv and Washington about his outside influence in the war."

Meanwhile, Musk supporters praised him for holding back and helping avoid a major escalation in the Russian war on Ukraine. Neither the criticism nor the praise of Elon Musk was warranted, as it turns out. Walter got it wrong.

Days after *Elon Musk* made its debut, Isaacson gamely stepped up and said he had committed an error that triggered an international incident. Rather than Musk's having instructed his engineers to shut down Starlink over Crimea, as Isaacson wrote, the coverage had already been dark, as required by U.S. law. U.S. sanctions against Russia blocked SpaceX from serving the Russian-controlled territory. So, Elon had refused a demand from Ukraine that Starlink switch on Crimean coverage because doing so would have violated U.S. law. He wasn't being a hero. He was following the rules, albeit doing so was unlike him.

At eleven o'clock the next night, Isaacson stepped up on social media to "clarify" the matter, saying, "The Ukrainians THOUGHT coverage was enabled all the way to Crimea, but it was not. They asked Musk to enable it for their drone sub attack on the Russian fleet. Musk did not enable it, because he thought, probably correctly, that would cause a major war." Whoops, he did it again: this wasn't the real reason Musk had to say no to Ukraine. Musk was abiding by U.S. law and bowing to sanctions against Russia.

Two days later at 5:30 a.m. (eastern time) on September 11, 2023, Elon Musk directly addressed his X following of 155 million people: "I am a citizen of the United States and have only that passport. No matter what happens, I will fight for and die in America. The United States Congress has not declared war on Russia. If anyone is treasonous, it is those who call me such. Please tell them that very clearly."

On September 13, Senator Warren went on CNN, clad in a Kelly-green, polyester-like blazer that looked like she'd borrowed it from a Whole Foods worker in the produce department. She was either unaware of Isaacson's skinback or had decided to ignore it. In her best Harvard professor's lecture tone, she thundered on air:

"No one is supposed to make foreign policy for the United States other than the United States government. It is not up to one billionaire to go off in secret and change our foreign policy."

Musk had done nothing close to this. In fact, he'd done the opposite. A day or two later, he added details, appearing by remote video on a giant screen onstage at a fan summit for the *All-In* podcast, which is hosted by four brainy, fabulously rich tech bros, including his good friend and fellow PayPal alum David Sacks. As hundreds of fans sat in the dark at Royce Hall on the UCLA campus, ready to applaud Musk's every word, his visage on-screen looked positively Orwellian. Elon told the crowd:

"We're not allowed to actually turn on connectivity to [Russian-controlled Crimea] without explicit government approval. So, we did not have the U.S. government [approval]. . . . We basically figured out that this was kind of like a Pearl Harbor–type attack on Sevastopol—on the Russian fleet at Sevastopol. So, what they're really asking us to proactively take part in a major act of war."

He added: "And, you know, while we certainly have huge support for the Ukrainian government, the Ukrainian government is not in charge of U.S. people or companies. That's not how it works." The room crackled with applause. Musk also told the crowd: "While I'm not President Biden's biggest fan, if I had received a presidential directive to turn it on, I would have done so. Because I do regard the president as the chief executive officer of the country. Whether I want that person to be the president or not, I still respect the office."

This is a lot more respect than President Biden and Senator Warren have shown for Elon.

The entire Starlink brouhaha ignored a few pertinent points. The satellite network is a privately owned property. It was built by SpaceX, in which Elon holds a controlling 42 percent stake, having funded it with $100 million of his own money. The Ukrainian government had praised Musk and SpaceX for Starlink's mission-critical role in restoring communications after hundreds of Russian rockets destroyed the country's tech infrastructure.

In fact, Starlink had provided upwards of $100 million in service to Ukraine and its military—free of charge, because Musk felt a sovereign country should be able to defend itself. At one point, the United States was close to signing an agreement to start paying for Starlink's service to Ukraine, but the deal fell apart amid news leaks and more anti-Musk controversy.

The highest nail gets pounded down first. And no good deed goes unpunished. Clichés stick around for hundreds of years because, so often, they are proven to be true.

Less than a week after Senator Warren went on CNN, Musk sent a tacit response to her admonishment that he should stay out of foreign affairs. He met in New York with Turkey's prime minister, Recep Tayyip Erdoğan, who asked him to build a Tesla Gigafactory in his country. Later the same day, Musk hosted, live on his own X platform, an hour-long conversation with Israeli prime minister Benjamin Netanyahu. They discussed AI and other topics.

At day's end, Elon Musk presented the Israeli leader with a new Tesla Cybertruck.

Elizabeth Warren has a thing for Elon Musk. In December 2022, she called for an SEC investigation of possible conflicts of interest between publicly held Tesla and privately held Twitter, two months after Elon acquired the platform. She reiterated this in April 2023. The senator was intervening in a matter that is the purview of the Tesla board of directors and the owners of Tesla stock. If shareholders are fretting about this, they can call for a board investigation, or file a resolution addressing it, or they can sell their stock and invest elsewhere.

The feds need not involve themselves in this. Go ferret out the next FTX cryptocurrency scam involving some whiz kid founder who has donated $40 million to Democrat causes so as to elude detection. But no: they prefer to go after Elon Musk.

Senator Warren reiterated her supposed concerns in July 2023. On July 17, at 3:02 p.m., she tweeted: "Since Elon Musk took over Twitter, I'm concerned @Tesla's board has failed to manage conflicts of interest from his role as CEO of Tesla & Twitter. Tesla's board has a legal obligation to serve its shareholders. I'm urging @SECGov to investigate." So solemn and pious.

Two days later, on July 19 at 11:27 a.m., Elon Musk responded on Twitter, sparing any punctuation: "Not you again" and then one minute later: "Can we please be friends please please." He was being ironic: saying one thing and meaning its precise opposite. Elon Musk sees Senator Warren for the grandstanding, self-serving enemy she is, and to him, this is war. And he is right. Investigate what? Senator Warren professes to worry about Tesla investors— yet Tesla's stock price was up 170 percent year-to-date when she posted her tweet.

One day later, on July 20, Reuters reported that Elon Musk's lawyers were preparing to subpoena Senator Warren and demand to see all her communications with the FTC and the SEC regarding Twitter and Tesla. It was a Musk power flex, turnabout as fair play. Therein lies the corollary to putting on a helmet when your enemies come after you: you also have to strike back. And turn defensive moves into offensive moves. This is what Elon would end up doing after the government essentially sued him for failing to hire refugees.

By the end of summer 2023, Elon Musk had become the target of another bully—the U.S. Department of Justice, which houses the Civil Rights Division, which houses the Immigrant and Employee Rights Section (IER). The IER filed a complaint against SpaceX with the Office of the Chief Administrative Hearing Officer, inside the Executive Office for Immigration Review, which itself sits inside . . . the Department of Justice.

So, one part of the Justice Department is taking action against Elon Musk and SpaceX, to be adjudicated by *another* part of the Justice Department. The term *justice* strains credulity. "Star chamber" and "kangaroo court" might be more fitting. Even more odd is the central point of the complaint filed by IER: SpaceX, from

2018 to 2021, supposedly discriminated against refugees by hiring, instead, U.S. citizens and approved residents with a secure legal status.

This was a case of Upside-Down World. Essentially suing a business owner for failing to hire refugees and asylum seekers, when U.S. law usually requires employers to verify that the workers they hire are U.S. citizens and legal residents. Additional regulations ban companies from hiring foreigners in sensitive tech jobs like many of those at SpaceX, which has satellite-launch contracts with U.S. intel agencies. As well, it is bad business to hire someone with an unstable residency status: you invest in training them, and they end up having to go back to their home country.

U.S. policies should encourage, as much as possible, the hiring of our own people. And those who already have won legal entry here: nine million legal immigrants in the United States are unemployed. Refugees and "asylees" are new entrants whose immigration and residency status are as yet undetermined—why would any firm hire a new worker with such uncertain prospects?

In the past decade, the IER office has pursued ten administrative cases of this nature and settled them without filing charges. Five of these cases were filed after Joe Biden became president. All of them involved small-time employers and were settled for small sums. But Elon Musk was treated differently. The official, high-handed statement from Justice, attributed to Kristen Clarke, assistant U.S. attorney general for civil rights, was: "Through this lawsuit we will hold SpaceX accountable for its illegal employment practices."

Here is one supposedly illegal practice that the complaint alleges: some of Elon Musk's public remarks were "discriminatory," such as when he said in a post on Twitter in 2020 that "U.S. law requires at least a green card to be hired at SpaceX, as rockets are considered advanced weapons technology." Musk was saying what he believed to be true, as advised by his lawyers, and now the government was trying to penalize his free speech by calling it "discriminatory."

Usually, when a bully as bloated and fearsome as the Department of Justice draws a target on you, your lawyers tell you to shut up, and you comply. As you should, because whatever you say can and will be used against you in a court of law. We all have seen *Law & Order* a thousand times. *Dun-dun!*

Elon Musk plays by another set of rules. At 8:44 p.m. on the day the case was announced, as if he no longer could hold back, he posted on X and drew 3.7 million views, explaining that SpaceX would be in violation of international arms trafficking laws if it hired anyone other than a permanent resident of the United States. "This is yet another case of weaponization of DOJ for political purposes."

Two days later, after letting the matter percolate while his followers took shots at the DOJ, Musk put out another message at 1:12 p.m. on August 26, 2023: "DOJ needs to sue themselves!" He posted this atop a note from a George Mason University economics professor, Alex Tabarrok, who drew a stunning sixty-six million views with this:

"The DOJ is suing @elonmusk and @SpaceX for focusing their hiring on US citizens and permanent residents. Do you know who else advertises that only US citizens can apply for a job? The DOJ." Attached was a screenshot of a job listing for a "recreation specialist" in the DOJ Federal Bureau of Prisons. "Conditions of Employment. U.S. Citizenship is Required."

One minute later, at 1:13 p.m., from @elonmusk: "I just can't . . . roflmao . . . the irony is too much," followed by two tilted crying laughter emojis. As you may know, "roflmao" translates to "rolling on the floor laughing my ass off." Elon is laughing in the faces of those who are trying to take him down. And so should we.

Consider for a moment what this must look like to Elon Musk. He is being pursued by the federal government of the United States, one of the largest, most powerful entities on the planet. A gargantuan, unrelenting, inexhaustible adversary run by a bunch of self-serving political hacks, in his view. In the case of the refugee complaint at SpaceX, what did it take to unleash this kraken when the offender is Elon Musk?

One single complaint from just one job applicant. One non–U.S. citizen who filed one of the more than a million job applications received by Space X in four years, to fill a total 11,500 job openings.

In February 2020, a job seeker named Fabian Hutter applied for a job posted on the SpaceX website. The notice said candidates must be a U.S. citizen, a lawful permanent resident, a protected individual, or a person made eligible by the State Department. Hutter's résumé clearly stated that he held dual citizenship in Austria and Canada.

And the weird thing is, rather than discriminate against this foreigner from the outset, SpaceX managers cleared him through a couple stages of interviewing. There was no evidence that his citizenship status affected the decision-making process. They turned him down because of inadequate answers about his motivation for working at SpaceX and a lack of creativity in discussing the Starlink constellation. And SpaceX ended up never filling the listed job, for a technical strategy associate. All of this is stated in SpaceX's legal response.

So, where is the discrimination? Yet Fabian Hutter filed a complaint with the Immigration and Employee Rights section on May 29, 2020, and IER took up the matter with a vengeance. Instantly, it warned SpaceX that the agency "may also explore any pattern or practice of discrimination" prohibited by U.S. law, the record shows.

IER demanded job records from SpaceX across thirteen categories encompassing almost forty subcategories. It wanted to see details on each one of seventeen hundred job openings for everything "from baristas to plumbers to highly specialized engineers," SpaceX reported. A copy of the job listing, the name, title, hiring date, start date, wages, all related documents, and the same details for the staff members who did the hiring.

The IER also requested "thousands of confidential records—including social security cards, passports, and birth certificates—for 3,500 SpaceX employees of every position across nine SpaceX locations nationwide," SpaceX said in its response to the IER complaint. "Yet IER has made no attempt to justify why such wide-ranging subpoenas are justified. . . . Its officious responses to date provide no explanation for why its current request . . . is specific and relevant to IER's purported investigations into SpaceX's hiring practices."

The Musk-owned company had staff spend more than a hundred hours responding to the IER query with more than a thousand pages of documents—and it's not enough! "Deficient in several regards," the agency's potentates told SpaceX lawyers about the company's response. The SpaceX filing says: "IER's enforcement application is the very definition of government overreach . . . based on an isolated, facially meritless national-origin-discrimination charge filed by a job applicant rejected for a position that was never filled, and who was never asked to provide any I-9 [citizenship] records himself."

Also this: "At every turn, SpaceX's good-faith efforts to cooperate with the legitimate scope of IER's investigation have been met with increasingly invasive, burdensome, and irrelevant documentary requests." IER's subpoena for more documents was "unduly burdensome given its lack of relevance." Thus, the agency was engaging in "circular logic—i.e., that the pattern-or-practice documents IER seeks are necessarily 'relevant' to any pattern-or-practice investigation IER can conjure up."

All along, SpaceX argued that it seeks the most highly qualified candidates while following U.S. laws regarding hiring, residency status, and secrecy requirements; and the company pointed out that it already employs hundreds of foreigners. There was no discrimination.

Plus, as a policy matter, why should the government order

SpaceX or any company to hire refugees and asylees—or any foreigner, ever, for that matter—if thousands of qualified Americans and permanent legal residents are applying for the same open jobs? The Immigration and Employee Rights Section had no dog in this fight at all. It is doubtful this case would exist if it involved anyone other than the highest nail, Elon Musk.

When Musk knows he is right, he retaliates with a vengeance. When he turns out to be wrong, he gains by having struck back, nonetheless. By reaching millions of fans, and unleashing thousands of comments in his support, all for punching a bully in the nose. The lesson for the rest of us is to err on the side of speaking out—you always can fix it on the fly. Standing up for yourself in a dispute that matters becomes more important, especially in a business world dominated by social media damnation for mere words rather than actions.

A week after the new investigation made news, Musk and SpaceX struck back. On September 15, they sued Attorney General Merrick Garland, and a chief administrative hearing officer, and an administrative law judge working for said chief administrative hearing officer. Members of Musk's kangaroo court, in other words.

The new SpaceX lawsuit, case number 1:23-cv-00137, was filed in the U.S. District Court for the Southern District of Texas by lawyers with Akin Gump Strauss Hauer & Feld, one of the largest law firms in the world. They argue that the case against SpaceX is unconstitutional, overseen by an administrative law judge who was unconstitutionally appointed because she cannot be removed by the POTUS, and who now was "unconstitutionally denying SpaceX its Seventh Amendment right to a jury trial," by keeping this case out of federal court and confined within the Justice Department bureaucracy.

The SpaceX lawsuit says it has hired hundreds of noncitizens; and that the DOJ "seeks relief on behalf of all individuals who self-identified as refugees and asylees—including individuals who may not qualify for either status." This "could potentially expose SpaceX to penalties and other sanctions under U.S. Export Control Laws, including ITAR," the International Traffic in Arms Regulations that control defense-related exports. "SpaceX is suffering ongoing 'here-and-now' injury because it is subject to coercive proceedings before an unconstitutionally structured agency," the company's attorneys state.

One month later, in October 2023, the Justice Department tried to pull an end around. The Executive Office for Immigration Review published an "interim final rule"—an oxymoron; how can an "interim" rule also be the final one? This rule dictated "that the Attorney General may, in his discretion, review decisions and orders" issued by administrative law judges like the one presiding over the SpaceX refugee-hiring case. Thereby granting the AG new powers.

This prompted SpaceX's attorneys to move for a preliminary injunction to halt the administrative action launched by the Immigration and Employee Rights section of the Department of Justice. They argued it was an unconstitutional awarding of powers that Congress never intended the attorney general to possess.

On November 8, the judge whom SpaceX had sued—Carol Bell, an administrative law judge of the Office of the Chief Administrative Hearing Officer—ruled in the company's favor. She found that SpaceX was entitled to an injunction because it was likely to succeed on the merits of its claim that this new order violated the Constitution of the United States. "Plaintiff will likely suffer irreparable injury if the administrative proceedings are not enjoined."

And there the case has ended, for now; until the bureaucrats at Justice find a new line of attack, which, undoubtedly, they will do at some point. Because, hey, this is Elon.

By this time, the Justice Department had already announced a second case against SpaceX. On August 30, 2023, just six days after the refugee-discrimination case against SpaceX was unveiled, the *Wall Street Journal* reported that Justice had opened a criminal investigation into whether Tesla had cheated shareholders by spending millions on building a new private home for its CEO. The SEC had begun a related civil investigation, as well.

Most compelling of all was the list of materials for this supposed construction: millions of dollars' worth of expensive, sophisticated, specially made, perfectly transparent glass. Reportedly to build a gleaming glass tower of transparency for Elon Musk, the man who freed Twitter, even though he throws an abundance of stones.

A gleaming glass tower could serve as a prominent promotional icon for Tesla and its famous CEO: a symbol of transparency. Every time Elon stayed overnight there, visible to the world as if residing in a glass cube suspended in the air like some stuntman magician, Tesla's brand might benefit from media visuals of this ritual.

The case instantly seemed bogus on its face. Other companies have authorized buying or even building a home for the CEO as part of the compensation package. This is a matter for Tesla shareholders, who can demand a board investigation or sell their stock if they dislike how the company is spending money. Why would the feds involve themselves in this?

At 10:23 p.m. on August 30, 2023, a Fox News clip ran on X, featuring anchor Jesse Watters decrying the glass-house probe: "Knowing Musk's sense of humor, the project's probably a lark. What's that euphemism about throwing stones? We don't know, but we have a hunch these investigations have less to do with glass houses and more to do with Biden exacting revenge on Musk for buying Twitter, the greatest psyop the Democrats have ever owned."

Well said. Although the glass-house slogan is an aphorism ("a pithy observation that contains a general truth," says the *Oxford English Dictionary*) rather than a euphemism ("a mild or indirect word or expression substituted for one considered to be too harsh or blunt when referring to something unpleasant or embarrassing").

This clip was posted by a controversial account called @Kanekoa

TheGreat, with more than half a million followers at the time (now over eight hundred thousand). It is part of a group known as We the Media, which includes influencers in the QAnon movement of conspiracy theorists. Disregarding for a moment Elon's observation that a lot of conspiracy theories are coming true lately. He has interacted with @KanekoaTheGreat at least eighteen times since early 2023, says a summary by the AI search site Perplexity.

Including this one: two hours later, at 12:22 a.m., Elon responded to the @Kanekoa post: "I'm not building a house of any kind, let alone a glass one!" Then @dvorahfr - Déborah, with forty-six thousand followers, chimes in: "There were several articles in France that you were building a huge house in the Italian Alps."

Elon: "What? I'm not building a house anywhere."

@TexasLindsay (182,000 followers): "Pretty sure you're already living in the glass house right now, called X." Good one.

Elon: "More like a glass cathedral lol."

@TexasLindsay: Amen. [Praying-hands emoji, tearful-laughing emoji]

As of this writing, it is unclear whether the glass ever got delivered. It isn't yet known whether Elon did, indeed, intend to build a glass house as his home and changed his plans after the board balked. And it is unclear why anyone other than Tesla directors and shareholders should care. Although Musk was right to refer to a glass cathedral, based on the scale of the order.

This criminal investigation was sparked by only a few complaints from Tesla employees, just as it took only a single complaint from one foreign job applicant to spark the ridiculously broad investigation of SpaceX for alleged discrimination against refugees. A year earlier, in July 2022, Bloomberg had reported that Tesla was conducting an internal investigation of an unusually large order of a special, hard-to-get glass. It had been placed by a Musk lieutenant, Omead Afshar, who ran the Texas Gigafactory and who was said to be quitting the company. Its story said some workers already had been fired. (Afshar would move on to oversee production of the Starship at SpaceX.)

A year later, on July 11, 2023, the *Wall Street Journal* reported about a supersecret operation at Tesla known as Project 42. It cited plans for a glass tower "envisioned in the shape of a twisted hexagon. Other images showed an expansive glass box that appeared to include a residential area." The plans must be for a glass house for Tesla's CEO, it was assumed. The possible project came to the direct attention of Tesla board members "after employees became concerned about how the company planned to use millions of dollars in specialized glass that it had ordered," the *Journal* reported.

"Concerned"? Why should they care?

This is something Tesla shareholders can address if it concerns them, so why is it a matter for the feds? Unless political retaliation were a motive. Then this move becomes more understandable— and even more reprehensible. Because for federal investigators, once they are set loose inside Elon's empire, scrutinizing one narrow thing opens the way for them to examine everything in their search for dirt.

Thusly, two months later, on September 20, 2023, the *Journal* ran a story on Page One saying the Glass House investigation had broadened into a wider look at perks that Tesla might have bestowed on its CEO and largest shareholder (Musk earned almost 13 percent of the company at this point). Headline: "DOJ Probes Musk Tesla Perks Since '17." Lead: "Federal prosecutors are scrutinizing personal benefits Tesla might have provided Elon Musk since 2017—longer than previously known—as part of a criminal investigation examining issues including a proposed house for the chief executive."

Now a grand jury was looking at the case, as well. And, as the old saying posits, a prosecutor can talk a grand jury into indicting a ham sandwich. Or a ham like Elon Musk.

Again, this matter lacks any pressing reason for an intervention by the federal government; it should be left to the Tesla board and shareholders. And no matter what perks Tesla paid to Elon, they pale in comparison with the huge gains in Tesla's stock price in the same period. Would that every CEO were caught up in a similar state of accusation.

Just as isolated complaints can bring the government down on Elon Musk, so did a relatively small number of accidents spark an intensive, two-year federal safety investigation of Tesla and its Autopilot self-driving software system. In August 2021, the National Highway Traffic Safety Administration opened a "broad investigation" of the Tesla Autopilot self-driving system. This was in response to at least eleven accidents in which Teslas using Autopilot "drove into parked fire trucks, police cars and other emergency vehicles," the *New York Times* reported.

Ten months later, on June 9, 2022, the *Times* reported that the NHTSA was "significantly expanding" its investigation. Now it was aware of thirty-five crashes while Autopilot was in use, "including nine that resulted in the deaths of 14 people." This, even though the NHTSA "said it had not determined whether Autopilot has defects that can cause cars to crash while it is engaged."

After almost a year of searching, NHTSA investigators had uncovered zero evidence that the Tesla system is dangerous—yet they were expanding their probe anyway. To cover 830,000 Teslas across all four models (S, 3, X, and Y) sold in the seven years from 2014 to 2021.

A year later, on June 10, 2023, the *Washington Post* published an exposé saying NHTSA data showed that a total of 736 crashes since 2019 had involved Autopilot mode, "far more than previously reported." Headline: "17 Fatalities, 736 Crashes: The Shocking Toll of Tesla's Autopilot." Shocking? Seven hundred thirty-six crashes in eight years out of two million Teslas sold in that time, in a nation with two million car accidents per year.

Also, the *Post* reported breathlessly, while just three traffic deaths had been definitively linked to Autopilot previously, the agency now cited seventeen fatalities, eleven of them since May 2022. Seventeen deaths in four years. This compares with roughly forty thousand traffic fatalities nationwide every year. The NHTSA, instead of focusing its efforts on that bigger picture, prefers to target Tesla. This is an inefficient use of resources, unless it is part of a broader strategy to mess with Elon Musk. In every way possible.

Plus, the rise in total Tesla accidents may simply be a result of having more Teslas on the road. The company sold a total of just shy of 530,000 models from its start in 2013 to 2018. In the four years thereafter, Tesla sold more than five times as many cars, an additional 2.837 million EVs from 2019 to year-end 2022. So, of course, the number of accidents went up. Even at the higher total of 736 crashes of Tesla cars on Autopilot, the rate of accidents is far lower than for all cars in the United States, overall. Let's do the math:

U.S. total: two million accidents per year of a total 290.8 million cars on the road.

This equals one accident for every 145 cars. Annually.

Tesla total: 736 accidents out of 2.837 million cars on the road in four years.

This equals one accident for every 15,418 cars. Annually.

Furthermore, Tesla's official Vehicle Safety Report shows that Teslas with the Autopilot system collectively drove five million to six million miles between each single accident. This is ten times the distance traveled without an accident for all cars in the United States. It also is four times as long as a Tesla that drives without the use of Autopilot software.

So, why are federal regulators cracking down so hard on Tesla? Musk wears his ego on his sleeve, and he readily plays up his hopes for Tesla EVs and the Autopilot system as a safer, 100 percent replacement for the human driver someday. NHTSA regulators are likely to try to prosecute Musk for hype and penalize him for talking too much. If they think they will succeed in silencing Elon Musk, they are bat fucking crazy.

TEASE YOUR CRITICS AND TORTURE YOUR ENEMIES.

Declaring war on short sellers

Whether our world is a sophisticated simulation (very likely, in Elon's eyes) or the one and only base reality (a one-in-billions chance, he says), it is defined by a lot of fakeness—political correctness, false modesty, insincere politesse, and pandering to the press and the elites. Elon Musk lacks time for any of this. He bows to no man or woman, nor anything in between. He says what he thinks and believes, and rarely does he filter it or hold back in any way. He has "fuck you" money, and he acts like it. Wouldn't you?

One example is his feud with Mark Zuckerberg, founder of Facebook. They had been tangling with each other since 2016, when a $62 million SpaceX rocket, carrying a $200 million Facebook satellite, exploded on the launchpad at Cape Canaveral. Zuckerberg posted on Facebook that he was "deeply disappointed to hear that SpaceX's launch failure destroyed our satellite." This was a diss.

A year later, Zuckerberg said on a Facebook Live call that people (like Musk) who sensationalize the dangers of AI "try to drum up these doomsday scenarios. . . . It's really negative, and in some ways, I actually think it's pretty irresponsible." To which Musk countered on Twitter: "I've talked to Mark about this. His understanding of the subject is limited."

In March 2018, Musk tweeted, "What's Facebook?" and deleted the accounts of Tesla and SpaceX as #DeleteFacebook was trending. This, in response to reports that a data firm called Cambridge

Analytica had exploited lax privacy policies at Facebook to gain access to the files of upwards of ninety million people without their consent, which it then used to craft political advertising in the 2016 election.

Musk was in good company. Brian Acton, the co-founder of WhatsApp, helped start the backlash by tweeting, "It is time. #deletefacebook." This was bold, given that he had personally reaped $3.1 billion when WhatsApp was sold to Facebook for $19 billion in 2014. Apple co-founder Steve Wozniak canceled his Facebook account, saying, "With Facebook, you are the product."

In 2022, Musk tweeted: "Facebook gives me the willies." In early 2023, he said Meta's Instagram platform depresses users, and WhatsApp "cannot be trusted."

When news broke in June 2023 that Facebook's parent company, now named Meta, was preparing to release a new Twitter copycat called Threads, Musk lamented on Twitter that the world is becoming "exclusively under Zuck's thumb with no other options." A user cited Zuckerberg's jiujitsu training, and Musk countered on June 20, 2023: "I'm up for a cage match if he is lol."

The next night, Zuckerberg decided to man up: "Send me location," he wrote on Instagram. Musk called and raised: "If this is for real, I will do it." He joked on Twitter, "I have this great move that I call 'The Walrus', where I just lie on top of my opponent & do nothing."

Zuck is five foot seven and weighs 155 pounds drenched; he had trained for two years and completed his first jiujitsu tournament a month earlier. Musk is six foot one and weighs 200 pounds or more and jokes about his love for doughnuts. And a meme was born.

Elon clearly was being lighthearted about this, but Zuckerberg took him seriously. Thus making the joke funnier.

The new Threads app went live on July 5, 2023, drawing worldwide media coverage and landing a hundred million downloads in five days. The "Twitter Killer," the media called it. Hours later, a

Twitter lawyer fired off a letter to Mark Zuckerberg, accusing Meta of hiring dozens of fired Twitterati and engaging in "systematic, willful, and unlawful misappropriation of Twitter's trade secrets and other intellectual property."

On July 9, Musk tweeted, "Zuck is a cuck," and proposed "a literal dick measuring contest." Channeling his inner twelfth grader. A day later, Musk bashed Facebook: "Censorship pays them well."

Soon, Musk was tweeting about the setting for the fight, training with former UFC champion Georges St-Pierre, and updating his posse, posting on August 6: "Zuck v Musk fight will be live-streamed on X. All proceeds will go to charity for veterans." Zuckerberg: "Shouldn't we use a more reliable platform that can actually raise money for charity?" Oh, snap!

This was a snide reference to the infamous crash, the previous May, of Twitter servers as millions of users tried to listen live on the Twitter Spaces platform when Florida governor Ron DeSantis announced his run for the Republican nomination for president.

On August 11, Musk tweeted that the fight would occur at "an epic location" in Italy (the Coliseum), that it would be live-streamed on both X and Meta, and that "everything in camera frame will be ancient Rome, so nothing modern at all." Dana White, president of UFC, told TMZ the fight would break all pay-per-view records.

Two days later, Musk reached out by personal text message to Mark Zuckerberg, offering to do a "practice bout" at his house the following week. Zuck has his own octagon fight ring.

Zuck responded brittlely, "If you still want to do a real MMA fight, then you should train on your own, and let me know when you're ready to compete. I don't want to keep hyping something that will never happen, so you should either decide you're going to do this and do it soon, or we should move on."

Elon: "I will be in Palo Alto on Monday. Let's fight in your Octogon [sic]." And: "I have not been practicing much. . . . While

I think it is very unlikely, given our size difference, perhaps you are a modern day Bruce Lee and will somehow win."

When news of this exchange leaked, it spawned funny memes on Twitter, showing Photoshopped images of Zuck hiding inside his home as Musk knocks on the front door.

Later the same day, Zuckerberg ended this dance: "I think we all can agree Elon isn't serious and it's time to move on. . . . If Elon ever gets serious about a real date and official event, he knows how to reach me. Otherwise, time to move on. I'm going to focus on competing with people who take the sport seriously." So there!

This provided an opportunity for Musk to torture Zuck some more. Musk responded by tweeting, "Zuck is a chicken." Now channeling his inner seventh grader.

It is fun to watch Elon run roughshod over the conventions of so many card-carrying members of the boring, repressed, preachy Establishment. You marvel at the boulder-sized balls on this man, and his ability to find humor in otherwise threatening attacks. And to give as good as he gets.

Thus, Musk can be an inspiration to us in how to handle critics and controversies, a guide for how we can stand up and be heard. Even if this makes you unpopular. Elon Musk cares little about being popular and clearly revels in being heard. We can operate in the same way, at work and, perhaps, in our most nettlesome and difficult relationships in life, whatever they may be.

If someone in your life gives you static, you can learn to let this amuse you, at their expense. You can choose to be the one who pisses off the other side, rather than the one who gets hurt and offended. This Elon Effect ripples through his millions of followers. He posts something on X, and hundreds of comments are posted in response from lesser lights, eager to stand up and add something to his conversation.

Then again, to achieve great things and invent a better future for the world, does Musk really have to be this way? To smack back so hard, and say hurtful things without regard for their impact, to be so unabashedly willing to be the Greater Asshole to get what he wants?

My inclination is to hope otherwise, that greatness falls short of requiring the level of obsession, contempt, and brutishness that we see in Elon Musk. Enjoyable as it is to watch it unfold. Then you consider other great achievers—Steve Jobs, Pablo Picasso, Bill Gates, Mark Zuckerberg, Michael Jordan, Tom Brady, the mercurial TV chef Gordan Ramsay. Even Donald Trump. Jerks every one of them, really. Yet all of them so effective.

Elon reserves special, withering enmity for the mendacious, destructive short sellers who have been his mortal enemy for a decade. They aim to profit from a sharp decline in the stock price of a target company—in this case, Tesla—and some of them traffic in lies and rumors to encourage this to happen.

Tesla, and by extension Elon Musk himself, has drawn the ire and fire of some of the biggest badasses to ever short a stock. They include Michael Burry, the brainy bettor made famous by the book and film *The Big Short*, who earned billions on the collapse of housing prices in the 2008 crash; David Einhorn of Greenlight Capital; and James Chanos of Kynikos Associates, whom I first interviewed in the 1980s.

The latter two men are New York City–based billionaires, and both have gone far beyond simply calling TSLA an overvalued stock. They have fought dirty, accusing Elon Musk of fraud, lies, and sacrificing driver safety to inflate Tesla's stock price.

In the ranks of investing, short sellers are an odious breed with a dark cloud hanging over their heads. They bet on failure rather than success. Yet capitalism is optimism monetized (a saying I coined as the managing editor of *Forbes* magazine). We choose to invest in something only when we have hope that it can grow. And hope is a decision.

Advocates of short selling say it serves as an important restraint on overexuberance in the markets, exposes accounting fraud through rigorous research, and provides liquidity to the markets. More often, however, short sellers are a tax and drag on stocks. They have crushed small, innovative companies that might have been able to survive and go on to thrive. They file bogus company tips with the SEC, then whisper to a reporter that the SEC is investigating the company, then hammer down the company's stock as it falls on the news.

The short seller's preoccupation with misfortune, destruction, and negativity utterly violates the Ethos of Elon. He errs on the upside of optimism, as he told Joe Rogan in their first interview back in 2016 (see lesson 1).

This may be why Musk takes matters so personally on this front. Most CEOs and Wall Street denizens figure that truth and the market will prevail in the long run, so they ignore short sellers and focus on business. Elon Musk chooses, instead, to go to war. He has called short sellers "jerks who want us to die," "the scum of the earth," and "value destroyers." Also saying: "I think short sellers should be forced to wear clown suits" and that they are "betting against America." And, indeed, they are—and you should never bet against the United States.

Thus, Musk has set the standard for CEOs of target companies in forging a scorched-earth counteroffensive to fight off short sellers. Call them out, give them unmitigated hell, razz them and ridicule them incessantly, and celebrate when your stock rises and the shorts take it in the shorts, like a kick in the balls. Because they deserve it.

His chosen theater is the former Twitter, which he made his bully pulpit long before acquiring it in October 2022. Elon tweets spontaneous thoughts and one-liners, often at the expense of his adversaries, and all of it in front of millions of followers on X. The largest part of Musk hostilities plays out for all to see. His trolling tweets draw the ire of his enemies and spawn hundreds of comments and countercomments from his fans, thereby holding up his targets for still more ridicule.

Musk has vowed: "I'm going to make short sellers pay." And he has. Short sellers lost upwards of $12 billion on Tesla from its IPO (initial public offering) in 2010 through 2018. They lost another $3 billion or so in 2019—and a stunning $40 billion, collectively, betting against TSLA in 2020, when the stock climbed 743 percent. The shorts lost another $10.3 billion combined in 2021, as Tesla shares rose another 50 percent.

They were able to recapture $16 billion in profits for the full-year 2022 on a combined bet of almost $20 billion, but by mid-2023, short sellers were back down another $13 billion.

Elon himself perfectly summed up the mission of short sellers in February 2023, in an email to CNBC: "Too often, sophisticated hedge funds have used short selling and complex derivatives to take advantage of small investors. They will short a company, conduct a negative publicity campaign to drive the stock price down temporarily and cash out, then do it all over again many times. The term for this, as you may be aware, is 'short & distort.'"

The shorts "take advantage of small investors" by driving down the price of the shares the small investors hold. They often sell shares they borrow from brokerages including Fidelity and Schwab, which are holding the stocks for the small investors. Wall Street rakes in billions in annual fees from hedge funds for loaning out the shares in client accounts—even though the hedge funds are intent on beating down the price of those stocks.

This is what the shorts have tried to do to Tesla for years. The business media have always been complicit in helping short sellers swarm against a target company, particularly pixel pundits on CNBC and writers for *Barron's* and the Heard on the Street column in the *Wall Street Journal*. They love a good rumor.

Especially starting in 2018, as Tesla started making real progress, the shorts were doing all they could to create bad news for the stock, whether fair and accurate or a concocted pack of lies. They fanned the flames of anything that might bode ill: production delays, $12 billion in losses from 2010 to 2018, and any negative publicity they could find about Elon Musk.

In 2018, Musk's resentment of short sellers hit a new peak of pique, and his hell-bent intention to smack them down got him in trouble with the SEC. Tesla was struggling at the time, running into production delays and automation problems in trying to produce its new Model 3, and racking up billions in losses. Meanwhile, Musk was overpromising on plans for a Tesla semi and touting schedules that raised doubts on Wall Street.

Bettors against TSLA stock had put up more than $10 billion to sell short upwards of 20 percent of the publicly traded shares of Tesla. This is deleterious to a publicly held company. It creates volatility in the stock price and undermines confidence in a company's prospects, and it can preoccupy company executives and distract them from running the business. Further, the shorts create doubts about the company among its partners, suppliers, customers, and employees.

On April Fools' Day 2018, a Sunday, when the stock market is closed, Elon Musk took to his favorite platform at 6:02 p.m. eastern time to dispense some gallows humor: "Tesla Goes Bankrupt," read the headline, followed by a dateline of Palo Alto, California, April 1, 2018. As in, April Fools' Day. It was followed by this: "Despite intense efforts to raise money, including a last-ditch mass sale of Easter Eggs, we are sad to report that Tesla has gone completely and totally bankrupt. So bankrupt, you can't believe it."

This is a stunning, irresponsible thing to say for any CEO of a publicly held company, which is subject to federal regulations regarding public disclosure of material events. It is especially startling when it comes from a company that is under ongoing assault from the shorts. Elon went on, anyway, tweeting a tongue-in-cheek tirade.

There are many chapters of bankruptcy and, as critics so rightly pointed out, Tesla has them *all*, including Chapter 14 and a half (the worst one).

6:02 PM · Apr 1, 2018

Then he tweeted a photo of himself, pretending to be passed out. A cardboard sign on his chest bore the hand-scrawled word *Bankwupt*. As in baby talk. The tweet read: "Elon was found passed out against a Tesla Model 3, surrounded by 'Teslaquilla' bottles, the tracks of dried tears still visible on his cheeks. This is not a forward-looking statement, because, obviously, what's the point? Happy New Month!"

When trading in Tesla shares opened on Monday morning, April 2, they took a dive and ended up down 5 percent on the day. They were back up by Friday. Then on April 10, the Goldman Sachs analyst following Tesla put out a report reiterating his "sell" rating on the stock. On Twitter, a Tesla shareholder said, "This doesn't make me feel warm and fuzzy," and Elon responded: "Place your bets."

The next day, CNBC.com ran a story citing Tesla as the most shorted stock on the market, noting that bets against Tesla had soared 28 percent in the past month to almost $11 billion. The chunk of Tesla shares sold short now exceeded a startling 25 percent of the company's stock.

On April 13, Gayle King of *CBS Morning News* visited Elon, with a camera crew in tow, at the Model 3 plant in Fremont, California. Elon had spent nights sleeping on the factory floor and working around-the-clock to fix production-line problems. He told her he was in "production hell." "I'm definitely under stress, so if I seem like I'm not under stress, then I'm gonna be clear, I'm definitely under stress." He explained his April Fools' tweet thusly:

"There were all those media articles saying that Tesla's going bankrupt. So, I thought, 'Well, I'll just do an April Fools' joke that we did go bankrupt. . . . I mean, it's April Fools'. People should, like, lighten up. Okay?"

Lighten up: part of the Ethos of Elon. And it seems especially apt in these times.

Around the same time (April 2018), Musk began clashing publicly with James Chanos of Kynikos Associates. Jim is a storied stock basher whose deep research had uncovered numerous overvalued, scandal-laden companies in the past four decades. He has been called the LeBron James of short sellers and a "catastrophe capitalist."

He won renown at the beginning of his career in the 1980s, finding fault and accounting flaws in the books of a piano maker named Baldwin-United, which owned a suspect insurance subsidiary, oddly enough. At the time, the *Wall Street Journal* ran a Page One profile of Chanos. I was a *Journal* reporter in New York, covering the Commodore computer company. And Commodore was another target of the shorts. So, I met with Jim, and he helped me pore over the Commodore balance sheet, in search of something wrong. I always appreciated the favor.

From that early win, Chanos went on to be an early doubter of Enron, which later collapsed in one of the largest accounting scandals ever. It was an energy production company that earned rapacious profits via a "black-box" trading unit in energy futures, which turned out to be trading back and forth with itself, basically. He also bet big against China when it seemed invincible, in 2010, admitting later that this backfired.

But Tesla would turn out to be James "Ahab" Chanos's Moby Dick. By April 2018, he had been short Tesla for several years, and Musk tweeted that Chanos was "probably the world's most inaccurate short-seller." On April 26, 2018, Chanos went on CNBC's *Squawk Box* to talk about his own book. He said Musk "may be misleading investors" and "I think Elon Musk has crossed the

Rubicon in terms of making statements to investors that he might rue later."

Chanos was shorting TSLA in a $100 million bet, 5 percent of his total investor funds. He had been short Tesla since the fall of 2015—and losing money on it for years. In 2016, he branded Tesla "a walking insolvency." Chanos was on hard times in a relentless bull market. He wanted vindication—and Tesla was his vehicle for seeking it.

His firm, once at $6 billion in assets under management in 2008, had dwindled to $2 billion in ten years. His most bearish fund, Ursus (Greek for "bear"), by this time was down 70 percent since 2009. Of thirteen companies Chanos had targeted for short sales in the previous three years, only five of them had fallen sharply in value and paid off, profit-wise. And his investment funds were down 10 percent to 20 percent so far in 2018.

A few months earlier, he had likened Tesla to Enron, which collapsed in 2000 in a tangle of fraudulent self-dealing. He told one audience: "Every bull market has its poster children. Tesla is one of the bad ones."

In early May 2018, Musk hosted a disastrous live briefing with Wall Street analysts who follow Tesla stock and advise their clients whether to purchase it. After the close of trading on Wednesday, May 2, Tesla reported its first-quarter earnings, an upside surprise. But the focus instead was on Elon Musk's behavior on the call.

Most senior execs of publicly held companies strain to be polite to Wall Street analysts, viewing them as salespeople for their companies' stock. Why risk insulting them? Elon Musk, by contrast, takes on an adversary wherever he sees one. On the Tesla analyst call, Elon starts off with an unrehearsed opening statement that runs for almost ten minutes, then takes questions from analysts, warning them: "We're going to go as long as there are good questions to answer."

The next five analysts in a row ask about arcane matters rather than the big picture. Then the sixth questioner is up. Toni Sacco-naghi of Sanford C. Bernstein, a frequent guest on CNBC. At this moment, he has a "hold" on TSLA, and on Wall Street a "hold" rating is a polite way of saying "avoid this stock." To Elon Musk, this is the same as putting a "sell" on his stock. This means Toni Sacconaghi is his enemy. Sacconaghi starts asking more arcane questions with a negative bent, and soon Elon interrupts him. "Excuse me. Next," Elon blurts out. "Boring, bonehead questions are not cool. Next?"

Operator: "Thank you. Our next question comes from Joseph Spak with RBC Capital Markets." Nervously, Spak takes the mic:

"Ah. Thank you. Um, the first question is, um, uh, related to the Model 3 reservations," and soon there is a click and a pause of twelve seconds as Elon goes offline, then comes back on-air: "We're gonna go to YouTube. Sorry, these questions are so dry. They're killing me."

Thereupon, Elon has just dissed two prominent analysts in a row, to take a question from a rank-and-file Tesla shareholder with followers on YouTube. Worse, he then lets the YouTuber ask a dozen questions, and they were, indeed, much more interesting. This rude breach of Wall Street protocol made headlines on CNBC and elsewhere. It was labeled "bizarre," and the critical response pushed down Tesla shares by 5 percent in after-hours trading in the middle of the analyst call. Maybe Elon was hiding bad news.

The next morning, Tesla stock was down almost 10 percent. By some estimates, this bungle lopped $2 billion off the total value of the EV maker. Some $700 million of this was reaped as profit by short sellers, Reuters reported. Barron's headline: "Tesla Earnings: Musk Has Problem with 'Boring' Questions, Market Has Problem with Snarky CEO." The story quotes one analyst calling it "one of the most bizarre earnings calls we have ever heard."

Two mornings later, Elon Musk doubled down and assiduously avoided making any apology. And he took another shot at the shorts, firing an opening salvo at 5:20 a.m. eastern time: "The 'dry' questions were not asked by investors, but rather by two sell-side analysts who were trying to justify their Tesla short thesis," Musk explained. Whereas the YouTube questioner "represented actual investors, so I switched to them."

Two hours later, Musk went on a Twitter run:

7:12 a.m.: "Please ignore this thread unless you're interested in a tedious discussion about Tesla stock."

7:35 a.m.: "First, it's important to know that Tesla is the most shorted (meaning most bet against) stock on the market & has been for a while. The 2 questioners I ignored on the Q1 call are sell-side analysts who represent a short seller thesis, not investors."

7:55 a.m.: "The reason the Bernstein question about CapEx was boneheaded," Musk wrote, was because the question had already been answered in the investor letter that went out beforehand.

8:04 a.m.: He further explained why the RBC analyst's question was "absurd."

8:34 a.m.: Elon makes a small concession. "Once they were on the call, I should have answered their questions live. It was foolish of me to ignore them."

Half an hour later, Musk drops a taunt bomb on Twitter: "Oh and uh short burn of the century comin soon. Flamethrowers should arrive just in time." And twelve hours on, at nine o'clock at night: "Looks like sooner than expected. The sheer magnitude of short carnage will be unreal. If you're short, I suggest tiptoeing quietly to the exit."

Sick burn. And entirely true. In that, Elon Musk did, indeed, have a shipment of flamethrowers arriving the next month, delivering on a joke he had made the previous December. Back then, he had tweeted that if the Boring Company sold fifty thousand hats, he would start selling the "Boring Company flamethrower." Just because they were cool.

A few days later, on May 7, 2018, Elon Musk personally bought $9.85 million worth of Tesla shares "to force a burst of the short-covering, which caused Tesla's stock price to increase from $297.50 to $302.77," as a federal judge's opinion would describe in a later lawsuit.

Meanwhile, on May 18, James Chanos did a podcast interview with trader Barry Ritholtz and told him: "I think the stock may not be worth anything on a pure financial analysis basis . . . it is a hopes and dreams stock that the investors have pinned, really, whatever their expectations are on a future—a green future globally—they have put it on this stock. And on this CEO, who has done a really good job in promoting that very vision."

By mid-June, TSLA shares had risen an additional 20 percent. On Twitter on June 17, 2018, Elon Musk further threw down the gauntlet for the shorts: "They have about three weeks before their short position explodes."

The next day, Musk personally bought a second batch of Tesla shares worth another $9.85 million to help offset any downdraft in response to news that Tesla was cutting forty-five thousand workers (9 percent of the payroll). Overall, Musk had pumped $25 million of his personal wealth into buying 72,500 shares of his company. A show of faith.

On June 21, 2018, James Chanos went on the attack again. He reactivated a pseudonymous Twitter account that had been dormant for six months: @WallStCynic, also known as Diogenes. A pretentious title: Diogenes, born twenty-three hundred years ago, was the leader of the Greek movement called the Cynics, just as Kynikos is the Greek word for "cynic." Chanos started trolling Tesla and Elon Musk almost daily. His opener:

"I leave you all for six months, and look what happens." He razzed the carmaker and its thin-skinned CEO. "Again, please don't park your Model 3 in the sun or rain, adjust the windows or wipers, or leave your car when parked." An allusion to various reported problems with the new Tesla model.

In early July 2018, Musk lashed out in a tweet storm fulminating at the media and short sellers. He said Chanos was "a professional Tesla short" and "not a fan of innovation," and he accused a reporter for *Business Insider* of puppeting Chanos's anti-Tesla arguments. Two weeks later, Chanos struck again, going on CNBC's *Fast Money Halftime Report* to say: "What bothers me is not so much the personal stuff and the personal attacks. I'm used to that." So brave of him. "It's the willingness to say things that I think he knows are a stretch, to be polite."

Chanos was being anything but polite. Meanwhile, also in July, Elon Musk clashed with a new adversary who had insulted him: Vernon Unsworth, a stranger to him online who oversaw the rescue of twelve boys and their football coach from an underwater cave where they had been stranded for ten days. Musk had delivered a mini-submarine to the site of the cave, in Tham Luang Nang Non, trying to be helpful.

Unsworth criticized this in an interview on CNN, calling the move a PR stunt and saying Musk should "stick his submarine where it hurts."

Two days later on Twitter, Musk fired three salvos in retaliation, unaware, he said later, of Unsworth's lead role in the cave rescue. "Sorry pedo guy, you really did ask for it," he tweeted. When a follower asked about this, Musk responded: "Bet ya a signed dollar it's true."

A signed dollar: this is a bet I made with my reporters dozens of times when I was at *Forbes* magazine, as we argued over facts and spin. One of my inked dollars once showed up in the cash register of a 7-Eleven in San Francisco. Which was a little insulting, frankly.

When a BuzzFeed reporter contacted Elon Musk for comment, he emailed back, noting that Unsworth had lived in Thailand, which in some places was infamous for child prostitution. This led the UK tabloid the *Sun* to publish a story on July 20, 2018: "Elon Musk's Bizarre Tweets Are Raising Red Flags on Wall Street as BILLIONS Are Wiped Off Shares in the Billionaire Inventor's Companies." The story said a venture capital investor, Gene Munster, had written an open letter complaining that Musk was "fueling an unhelpful perception of [his] leadership—thin-skinned and short-tempered."

Good point, actually. After an uproar on Twitter, Musk deleted the tweets and apologized to Unsworth, saying, "His actions against me do not justify my actions against him." Unsworth later sued Musk for defamation in federal court in Los Angeles, seeking $190 million in damages: a ridiculous number on its face. In December 2019, after a four-day trial, a jury took all of ninety minutes to exonerate Elon Musk. Musk testified that he thought Unsworth was just "some random creepy guy" who was "unrelated to the rescue."

He added: "I assume he [Unsworth] did not mean literally to sodomise me with the submarine, just as I didn't literally mean he was a paedophile," as the *Sun* in the UK reported it.

Then on July 25, 2018, reports surfaced that a particularly toxic Tesla critic on Twitter, @MontanaSkeptic, had shut down his pseudonymous account after Elon Musk personally contacted the poster's boss. This sparked a backlash and helped set off the entire TSLAQ movement, a posse of virulently anti-Tesla short sellers.

TSLA is the company's stock symbol, and the letter Q is attached to a dead stock symbol by the New York Stock Exchange and Nasdaq after a company goes belly-up. As the shorts want Tesla to do.

Musk, admittedly, gave short sellers plenty to criticize. He issued overly confident forecasts on production and financial results. He always reached too far, because this way he got a lot farther even if he fell short of bold goals. But the shorts then overplayed the problems: isolated reports of battery fires, any traffic accident, a contrived road test of a Tesla mowing over a child-sized dummy in the middle of the street, missed shipment projections, federal investigations of Tesla marketing claims and software upgrades, and Musk's clashes with politicians and the media.

On July 31, 2018, Bloomberg reported that famed short David Einhorn of Greenlight Capital was giving up his Tesla lease. Elon went on Twitter that night at 3:46 a.m. to serve up the sarcasm, saying, "Tragic. Will send Einhorn a box of short shorts to comfort him through this difficult time." On August 10, David Einhorn, having received a shipment of shorts from Musk, went on Twitter and gamely tried to joust on Musk's chosen platform, declaring, "He is a man of his word! They did come with some manufacturing defects." This was a jab at short-seller reports of production flaws on the new Model 3.

Musk took another jab at Einhorn, telling him to don the shorts and "post a selfie." In the same month, Elon took aim at James Chanos again. He called Chanos a "pedo guy"—again with this! Apparently, alleging this perversion aspersion is a favorite form of put-down in the Musk arsenal of insults. Chanos threatened a lawsuit against Musk but never filed one.

And on August 7, 2018, another Elon tweet created another controversy—this time, a huge one. Fed up with short sellers and their more than $12 billion in outstanding bets against Tesla stock, Elon tweeted a shocker:

Elon Musk ✔ 🇽
@elonmusk   Subscribe   ···

Am considering taking Tesla private at $420. Funding secured.

12:48 PM · Aug 7, 2018

Elon Musk ✔ 🇽
@elonmusk   Subscribe   ···

Shareholders could either to sell at 420 or hold shares & go private

2:13 PM · Aug 7, 2018

"Funding secured": those two words would raise the ire and finger-wagging of the Securities and Exchange Commission. If Elon Musk had, indeed, lined up funding for a go-private offer for Tesla, he would have had to review it with the board and disclose this to shareholders as a material event.

Tesla shares popped on the Musk tweet, producing further losses for the shorts. The stock had been at the pre-split level of $340, and shares jumped 11 percent to $380 by the day's end. Jim Chanos was on his annual summer sabbatical in Greece, and still he managed to sell short an extra load of Tesla shares after Elon's shocking tweets.

At first it looked like a prank: the price of $420 cited by Elon invoked a popular street reference to smoking pot, 420. Later the same day, Musk put out a message to Tesla employees, saying this possibility of going private was legit. The note told them that "as the most shorted stock in the history of the stock market, being public means that there are large numbers of people who have the incentive to attack the company."

Tesla stock went back down, and short sellers made the most of this, reaping a billion dollars in profit in just two weeks after the August 7 "funding secured" tweet from Elon Musk. Their victory would be fleeting.

In mid-September 2018, *Institutional Investor* ran a long profile of Jim Chanos: "How Jim Chanos Uses Cynicism, Chutzpah—and a Secret Twitter Account—to Take on Markets (and Elon Musk)." Deck: "The LeBron James of short-selling talks Ponzinomics." In the article, Chanos likens Tesla to the Theranos fraud and the shady drug company Valeant.

Sample sound bite: "This is the first instance where I think we are seeing a possible fraud unspool itself in real time, with social media commentary." And: "Crazy companies are trading at really crazy valuations now, on top of their bad businesses. That's kind of exciting. Tesla—I mean, that's some monster valuation for a company that might be bankrupt."

Tesla's "monster" stock market value in September 2018, when the article ran, was just north of $40 billion. Three years later, in October 2021, TSLA would top *$1 trillion*: up twenty-five-fold in three years. How much more wrong could Chanos and the short sellers have been?

The SEC filed a lawsuit against Musk on Thursday, September 27, 2018, alleging "a series of false and misleading statements regarding taking Tesla, a publicly traded company, private." That was case number 18-cv-8865 in the Southern District of New York. Simultaneously, case number 18-cv-8947 was filed against Tesla itself. It alleged that the company failed to implement controls to assess whether its CEO was disseminating information on Twitter that, instead, should have been filed first with the SEC under the antiquated Securities Exchange Act of 1934.

The day after the SEC filed the two lawsuits, shares of Tesla tumbled 14 percent amid fears that the SEC might try to remove Musk from Tesla entirely. Musk and Tesla settled the two SEC complaints two days later, on a Sunday, without admitting or denying guilt. Each party agreed to pay the SEC $20 million apiece. At the time, Musk's net worth was at $25 billion, and the fine amounted to eight ten-thousandths of 1 percent of his wealth.

Elon also agreed to step down as chairman for three years and hand the title to an outside board member, add two independent board members, and establish a new committee of outside directors to impose safeguards "to oversee [his] communications."

The next day, on a Monday, Tesla shares rose back up 17 percent on the settlement. The SEC promised to give the $40 million in fines to "harmed investors." Meaning: short sellers and tort lawyers. This had to have galled Elon Musk greatly, and five days later, he let this show. At 4:16 p.m. on October 4, 2018, he bit the hand that had just slapped him, tweeting about the SEC:

"Just want to [say] that the Shortseller Enrichment Commission is doing incredible work. And the name change is so on point!" And minutes later: "Sorry about the typo. That was unforgivable. Why would they be upset about their mission? It's what they do."

This scandalized the obedient business media. Here is how Bloomberg covered it: "Elon Musk insulted the Securities and Exchange Commission days after settling a fraud lawsuit with the U.S. agency, potentially imperiling a deal that allows him to remain Tesla Inc.'s chief executive officer." Note: the deal never was in peril.

The SEC required Tesla to add two new outside directors, so Musk filled one seat with a close friend: Oracle software billionaire Larry Ellison. Ellison had put up $1 billion for a Tesla stake, and when reporters asked why, he responded: "Why should I believe you, as opposed to my friend Elon? We're out here watching this rocket land, which I think is really cool, and you're there in front of your Apple Macintosh, and typing up an article saying Elon's an idiot. This guy's landing rockets. He's landing rockets on robot drone rafts in the ocean. And you're saying he doesn't know what he's doing. Well, who else is landing rockets? You ever land a rocket on a robot drone? Who are you?" *Touché.*

Ellison's $1 billion investment in Tesla had soared thirteenfold to $13 billion in the next year, all of it at the expense of short sellers.

In April 2019, Musk clashed anew with short sellers. David

Einhorn put out an investor letter saying, "The wheels are falling off—literally." Bada-bing! He claimed Tesla was "on the brink," demand for its cars was ebbing, and it was looking like Lehman Brothers in late 2008, when it collapsed and turned out to be one of the greatest short calls Einhorn ever made. A decade later, he was still dining out on it.

The same month, Musk struck back at another short seller, and his assault would rile up the TSLAQ pack. Tesla filed a lawsuit and a request for a restraining order against one short named Randeep Hothi, who was behind the Twitter account @skabooshka.

Hothi had spotted a new Model 3 on the highway, which seemed to be undergoing a test of the Autopilot self-driving system. He followed it in his car and filmed it, almost crashing into the Model 3, the Tesla court filing claimed. The complaint also said that two months earlier, Hothi had had a scuffle with Tesla employees in a parking lot at the factory in Fremont, California, and sped off in his car and almost struck a worker.

The attempted restraining order outraged the TSLAQ posse, and members raised $100,000 for a defense fund for Randeep Hothi. The effort was led by another Musk target: @MontanaSkeptic, also known as Lawrence Fossi, who had ceased attacking Musk back in July 2018 after Elon called the guy's boss. The enemies you make stick around longer than you want.

Tesla filed a lawsuit seeking a restraining order against Hothi and dropped the case when Hothi demanded discovery. Elon Musk, meanwhile, sent an email to Hothi's employer, claiming Hothi had harassed and almost killed a Tesla worker.

So, Randeep Hothi sued Elon for defamation in August 2020. A judge refused to dismiss the case in January 2021, and the two men finally settled in April 2023—for a payment of just $10,000 from the billionaire to @skabooshka. One-tenth of what Hothi had raised for legal fees. A Pyrrhic victory for each side, and a financial win for the warring lawyers, as always.

In July 2019, Tesla announced reaching a major milestone: its promised goal of producing five thousand new Model 3s per week. The shorts had insisted this never would happen. A month later, the EV maker reported its first profit in two years. In November 2019, Elon Musk came to blows once again with two of his most formidable nemeses: Chanos and Einhorn. Musk tweeted about Chanos: "So many reporters gave Chanos airtime when he called Tesla a worthless fraud. Now that he has been proven wrong, silence."

As for Einhorn, he increased his attacks on Musk. In his quarterly letter to his investors, Einhorn wrote that "TSLA appears to continue to spin positive PR ahead of the safety and fair treatment of its customers." He said, "Elon Musk knowingly orchestrated a significant fraud by arranging the $2.6 billion acquisition" of SolarCity, a company run by Musk's cousins (which was disclosed). "For now, the accepted reality appears to be that Elon Musk is above the law."

Elon returned fire in the wee hours of November 8, 2019, posting a letter on Twitter at 2:24 a.m. eastern time. He accused Einhorn of making "numerous false allegations against Tesla," saying, "It is understandable that you wish to save face with your investors, given the losses you suffered from Tesla's successful third quarter."

He concluded: "Finally, please allow us to send you a small gift of short shorts to help you through this difficult time."

At year-end 2019, Tesla revealed that it had shipped 367,500 cars for the year, a company record—and Elon took it to the shorts again. In December 2019, one of the world's largest pension funds, Japan's $370 billion Government Pension Investment Fund, issued a ban on letting its shares be loaned out to short sellers. Musk applauded the move, tweeting at 3:33 in the morning of December 3: "Bravo, right thing to do! Short selling should be illegal."

In January 2020, TSLA shares suddenly jumped 80 percent higher in a single month, crushing the short sellers. This prompted a story in the *Wall Street Journal* on February 9, 2020: "The Agony of the Tesla Bears: $8.4 Billion of Losses in Five Weeks." It mentions another Elon Musk tweet in recent days: "This past week, he tweeted three fire emojis as Tesla's share price skyrocketed, which some speculated was a reference to how shorts were getting burned."

This fierce rise in the stock price was in part a result of the short sellers' own bets. As the share price rose and some shorts panicked and raced to buy Tesla stock before it could go up even more, their new demand sent the price of Tesla up higher still. A "short squeeze." By July 1, 2020, TSLA shares had tripled in price, and short seller losses were soaring amid more short squeezes. One day later, Musk took another shot at the SEC on Twitter, making a tacit reference to a profane street-language invitation:

"SEC, three letter acronym, middle word is Elon's."

For the uninitiated: S(uck) E(lon's) C***. Ross Gerber, a wealth advisor and a Tesla bull with more than three hundred thousand followers on Twitter, stepped in to post a warning to the CEO: "Dangerous." Elon shot back, "But sooo satisfying."

Four days later, Elon Musk went on Twitter to rub it in, offering shiny red satin short shorts for sale. On the back was the initialism "S3XY," for "sexy," and for the four models in the Tesla line: the S, Model 3 (the reverse E), X, and Y. He offered an online link for orders—and so many followers instantly clicked on it that they crashed the Tesla website.

By year-end 2020, short sellers had lost a massive $40 billion for the full year. It likely is one of the largest losses ever on one short-seller target in a single year. It was more than Jim Chanos could bear. (See what I did there?) As the year ended, he admitted he had slashed his exposure to Tesla by covering a big portion of his bets and taking his losses. As he told Bloomberg: "It's been painful, clearly." If he were to meet Elon Musk personally, he says he would tell the man: "Job well done, so far." That was the closest Chanos could come to conceding defeat. And . . . he would be back.

As 2021 began, on February 4, Elon invoked nuclear bomb

inventor J. Robert Oppenheimer, who, while watching the first ever atomic bomb explode in a test, thought of Hindu scripture: "Now I am become Death, the destroyer of worlds." On Twitter, Musk bragged: "I am become meme, Destroyer of shorts."

More than two years later, with still more successes racked up by Tesla, Elon would resurrect the Oppenheimer tweet on July 22, 2023. *Oppenheimer* was now a hit movie, competing at the box office with *Barbie*, which spawned a portmanteau as meme: Barbenheimer.

The shorts lost another $10.3 billion combined in 2021, as Tesla shares rose another 50 percent (according to CNN.com). In 2022, hostilities between Musk and the shorts—and the SEC—continued. In February, news headlines said the Justice Department was investigating two prominent Tesla short sellers. Elon emailed a CNBC reporter about this:

"I am greatly encouraged by the Justice Department investigating short sellers," he wrote. "This is the something the SEC should have done, but, curiously, did not."

Two weeks later, Musk took his war on the SEC to another phase, accusing the agency of harassment since his settlement over the "funding secured" tweet five years earlier. He made a new filing with the federal judge overseeing his settlement with the agency. A Musk lawyer wrote that the SEC had "broken its promises" and had been "weaponizing the consent decree by using it to try to muzzle and harass Mr. Musk and Tesla."

The Musk complaint noted that the SEC, more than four years after initially settling with Elon Musk, still had failed to pay out the $40 million in damages collected from Musk and Tesla. It was supposed to go to Tesla shareholders who supposedly were "damaged" by Musk's tweet.

Two days later the SEC responded, saying Musk and his lawyers had never brought up any concerns about the payout previously, and that a distribution system was still being set up.

The shorts were able to recapture $16 billion in profits for the full-year 2022 on a combined bet of almost $20 billion. Tesla stock fell 65 percent on the year, the Nasdaq stock index fell 33 percent, and the S&P 500 fell 18 percent. But by the end of 2022, Tesla had manufactured almost 1.4 million EVs: 1,369,611, to get precise about it. Which is something that Elon would do.

In January 2023, Elon Musk and Tesla were the defendants in a lawsuit alleging securities fraud, filed by a class of shareholders in federal district court in San Francisco. This related to the fallout from Musk's "funding secured" tweet back in August 2018. Tesla lawyers tried unsuccessfully to move the trial out of San Francisco, where Musk was hated by thousands of Silicon Valley liberals for buying Twitter and letting Donald Trump back on the platform.

The trial lasted three weeks. The lead plaintiff, Glen Littleton, said he lost $3.5 million when he sold out of Tesla after the Musk tweet. As Musk took the witness stand, the opposing attorney asked him about short sellers and Tesla, and Musk went smart-mouth:

"I think most people don't know what short seller means. It's sort of—is it sort of a seller of small stature? Is it like medium and tall sellers?" he told the jury. He went on to say that selling short is "a means for, in my opinion, bad people on Wall Street to steal money from small investors." Musk also told the jury, "Just because I tweet something does not mean people believe it or will act accordingly." Words to live by.

On Friday, February 3, 2023, the federal jury cleared Elon Musk of the charges. Tesla went on to fall 20 percent in April, emboldening the shorts, but the next month it went on a tear, gaining 60 percent by mid-June.

With the stock up 110 percent year-to-date by this time, short sellers had piled up another $13 billion in losses for the year thus far. That was a loss of 80 percent from where they first placed their bets. They were down $5 billion in the first half of June, and they lost $816 million in a single day as TSLA's price rose 3.5 percent, research firm S3 Partners told MarketWatch.

TSLA shares, which had started the year at $108 apiece, hit almost $300 a share by July, and they were still above the $230 mark by November. On November 17, 2023, the *Wall Street Journal* ran a Page One story on James Chanos and the muted announcement that he was closing up his short-seller shop for good. Chanos's hedge fund had had $6 billion under management in 2008, the *Journal* reported, and now it was down to $200 million. Two days later, Chanos vented on his X account, @WallStCynic.

"For those of you asking why I don't address some of my harshest critics directly," he wrote, "please understand that I give those with clear signs of mental illness wide berth, and you should too." He mentioned "Cult Member[s]" who believe "rockets exploding are a 'success'" and said, "Your ignorance and resentment is [*sic*] tiresome."

Sour grapes from a master of the universe on Wall Street. A week later, I published an op-ed on Newsmax.com, "Betting on Doom Is a Losing Proposition." Second paragraph: "This marks an ignominious end for one of the smarter, cockier and more self-righteous short sellers ever to practice the dark art of betting on destruction. Chanos, as part of the job, trafficked in aspersions, rumors, and, at times, assertions of chicanery where none existed."

Apparently, this struck a raw nerve. Jim Chanos responded with fury on Elon Musk's platform, impugning my ethics, questioning my intelligence, and insisting that he actually had been a market bull since 1996. As if! Sounding like a mean girl, Chanos tweeted to his almost two hundred thousand followers: "Wow, Dennis. I'm not sure what is worse . . . your inability to understand basic financial concepts, or your lack of journalistic integrity."

He argued that since 1996, he had "in effect been long the market, and short individual stocks." Knockout punch: "And if you had reached out to me before writing such an embarrassing column, I would've explained that profitable concept in a way that even you might've understood."

Condescending and a little silly: Jim Chanos made his career as a dark prince of short selling, so he should just own it. Frankly, I was surprised he had deigned to notice my column at all, let alone respond to it, even disparagingly. But why is it that the richest, most powerful men also have the thinnest skin? James Chanos and Elon Musk included.

Chanos quit the game, and Elon Musk and Tesla arguably are the biggest factors in his retreat. But the short sellers, who qualify as Elon's number one enemy, may never stop dogging him. Every time Tesla shares spike nicely, some detractors will descend in an attempt to push the price back down. It is just as certain that Elon Musk will counterpunch them at every turn, making fun of them and holding them up to ridicule before his millions of followers.

This is as it should be. Short sellers bet on darkness and doom, and this is anathema to the Musk mystique. Elon lights a candle and errs on the side of hope. Everyone else can fare better in life by doing the same.

MOST PEOPLE ARE LOAFERS. WORK HARDER THAN YOU EVER HAVE BEFORE.

Emailing staff after midnight, telling them to show up at 2:00 p.m. with proof of coding

Elon Musk works a lot harder than the rest of us. Maybe this is why his net worth is at twelve digits. Actually, no: superhard work might have gotten him to the first ten digits ($1 billion), enough to live as lavishly, safely, and securely as any person could ever desire. And still support eleven children and their three different moms. And give away most of his wealth to good causes.

To work so furiously even after passing that ten-digit milestone shows that Musk is pursuing something much larger than wealth itself.

It is an undeniable truth: Elon Musk works twelve hours a day or more, seven days a week, in pursuit of things that can make the world a better place. At the start of his career, he took two weeks of vacation—in twelve long years of labor. He takes off only three or four days a year and puts in 120-hour workweeks. For years, he slept only three or four hours a night; more recently he shoots for six hours with the help of Ambien, after an intervention from sleep champion Ariana Huffington a few years ago.

Elon brandishes his work ethic as an element of leadership-by-example. He always has made a big deal about how hard he works, as a way to inspire employees at the companies he oversees. He wants them to know he will never ask of them more than what he is willing to give to their common corporate cause. And because

Musk himself works incredibly, maniacally hard, this enables him to ask the same of the people who work for him. Loafers need not apply.

In 2010, a baby-faced Elon did an interview with Bambi Francisco Roizen of Vator News, and she asked him three tips for entrepreneurs. He told her you must be focused on something you are confident will have high value to others and be "really rigorous in making that assessment," able to differentiate between believing in "new ideals and sticking to them, versus pursuing some unrealistic dream that doesn't actually have merit."

Be "extremely tenacious," Musk advised, and, "You just have to put in, you know, eighty-hour, eighty- to hundred-hour weeks, every week." Simple math: "If other people are putting in forty-hour workweeks, and you're putting in hundred-hour workweeks, then even if you're doing the same thing," he said, "you will achieve in four months what it takes them a year to achieve."

To which Bambi admiringly replied, "I like your work ethic."

In the summer of 2018, when Tesla was battling short sellers and struggling mightily to meet a much-promised Musk target of producing five thousand new Model 3s per week, Musk famously slept on the factory floor overnight for three weeks straight at crunch time at the Tesla plant in Fremont, California. He spent the entire twenty-four hours of his forty-seventh birthday at the worksite, never stepping outside once. He told this to reporters for the *New York Times*, which on August 16, 2018, ran a story on a "tearful interview" with him, as the media described it. He opened up about the pressures and turmoil at Tesla and the immense hours he was putting in at the Fremont factory.

Arianna Huffington, the liberal socialite, entrepreneur, and sleep advocate, read the *Times* piece and saw it as a plea for help. One day later, unsolicited, she published an open letter to Elon on her website, Thrive Global.

She told him, "You've exhausted yourself working 120-hour

weeks at the expense of seeing your children and your friends. You've had days-long stretches where you shut yourself inside the Tesla factory and don't even go outside. You don't take vacations. There's no way you can connect with your amazing vision and creativity when you don't give yourself time to reconnect not just with those you love but also with yourself and your wisdom."

And this: "Working 120-hour weeks doesn't leverage your unique qualities, it wastes them. You can't simply power through—that's just not how our bodies and our brains work."

Huffington went on to tweet this to Elon publicly on August 17, 2018, imploring him, "Dear Elon, please change the way you work to be more in line with the science around how humans are most effective: You need it, Tesla needs it and the world needs it." She attached an online link to her open letter.

Who asked her? Musk had little patience for this slacker advice. He tweeted back two days later at 5:32 in the morning, 2:32 a.m. where he was on the West Coast. "Ford & Tesla are the only 2 American car companies to avoid bankruptcy. I just got home from the factory. You think this is an option. It is not." Elon getting right to the point, if less than charmingly so. At the Fremont factory right then, the last thing he needed was a reexamination of work-life balance. What he wanted was for everyone at the plant to sit down, pick up an oar, and row.

He was sleeping on the factory floor to inspire his employees, and Arianna was cramping his style. Five years later, on a call with Wall Street analysts in October 2023 to discuss third-quarter financial results for Tesla, Musk went off-script. He told his listeners he slept on the floor back then for his workers: "Whenever they felt pain, I wanted mine to be worse."

To him, extremely hard work is the X factor that will determine a person's success at achieving what everyone else sees as impossible. Nobody will get anywhere if everyone sloughs off and rejects hard work. People will, instead, stay mired in mediocrity and underachievement, and they will be fine with it. This is how they got there in the first place. Elon Musk views the business world as an arena devoted to hard work. Why else would he come here to the United States, where enterprise and sweat equity are rewarded with the bountiful fruits of your labors?

He puts his work ethic above most everything else but his children, and even that exception may be debatable, as is true for many successful executives who also are fathers. We see an awful lot of images of Elon, hip-toting the towheaded toddler he calls X, and the media love it—but when is he ever seen with the rest of his posse of offspring? Rarely, if ever.

Musk's obsession with work flies in the face of the American Way of late. The current popular view of hard work might be boiled down to one word: "Suckers!" An inbred cultural resistance to working all out has festered for decades, as if, somehow, we are being misled or exploited by the owners of capital who were so demonized by Karl Marx. This, after two centuries of *extremely* hard work. Maybe those two things are related.

Hard work is a lost art in America—and America once was the hardest-working nation on Earth, really. For our first two hundred years, we extolled the virtues of hard work and the American Puritan ethic. We admired work and celebrated it and viewed it as the honorable, heroic path to creating our own wealth and handing it off to our heirs. And then . . . something went wrong. And awry. The United States, once the land of opportunity, began to sound more like the land of envy.

Instead of seeing a person's wealth as a reflection of hard work, Americans started to see it as an inherent injustice. "The rich are not paying their fair share," the slogan went. Yet in 2022, the top 1 percent of earners raked in 22.2 percent of income and paid in 42 percent of all income tax revenue; the bottom 50 percent earned 10.2 percent of income and paid 2.3 percent of tax collections. Despite this, politicians preach about the woes of "wealth inequality" and criticize those at the top for failing to pay their "fair share" of taxes.

The charge falls flat when applied to Elon Musk, who paid a massive tax bill of $12 billion to the United States in 2021, the highest individual tax payment in our nation's history. This was more than the annual taxes paid by all of the residents in two states combined: Vermont ($4.5 billion in federal taxes collected) and Wyoming ($4.7 billion). It also was more than the total federal tax collections in each of eleven other states: Wyoming, Alaska, Montana, North and South Dakota, West Virginia, Maine, Hawaii, New Mexico, Mississippi, and Idaho.

Rewards are possible for us, too, if we are willing to work hard enough and are smart about it. This is why each of us, in our jobs and in our lives, should always go the extra mile, and perform at as high a level as possible in the bid to achieve success and connection. We should do this if we are in a leadership position because, like Elon Musk, we should lead by example and work harder than our underlings. Or we should do this because we are rank-and-file players who want to get picked to join a good leader's team.

Working harder is even more important as artificial intelligence spreads like a virus throughout the economy and grows smarter and smarter with each passing month and year. Some 30 percent of the work involved in each job now can be done by AI without human involvement, as opposed to 30 percent of all jobs in their entirety, and this portion will increase.

Those of us who use that freed-up time to summon new creativity and devise new sources of revenue and growth will have better chances of surviving the workplace devastation that AI will wreak on the world. Those who slack off and play videogames will get left behind. Mounting evidence shows this has been happening for the past ten years or more.

A lot of Americans have forgotten how to work hard, or they have given up on it. One Gallup poll, taken in September 2022 and updated in May 2023, found that fully half of workers privately admit to "quiet quitting," staying in their jobs and sloughing off. They lack the balls to just up and quit and search for a better job to make a positive change in their lives, choosing to languish, uninspired and unproductive. The sad truth is that fewer people are working now than in the past fifty or so years, as a percentage of the total population. Those who are still working are putting in fewer hours and pushing for even fewer hours still and fewer days in the office.

In 1850, the average worker in the United States put in up to 3,650 hours per year at work, an average 70-hour week fifty-two weeks per year. A century later, by 1987, U.S. workers were putting in less than 2,000 hours total, which works out to 37.5 hours per week, fifty-two weeks per year. By 2022, we were down 5 percent more, to 1,892 hours per year, about 36 hours per week.

This means we work almost six hundred hours a year less than the average worker in India, which equates to 24 percent less work per year. We trail even the long-dormant, all but moribund economy of Japan, where the median age of the population is almost fifty, while the median age in the United States is only thirty-nine. We are younger, yet working eleven hours less per year than the Japanese.

Men are the biggest part of this dropout problem. In the past two decades, the largest addition to the ranks of the non-working came from men who left the workforce and stopped looking for any job at all. In 1970, 80 percent of working-age men in the United States held full-time jobs, powering a national GDP of $1 trillion a year. Fifty years later, the U.S. economy was twenty times larger at $21 trillion GDP, yet the participation rate for men had fallen to just 69 percent in January 2020, and to just 66.2 percent in April 2020 amid the Covid lockdowns (according to the Richmond Fed).

Women, in the same span, went from a Labor Force Participation

(LFP) rate of 43.3 percent in 1970 to 57.8 percent in January 2020. It dropped almost three points amid the Covid crisis to 54.6 percent in April 2020, according to data from the St. Louis Fed.

Thus, men's participation rate fell by 14 percent overall, as women's LFP rate rose 26 percent in the same fifty-year span. Moreover, this decline in male labor participation goes deeper than just older men who retire; the slide is also occurring in the "prime age" group of twenty-five- to fifty-four-year-olds. Their rate is down from 92 percent in 2000 to 89 percent in 2019, and 87.6 percent during the Covid lockdown. The indolence is worst among the youngest men, and this bodes ill for the future of work. Here is the bleak picture painted by government reports and academic studies:

Young men work less than their fathers and grandfathers did. More of them have left the workforce than in fifty years. Twice as many go an entire year with zero hours of work now, compared with the year 2000. They sit at home and fail to help out around the house, playing videogames four hours a day, and one-third of them take opioids or have a criminal record.

In 2015, men ages twenty-one to thirty worked 203 hours less in total paid time than this age group worked in 2000, a drop of 12 percent in that span. In 2016, fully 15 percent of men ages twenty-one to thirty had worked *zero hours* in the previous year, and this was double the portion back in the year 2000. As one study understated it: "Not only have the hours (worked) fallen, but there is a large and growing segment of this population that appears detached from the labor market."

These idle men are a lazy and lallygagging lot, government data show. Though they lack a job, they spend only forty-nine minutes more per day on "household activities" than men who work full-time. And these non-working males spend less time "caring for household members."

In fact, the biggest difference in time usage between employed men and these non-participators is "leisure and sports," according to the American Time Use Survey in 2019.

The layabouts spend almost four hours more on fun *every single day* than working men. Primarily, they are playing videogames. Quite literally. These goldbrickers are already getting lost in simulations inside the simulation.

Startlingly, the vast improvement in game graphics and realistic play in the past twenty years is cited as being responsible for 75 percent of the precipitous drop in total work hours for men ages twenty-one to thirty. This, in a study published in February 2021 in the *Journal of Political Economy*. Their reduction of more than 200 hours, or 12 percent of working time, from 2000 to 2015 is much steeper than the 8 percent decline (163 hours) for men ages thirty-one to fifty-five in the same period.

In the meantime, the time these young men spent on videogames and other online recreation increased by a stunning and disturbing 60 percent from 2004 to 2017. The journal study cites gaming and online leisure as contributing to a 2.2 percent decline in working hours among young men, responsible for three-quarters of the reduction in working hours over all in this cohort.

Elon Musk plays videogames, too, but he still works ten or fourteen or eighteen hours a day.

The study discusses other factors, too. One 2014 survey estimated that one-third of non-working men have criminal records. Almost half of non-working men reported taking pain medication on a daily basis, and one-third of all male non-workers are on prescription painkillers like opioids, says a 2017 article by Princeton University's Alan Krueger.

...

Among all able-bodied, working-age Americans today, almost 40 percent of them are idle and at home on the sofa. In January 1970, when less than half of women worked in jobs, the national LFP rate was at 60 percent of all able-bodied, working-age Americans. The rate peaked at 67 percent some thirty years later, in 2000, and by January 2020 it was down to 63 percent. Then it fell to just 60 percent in the Covid trough of April 2022, a level last seen in 1970; it rose to 62.8 percent by late 2023.

Meaning 37.2 percent of us are able-bodied, under age sixty-five, and sitting at home at a time when the media and our leaders keep insisting a "labor shortage" afflicts America and that only millions of new immigrants can fix this. What's up with that? If we worked harder as a people, if more of us deigned to land a job when, clearly, millions of unfilled jobs are available, no labor shortage would exist. Two corollaries to this: if more employers were more generous in their approach to compensation and raises and employee stock plans, more Americans would go back to work; and if government offered better tax breaks for retraining and hiring the idle, more companies would invest in this goal.

The cynical erosion of our work ethic in more recent years has accelerated since the Covid crisis that roiled the world from 2020 to 2022. The U.S. government handed out $2 trillion to businesses and individuals in just one year's time. This produced a live, nationwide test of two conservative economic arguments: that inflation results from government's expanding the supply of dollars chasing after an unchanged supply of goods; and that handing people too much free money gives them an incentive to work less. Both would prove to be painfully true.

The U.S. government paid out a total of more than $800 billion to households from March 2020 to March 2021, in three tranches. For a family with two tax filers and two children, this amounted to an extra $11,400. This was a huge increase when median household savings stood at only $5,300. And when more than one-third of Americans had too little cash to handle a $400 emergency, a Federal Reserve study shows.

On top of this largesse, the Small Business Administration distributed another $1.2 trillion in grants and loans to businesses in the same period, with the intent of forgiving the loans to keep the locked-down businesses afloat. A total of $200 billion likely went to fraudulent recipients, a report by the SBA's Office of Inspector General found in June 2023.

In the aftermath of this windfall, in exchange for slashed productivity or zero increase in output, employers now have a hard time getting their staffs to show up at the office. At all. In the fall of 2023, Amazon empowered its thousands of managers to start firing people who refused to show up just three days every week. Wimps. One year later, in September 2024, Amazon upped the ante: "corporate employees"—some 300,000 people—must resume showing up in person at the office five days a week by January 2025. This must be so difficult for them.

Elon Musk lacks patience for such precious ways. On a call with Wall Street analysts to review Tesla's financial results for the third quarter of 2023, Musk went off-topic to say that the work-from-home advocates give off "real Marie Antoinette vibes." Factory workers, restaurant servers, and delivery people have to be there in person, he told his listeners, adding:

"How detached from reality does the work-from-home crowd have to be? While they take advantage of those who cannot work from home."

For the better part of two hundred years, our nation prized the goal of equality and handing every individual an equal opportunity for success, and the rest was up to us. Politicians today preach "equity" rather than equality, divvying up identical portions of the fruits of labor and distributing them evenly to everyone, regardless of how many or few hours they contributed.

This political and media focus on "equity" further contributes to the antipathy against hard work. If everyone is entitled to receive an equal share of the upside, even the fuck-offs who contributed almost nothing to production, why bother working harder than anyone else? We learned this in grade school when we were taught the legend of Jamestown and Captain John Smith in the early seventeenth century. Remember?

The term *American Dream* was coined by James Truslow Adams in 1931 in his book *The Epic America*, which billed hard work as the foundation of same. Forty years later, the word *workaholic* came into vogue as a cautionary label. In the 1980s, "work-life balance" became a thing, and by 1990, Boomers had yielded to Generation X, or the "slacker generation," born between 1965 and 1980. A decade later this group was supplanted by a far bigger generation, the Millennials, born between 1981 and 1996.

The Millennials sought a higher purpose in their pursuits at work and were more adamantly focused on work-life balance. Read: less work, more life. Raised on tech, they parlayed remote work and flexible hours into serving themselves rather than their employers. Now they yearn for work-life "integration," which basically means they want to make their lifestyle the number one priority and find work that can fit around that. Which seems out of balance.

Generation Z (born between 1997 and 2012) is just now beginning to enter the workforce. Technology is intrinsic to their lives, and they have never been without it. Inclusivity and diversity and "social justice" are the lingua franca of their day. That is nice, for them. Albeit this preoccupation with work-life "balance" and a leisurely lifestyle, among all three younger generations to succeed the Baby Boomers, may lack sufficient regard for ambition, wealth creation, and working overtime to buy, say, a new home.

This is the mindset that Elon Musk encountered in late October 2022, when he took over Twitter. And this is why Twitter employees were about to get a shock to the system. All told, Twitter had run up almost $4 billion in net losses in eight of the previous ten years (2012 to 2021). This, despite logging more than $20 billion in sales in that period. It had two profitable years in (2018 and 2019) but was back in the red the next three years in a row, including a $300 million loss in 2022 as Musk stepped in.

Despite this woeful performance, Twitter's incumbent staff of eight thousand people comprised a well-paid, pampered, and self-satisfied lot. Median compensation for all workers was at a jarring $236,000 a year. This means half of them earned *more* than that sum. Their stock options cost $900 million a year.

On Wednesday, October 26, 2022, two days before a court-imposed deadline requiring Musk to close the Twitter deal, he strolled into headquarters in downtown San Francisco while carrying a large white porcelain sink. He posted video of himself entering the Twitter lobby, tagged with the puckish pun, "Entering Twitter HQ—let that sink in!" Elon also changed his Twitter name to "Chief Twit," for a time.

The next day, even before closing the deal, Elon fired a phalanx of senior officers that included CEO Parag Agrawal, CFO Ned Segal, legal and policy chief Vijaya Gadde, and general counsel Sean Edgett. And on Friday the twenty-eighth, the acquisition formally went through.

The following Thursday, November 3, a company-wide email went out to Twitter staff, telling them that, by nine o'clock the next morning, they would receive an email with the subject line "Your Role at Twitter." The next day, in a single, instant 50 percent whack, half the people on the payroll got emails telling them, "Today is your last working day at the company."

Ultimately, six thousand would get the gate, an 80 percent cut, as well as forty-four hundred of the fifty-five hundred contractors Old Twitter had employed, another 80 percent cutback. As Musk explained at a *Wall Street Journal* conference in London in May 2023, "There were a lot of people that didn't seem to have a lot of value. I think that's true at many Silicon Valley companies," where "significant cuts" could be made while "in fact increasing their productivity."

He elaborated: "Twitter was in a situation where you'd have a meeting of ten people and one person with an accelerator and nine with a set of brakes."

Anyone who has managed workers knows the 80/20 rule: only 20 percent of the staff works really hard and produces 80 percent of the value of the whole group. They do so by working let us say twice as hard as the slackers to produce four times as much of the value. And those 20 percent are the ones you keep tapping for still more work, because they get it done. Instead of creating obstacles and problems.

Musk imported several dozen managers from Tesla and SpaceX, in a move that would bring yet another federal investigation. Bosses started advising people to work twelve-hour days, and top Tesla engineers vetted the engineers at Twitter to pick the best ones. The reductions, swift and remorseless, would rivet Silicon Valley: How could Musk axe 80 percent of staff and keep the platform running unhindered? In the next year, Twitter's monthly users would double to 550 million people worldwide, with only a fraction of the old staff.

In the second week of Musk's tenure at Twitter, at 2:39 a.m. eastern time on Wednesday, November 10, Elon sent out his first email to his newly acquired employees. In 276 words, he apologized for his first message being so blunt and warned "the economic picture ahead is dire." In the fifth of seven paragraphs, he drops the mother of all bombs, telling them:

"The road ahead is arduous and will require intense work to succeed. We are also changing Twitter policy such that remote work is no longer allowed unless you have a specific exception." Which Elon must approve. "Starting tomorrow (Thursday), everyone is required to be in the office for a minimum of 40 hours per week." He ends by saying: "I look forward to working with you to take Twitter to a whole new level. The potential is truly incredible!"

Elon leads all of his companies this way: he paints a dire picture to unite his teams and steel them to be valiant and work even harder under this do-or-die, existential threat.

The next day, Thursday the eleventh, Elon gave the staff at Twitter headquarters twenty minutes' notice and, at 2:00 p.m., held his first public meeting with employees since the takeover. The intense, quirky session lasted almost an hour, and a transcript was leaked to the Verge. He starts by emphasizing the "immense" potential of Twitter as "an incredibly valuable service to the world . . . where you have a battleground of ideas that can hopefully take the place of violence in a lot of cases. So, people can just be talking instead of physically fighting."

Which sounds funny now, after Musk went on to challenge the much smaller Mark Zuckerberg to a UFC match.

"I think we could actually be a force for peace, which would be amazing," Musk tells the crowd. This will require reaching a billion people, and creating more dialogue among different countries, and expanding as a multimedia platform with more video, and challenging YouTube for influencers, and adding payments to the platform.

"And payments really are just the exchange of information," Musk tells his new recruits. A moderator asks an employee's question, and Musk turns to verification of accounts as a way to block millions of bots from invading the site, then a short-form video, then how long it usually will take him to respond to an email from them. He adds:

"And I'm also for like, 'Hey, let's have some fun and let's have some adventure here.' Let's just try some crazy stuff. And if it doesn't work, we'll stop it. And if it does work, we'll amplify it. But I think that's really fun and exciting."

His audience, it was clear, felt otherwise. A questioner asks about YouTube personalities, and Musk instantly says Twitter should offer them 10 percent higher compensation and see how it goes. "Let's do that. Okay, great. So, you will do that?" Inaudible exchange.

Musk: "Okay, collectively, you'll do it. Great. Please do it. Let's take action. I'm a big believer in having just a maniacal sense of urgency. So, if you can do it after this meeting, I would do it after this meeting. Just a maniacal sense of urgency. Like, if you want to get stuff done, maniacal sense of urgency. Just go 'aah!' Hardcore!"

Moments later, he mentions that "subscribers" might be a better label than "followers" on Twitter, which "sounds more like, do you have a cult or something? And I'm like, I guess I kind of *do* have a bit of a cult, but like, not everyone wants to be a cult member, you know?"

An extra subliminal message therein for his audience: join the cult or move on.

Then employees ask a few questions about working remotely vs. coming into the office, and Musk minces few words and tells them, "We need to be default in the office and for a reasonable amount of time. It's not like some crazy number of hours. I'll do crazy hours in office but I'm not asking everyone else to do crazy hours in the office." Leading by example, and using a qualifier: less than crazy hours *in the office*, which leaves plenty of time for work at home.

A worker asks what "the big vision" is. Musk answers: "Well, I mean, I don't know. I don't have a great answer to that. But I can tell you, philosophically, what works at SpaceX and Tesla is people being in the office and being hardcore, and a small number of people can get a tremendous amount done in that situation."

His team on the Tesla Autopilot system is all of 150 engineers, who outperform rival teams of three thousand people, he says, adding: "I'm a big believer that a small number of exceptional people can be highly motivated and do better than a large number of people who are pretty good and moderately motivated. That's my philosophy. Those who go hardcore and play to win, Twitter is a good place. And those who are not, [I] totally understand. But then Twitter is not for you."

Wow. Addressing them like grown-ups, and they were unprepared for this. Then an employee testily asks him, "Why is our leadership trying to increase attrition rate if we're already under-staffed and barely able to keep things running?" Whiner. Nega-tivity.

Musk: "I'm not trying to increase attrition, but I think we are not understaffed. I think we are overstaffed. That is my opinion, which you're welcome to disagree with."

Another employee returns yet again to the work-from-home peel-back: "Are you asking us to return to the office just to get on calls with other offices? . . . Why are you asking this?"

Elon loses patience: "Let me be crystal clear. If people do not return to the office when they are able to return to the office, they cannot remain at the company. End of story."

Got it yet? Nope. The worker responds: "That's not my question. Even if people return to the office, the offices are separate offices. We won't be in person anyways." Impertinent at best.

Musk again: "Yes, but you can still maximize the amount of in-person activity. Tesla is not one place either. Basically, if you can show up in an office and you do not show up at the office, resigna-tion accepted. End of story." Again with the end-of-story.

This prompted a Twitter employee named Yao Yue to tell her colleagues on Twitter: "Don't resign, let him fire you." This way they could draw severance payments. For this, Yue got fired days later. In October 2023, a regional director for the National Labor Relations Board filed a complaint alleging that X née Twitter had violated federal law prohibiting employers from punishing workers for communicating with workmates regarding their working con-ditions.

This seems an overreaction to the firing of one smart-mouthing employee, but, then, Elon Musk is the highest nail.

At a later NLRB hearing, Twitter defended its right to fire Yao Yue on the grounds of insubordination and said she was a supervi-sor who wasn't covered by law. On July 9, 2024, an administrative law judge threw out the NLRB complaint, siding with Twitter's argument that Yue wasn't covered by the rules the agency had invoked.

A week after his first in-person meeting with staff, Elon sent an after-midnight email on November 16, issuing a new challenge to his shell-shocked troops: they must commit to a new, "hardcore" culture at Twitter that will demand huge sacrifice and hard work. The company is shifting to an engineer-driven business that "will need to be extremely hardcore."

Those who leave will get three months' pay. For those who stay, "This will mean working long hours at high intensity. Only exceptional performance will constitute a passing grade." They must decide within twenty-four hours and vote by clicking an icon in Elon's email.

The next day, Elon got his answer. Hundreds more from the Twitter old guard quit. They trumpeted their noble departures on Twitter with salute emojis and #LoveWhereYouWorked.

Hours later, the liberal, government-supported radio network NPR ran a story headlined "Twitter Employees Quit in Droves After Elon Musk's Ultimatum Passes," writing "Twitter has been convulsed with chaos. . . . The new wave of departures is adding to fears that Twitter is losing critical expertise in . . . how it handles toxic and illegal content." Illegal content? There is almost no such thing, other than child porn and state secrets that would endanger the U.S. military.

Yet a group of Democrats in the U.S. Senate sent an open letter to the Federal Trade Commission, demanding an investigation of Twitter and saying Musk had "taken alarming steps that have undermined the integrity and safety of the platform." A hasty jump to judgment.

A media consultant told NPR, "Musk's new belief that employees should take a 'hardcore' approach to work is likely going to make things worse." He cited "so much research out there that says if you overwork people, it literally kills them," adding, "And now he's turning to the remaining people, many of whom I'm sure have terrible survivor's guilt, who have to sit there and work these obscene hours. . . . We are looking at one of the worst financial transactions in history, and possibly one of the worst executives in history."

Reality check: these people had cushy, unproductive jobs at a hip company, and they gladly accepted three months' pay to quit, yet the media regarded them as prisoners at a gulag.

A day later, after midnight where he was on the West Coast, Elon Musk sent out an email plea to programmers: "Anyone who actually writes software, please report to the 10th floor at 2 pm today. Before doing so, please email a bullet point summary of what your code commands have achieved in the past ~6 months, along with up to 10 screenshots of the most salient lines of code. Thanks, Elon." Pretty intense.

Then he followed up with two more emails, telling his programmers they must show up unless they have a family emergency, and saying to those who resided elsewhere, "If possible, I would appreciate it if you could fly to SF to be present in person. I will be at Twitter HQ until midnight and then back again tomorrow morning." Leading by example, again.

Nobody there was working harder than Musk, who, in the opening weeks of his takeover, once again took up residence at a company site to work all-nighters and crash overnight, whether on a factory floor or in an empty office. Albeit later he would reveal that he was sleeping on a sofa in an unused library, as he told his BBC interviewer six months hence.

Late one night a couple of weeks in, Musk once again played to his employees by emphasizing his commitment to laboring for long hours to do whatever it took to make Twitter work: "I've been at

Twitter SF HQ all night. Will be working & sleeping here until org is fixed," he tweeted. He later deleted the message, likely for legal considerations.

Remarkably, and ridiculously, this tweet would help spark a city investigation of the company. In early December, San Francisco city inspectors began investigating whether Elon had violated zoning regulations by setting up an illegal hotel at Twitter offices. All because he had set up beds so his people could put in longer hours and sleep on-site.

The city action was responding to a complaint filed by half a dozen disgruntled ex-employees whom Musk had just fired. San Francisco was battling a tattered image for rampant homelessness, high crime, and gruesome random murders that draw headlines around the world, but the city devoted inspectors to tackle the *real* problem: Elon and his minions sleeping on sofas overnight at the office.

Just weeks earlier, a ten-month-old infant crawling at a public playground had come into contact with stray fentanyl and had overdosed. Elon tweeting: "So city of SF attacks companies providing beds for tired employees instead of making sure kids are safe from fentanyl. Where are your priorities!?" Fair question.

For Elon Musk, buying Twitter was unwise, inefficient, and impulsive, and it was a standing invitation to hassle and harassment. From regulators, and politicians, and the media, and fired employees, and resisters who stayed. And all of this, for what? And why? The answers lie in the next chapter, and in the next lesson, coming right up.

FREE SPEECH IS EVERYTHING. STAND UP AND BE HEARD.

The Twitter Files and Musk's Montoya moment on CNBC

One year after Elon Musk bought Twitter, it was looking like a sucker's bet, perhaps the worst bet he had ever made. Even for a guy with more than $200 billion in net worth at the time, this had to hurt. A multibillion-dollar blow to one humongous ego.

After Musk paid $44 billion to buy his favorite digital playground on October 27, 2022, skittish advertisers fled the platform to wait and see what Elon would do to it. Ad revenue—Twitter's lifeblood—plunged 60 percent in the ensuing year. By October 2023, the market value of Twitter, now rebranded as X, had plummeted almost 60 percent to just $19 billion.

This was a loss, on paper, of $25 billion, and Elon Musk personally bore almost $20 billion of this red ink. The steep drop was even more painful in terms of where else that same $44 billion could have been invested. Had Elon Musk pumped $44 billion into Facebook stock, it would have soared to $125 billion one year later. Fuuuuuuck!

Not to worry: X, née Twitter, remains the single most important media platform in the world. It is a platform for citizen videos of urban warfare in the Israel-Hamas war; official, breaking-news statements of government officials and politicians; and investigative threads that are striking for their depth and expertise. X makes stars of unknown political newcomers, such as Vivek Ramaswamy.

On X, Tucker Carlson, fired by Fox News, started a new show

and garnered 120 million views for his first episode, and 60 million and over 100 million views for his second and third shows, respectively, and he continued to draw tens of millions more, no cable network required.

And on X, on December 10, 2023, a live Spaces call featured the disgraced conservative talk-show host Alex Jones, whom Elon Musk had just allowed to rejoin the platform after a ban imposed by the old regime five years earlier. Jones was joined, unexpectedly, by Musk, Ramaswamy, General Mike Flynn, and the controversial MMA fighter Andrew Tate, stanchion of toxic masculinity. X can make odd bedfellows.

That was just a warm-up for what followed on August 24, 2024: Elon Musk's two-hour live SpaceX call with Donald Trump, which drew more than 27 million listeners (almost triple the audience for a top-ten prime-time network show) and a billion interactions.

Musk insists that what he calls "X (fka Twitter)" (fka for "formerly known as") ultimately will be worth $250 billion, on a scale with the current valuations of Coke and Toyota. Buying Twitter accelerated a dream Elon has harbored for more than twenty years: X as "the everything app," a digital nerve center for hundreds of millions of people managing their own lives.

They will use it for banking and paying bills, collecting receivables, buying and selling stocks and ETFs, shopping online, buying tickets to concerts and sports events, listening to podcasts and music, watching TV shows and movies, and doing anything and everything they do online now on dozens of different websites. And all along, X will skim a teensy sliver of the financial exchanges. This would free the platform from relying on advertising sales that provide over 90 percent of the revenue at Google, Facebook, and most all social media platforms.

All of this, however, misses the real point. For Elon Musk, buying Twitter was about something more important than money, more important than mining intrinsic value inside a troubled company.

In truth, this deal was always about freedom of speech: unleashing it, restoring it, and paying homage to it. And teaching a civics lesson to the media, politicians, and millions of people who have lost sight of the First Amendment and its centrality to the American way of life.

Musk himself made this clear, famously and profanely so, on November 30, 2023, in a live onstage interview with Andrew Ross Sorkin, a *New York Times* editor and anchor on CNBC. It was the shot heard round the advertising world: Go fuck yourself.

Elon had been at the center of another media storm in recent weeks, over a single, supposedly antisemitic tweet from a random X user, which he had endorsed. The liberal censorship group Media Matters for America had capitalized on this by pressuring advertisers to abandon the X platform.

According to a defamation lawsuit filed by X in U.S. District Court in Texas, MMFA ginned up a biased story claiming X ran big brands' ads next to pro-Nazi content. This prompted Disney, Apple, CNBC owner Comcast, and a few other big brands to halt ads on X. Yet, in truth, as X lawyers later set out in a lawsuit filed against Media Matters in U.S. District Court for the northern district of Texas, the liberal NGO had manipulated search results to force these rare ad match-ups to happen. It used a bogus account that followed only thirty feeds, all of them pro-Nazi, and then a reporter clicked on the feeds so many times that fifteen times as many ads appeared per hour as usually occurs on X. This produced all of fifty such bad ad pairings out of 5.5 billion impressions on X that day. One ad was seen by only two users—and the Media Matters reporter on the story was one of them.

Media Matters denied these allegations, claiming the lawsuit was intended to bully X's critics into silence. In August 2024, U.S. District Judge Reed O'Connor rejected an MMFA request that would have led to his recusing himself from the case, which remains pending.

Amid these charges of antisemitism leveled at Elon Musk, he had just returned from a previously planned trip to Israel to meet with Prime Minister Benjamin Netanyahu. While there, Musk viewed gruesome videos of Hamas terrorists slaughtering Israeli civilians in the October 7 massacre. He wore a dog tag he had received on behalf of the hostages held by Hamas. It was inscribed: "Bring them home."

In the interview with Sorkin at the *New York Times* DealBook Summit, Musk sat across from him onstage at the Frederick P. Rose Hall at Lincoln Center in New York, he took hold of the dog tag and said: "And I said I would wear it as long as there was a hostage story remaining. And I have."

Then Sorkin asks him, "What was that trip like? . . . There's a public perception that that was part of an apology tour, if you will. . . . There was all of the criticism, there was advertisers leaving. We talked to [Disney CEO] Bob Iger today."

Elon: I hope they stop. Don't advertise.
Sorkin: You don't want them to advertise?
Musk: No.
Sorkin: What do you mean?
Musk: If somebody's gonna try to blackmail me with advertising, blackmail me with money, go fuck yourself.
Sorkin: But—
Musk: Go. Fuck. Yourself. [*Stunned, the audience titters nervously.*] Is that clear? I hope it is. Hey, Bob, if you're in the audience. That's how I feel. Don't advertise.

Consider the nerves of steel it must have taken for Elon to say this, publicly at an event sponsored by the *New York Times* and covered by CNBC, when advertising revenue is the main income source at X. Consider what it must have felt like to him at the moment: the rush of adrenaline to his solar plexus, the whooshing sound as blood pumped through his ears, the nervous excitement in his gut from having shocked the audience inside the hall.

Sorkin then asks him about the business model for X and a shift away from ad revenue, and Elon interrupts: "GFY." He goes on to say, "So, actually, what this advertising boycott is gonna do, it's gonna kill the company. And the whole world will know that those advertisers killed the company, and we will document it in great detail." And when the advertisers protest, he will tell them, "Tell it to Earth."

Go. Fuck. Yourself. For more than two hundred years, the media business has been driven by advertising revenue. And in two centuries, Elon Musk may be the only media mogul to publicly issue this invitation to intrusive advertisers that try to infringe on free speech.

If this had been anyone else refusing to be blackmailed by corporate money, he would have been lionized by the American media—they would have thrown around fawning phrases like "saving democracy." But, in reality, they care about free speech only for me, not for thee. And their antipathy toward Elon Musk runs deep.

Musk prizes the distinctly American, constitutionally guaranteed freedom to say what you want, about whatever you want, without being muzzled by government. Nor by, in his particular case, societal rules of protocol and political correctness. He calls himself a free-speech absolutist, and this means almost everything is allowed to be said without government intervention. Even hate speech and dreaded "disinformation" (lies) and "misinformation" (inaccuracies).

This emphatic stance has been part of his belief system for at least twenty years. It goes beyond the right to free speech. Musk believes that only by exercising free speech can we let ideas compete in the intellectual marketplace, in the media, in politics and policy, and in business. The CEO who stifles dissent and discourages debate ends up cutting off innovation and suffocating potentially great ideas. The executive who welcomes competing views before making the final decision inspires more confidence and sparks more creativity from those he leads.

President Trump has always taken this approach to welcoming divergent views and letting ideas compete, as POTUS and in his business career. In the public relations field, a founding father, Gershon Kekst, would let his senior executives fight it out at the conference table while he sat there wordlessly, speaking up only at the end to render a final decision. For Musk, rival ideas are welcome but must be expressed in a positive vein, offering alternative solutions rather than just pointing out a flaw. He lacks patience for woe-is-me Eeyores who express doubts without pitching a positive fix.

Never go to your boss with a problem: go to him or her with a solution.

On X and everywhere else, Elon Musk would rather thrash it out in front of everyone, with no holds barred and all insults and profanities allowed, than defer to government censors. The search for solutions and common ground is worth the risk of hurting someone's feelings. This can substitute for war, in his view.

This is anathema and scandalous to the fragile souls who now dominate the conversation on MSNBC, CNN, and other woke outlets, in the halls of Congress, on university campuses, and among Millennials and Gen-Zers in the workplace. And some members of this mob are doing all they can to take down Elon Musk and silence free speech on the platform he controls.

They fret about "harmful content" and call for restraints on X, in particular. "Harmful": as if words on a smartphone screen can leap out and smack us in the face. This is overdone—wimpy, even. And if this makes some folks want to flee to a "safe space," their lives have been too free of the hardship that provides perspective.

The litany of public officials calling for unconstitutional restraints on free speech is long and disturbing. In 2019, Kamala Harris, who later would take President Biden's place as the Democrat nominee in the 2024 election, advocated banning the Twitter account of then President Trump and said:

It should be taken down. And the bottom line is that you can't say that you have one rule for Facebook and you have a different rule for Twitter. The same rule has to apply, which is that there has to be a responsibility that is placed on these social media sites to understand their power. They are directly speaking to millions and millions of people without any level of oversight or regulation. That has to stop.

For a lawyer who was once the state attorney general of California, this shows a shocking level of ignorance of First Amendment protections. Government lacks any authority to oversee or interfere with social media content, whether it is accurate or misleading. Likewise, her running mate, Minnesota governor Tim Walz, in 2020 declared that misinformation and hate speech are unprotected by the First Amendment—patently false.

Former secretary of state John Kerry similarly dissed the First Amendment in September 2024 at the World Economic Forum's Sustainable Development Impact Meetings in New York. Kerry, who travels by private jet while preaching about the supposed climate-change crisis, publicly lamented that "the dislike of and anguish over social media is just growing and growing, and part of our problem—particularly in democracies—in terms of building consensus around any issue, it's really hard to govern today."

He added, "Our First Amendment stands as a major block to the ability to be able to just, you know, hammer it [a biased source of misinformation] out of existence. So what you need, what we need is to . . . win the right to govern by hopefully having, winning enough votes that you're free to be able to implement change." His chilling clincher: "And to me, that is part of what this race, this election, is all about. Will we break the fever in the United States?"

This Democrat desire to rein in certain kinds of speech already has gone too far. In September 2024, in California, Governor Gavin Newsome signed into law three bills related to AI "deep fakes." One of them, AB2655, went into effect immediately to apply to the presidential election and state and local elections.

AB2655 imposed a ban on AI-generated political parodies that mimic a candidate's voice and image, starting four months before Election Day and extending two months after. It requires platforms to restrain, label, or take down these parodies under penalty of fines and lawsuits filed by the state or private individuals. This is a clear violation of the First Amendment. It just is.

Several lawsuits challenging the new laws were filed instantly, including one by the Babylon Bee, a satirical website that relies heavily on parody, and another by Christopher Kohls, aka "Mr. Reagan," who produces political content. On October 2, a federal judge in Sacramento granted a request for a temporary injunction in the Kohls case. This blocked the new law from affecting the coming election. Happily.

Yet this de facto threat to our constitutional republic is spreading into Congress. Also in September 2024, a video popped up on X showing Congresswoman Alexandria Ocasio-Cortez, a member of the ever-shrinking liberal "Squad," saying this:

> You know, I do think that several members of Congress, in some of my discussions, have brought up media literacy, because that is a part of what happened here, and we're going to have to figure out how we rein in our media environment so that you can't just spew disinformation and misinformation. It's one thing to have differing opinions, but it's another thing entirely to just say things that are false, and so that's something that we're looking into.

Actually, AOC, saying things that are false is entirely protected by our right to free speech. Deal with it. It is no wonder that Elon Musk is so fervently devoted to the First Amendment: It is under attack like never before.

In our own personal lives, we can take inspiration from Elon Musk and map to his behaviors. Many of us take our First Amendment rights for granted, and we fail to exercise them. As more radical actors in our society mount a united campaign to overturn and rewrite our way of life, more members of the long-suffering silent majority must stand up, speak up, and make themselves heard.

Exercise your First Amendment right to freedom of speech, and do it daily. Elon does.

In his reverence for the First Amendment, Musk is driven by the zeal of a convert. Born in 1971 in South Africa, he immigrated to Canada in 1990 and moved to the United States in 1992 to attend the University of Pennsylvania. A decade later, at age thirty-one, he became a U.S. citizen. Thereby, he appreciates the First Amendment more than most Americans. It runs all of forty-five words and covers the four pillars that make us America: freedom of religion, speech, press, and peaceful protest. It says:

"Congress shall make no law respecting an establishment of religion, or prohibiting the free exercise thereof; or abridging the freedom of speech, or of the press; or the right of the people peaceably to assemble, and to petition the government for a redress of grievances."

Only 60 percent of Americans understand that even hate speech is protected by the First Amendment. More than one-third are unaware that it also protects film, artworks, music, books, and online commentary. Alarmingly, 36 percent of us say it is more important to prevent hate speech than it is to *preserve* free speech. One-quarter of people say hate speech should be outlawed entirely—a disturbing view. Another 37 percent of people are neutral on the idea. These anti-free-speech views are even stronger among the young.

Almost 60 percent of people believe political correctness hampers free speech, but fewer people are speaking up. Close to 40 percent of respondents said they have withheld expressing an opinion because they feared reprisal. Half have never shared a political opinion on social media. These stats are from the Freedom Forum Foundation's random-sample survey of three thousand Americans on their First Amendment beliefs, taken annually for the past twenty-five years.

...

Twitter made its debut in 2006, and it took four years for Musk to release his first tweet in June 2010. Ever since, the platform has been his favorite outlet for exercising his own form of unfettered speech. His spontaneous tweets have gotten him into trouble, long before he bought Twitter, and in spite of his repeated vows to cool it.

The "pedo" slur he hurled at a cave-rescue hero in July 2018 got him sued, though he won the case because . . . free speech! One month later, Musk put out the "funding secured" tweet that cost both him and Tesla each a $20 million fine paid to the SEC.

The topic of his swaggering Twitter presence came up again when Musk sat down for his record-breaking podcast chat with Joe Rogan. At the end of more than two and a half hours of talking, drinking whiskey, and smoking a pot-filled "blunt" that sparked worldwide headlines, Musk said he was off social media. Except for Twitter, "because I kind of, like, need some means of getting a message out, you know," he said, as the transcript shows.

Rogan: "Well, what's interesting with you, you actually occasionally engage with people on Twitter. What percentage of that is a good idea? Probably 10 percent, right?"

Musk: "I think it's on balance more good than bad, but there's definitely some bad. . . . There are a vast number of negative comments, so, for the vast majority of them, I just ignore them. Every now and again you get drawn in, it's not good. You make mistakes."

Joe Rogan comforts him: "We're all human, we can make mistakes."

...

By almost any measure, it was a mistake for Elon Musk to buy Twitter. The social media outlet had feeble finances for years before Elon took a shine to it. As 2022 unfolded, Twitter was on track to lose $3 billion in the coming year.

Despite this, Twitter stock in 2022 was priced at 88 times its revenue per share, compared with 5 times revenue per share for Facebook. Twitter traded at 180 times its per-share earnings, compared with 16 times earnings at Facebook. So, Twitter stock, pound for pound, was more than 10 times as expensive as Facebook stock.

Elon started buying up shares in Twitter anyway, drawn to it in part because he was such an enthusiastic user. When he announced his $54-a-share bid for the company on April 4, 2022, he made it clear in a letter he wrote to the Twitter board of directors that free speech was paramount:

Bret Taylor
Chairman of the Board,

I invested in Twitter as I believe in its potential to be the platform for free speech around the globe, and I believe free speech is a societal imperative for a functioning democracy.

However, since making my investment I now realize the company will neither thrive nor serve this societal imperative in its current form. Twitter needs to be transformed as a private company.

As a result, I am offering to buy 100% of Twitter for $54.20 per share in cash, a 54% premium over the day before I began investing in Twitter and a 38% premium over the day before my investment was publicly announced. My offer is my best and final offer and if it is not accepted, I would need to reconsider my position as a shareholder.

Twitter has extraordinary potential. I will unlock it.

This was in characteristically cocky leadership style for a man on a roll. Twitter's board responded a day later by adopting a "poison pill" that would flood the market with new shares if Musk or anyone else acquired a stake higher than 15 percent. This would vastly dilute and reduce the value of the shares that the unwanted suitor had just acquired.

On April 14, Musk sat down for an interview at the Tesla Gigafactory in Austin, Texas, with TED Talks owner Chris Anderson. In the recorded chat, Elon told him:

Twitter has become kind of the de facto town square. It's important to the function of democracy. It's important to the function of the United States as a free country and on many other countries and to help freedom in the world.

Musk also said, "This is not a way to make money. My strong intuitive sense is that having a public platform that is maximally trusted and broadly inclusive is extremely important to the future of civilization. I don't care about the economics at all."

And this beauty: "If I acquire Twitter and something goes wrong, it's my fault, 100 percent. I think there will be quite a few arrows."

Prophetic of him. And overstated on a key point: Twitter is only as vital to democracy as the people, their leaders, and the media decide to make it. In the United States, only forty million people are on X every day, meaning three hundred million Americans are elsewhere. Users are fickle. X may yet get left behind and become the next MySpace and all but disappear. Democracy will survive, somehow.

Ten days later, on April 24, Twitter directors reversed course suddenly and accepted the offer. Careful what you wish for, Elon Musk.

This came as the bottom was dropping out of the stock market. The tech-heavy Nasdaq index had peaked at 15,860 in November

2021, and by mid-June 2022 it was at 10,600, down 33 percent. So, Musk tried to bail on the deal in July, citing fake bot accounts and Twitter management's lack of transparency about them. Twitter stock, near $50 in April 2022, fell below $40, down 23 percent in that span.

Twitter, despite having first spurned Musk's offer as inadequate and bad strategy, then sued him in Delaware Chancery Court on July 12 to force him to go through with the deal. A Pyrrhic victory at best: Why force yourself on a suitor who no longer desires you?

But this being the case, if marriage is inevitable and you are the one being forced to go through with it, why not get out in front of this and act like it was your idea? Thus, after the Delaware judge refused to dismiss the case and set a trial date for October 2022, Musk acquiesced on October 4.

He closed the deal on October 27, surprisingly quickly, even for a shotgun wedding. At 9:10 eastern time that morning, he took to Twitter to make his first announcement as the new owner of the platform. It began:

Dear Twitter Advertisers

I wanted to reach out personally to share my motivation in acquiring Twitter. There has been much speculation about why I bought Twitter and what I think about advertising. Most of it has been wrong.

The reason I acquired Twitter is because it is important to the future of civilization to have a common digital town square, where a wide range of beliefs can be debated in a healthy manner, without resorting to violence. There is currently great danger that social media will splinter into far right wing and far left wing echo chambers that generate more hate and divide our society.

In the relentless pursuit of clicks, much of traditional media has fueled and catered to those polarized extremes, as they believe that is what brings in the money, but, in doing so, the opportunity for dialogue is lost.

That is why I bought Twitter. I didn't do it because it would be easy. I didn't do it to make more money. I did it to try to help humanity, whom I love.

After two more paragraphs, he concludes:

Fundamentally, Twitter aspires to be the most respected advertising platform in the world that strengthens your brand and grows your enterprise. To everyone who has partnered with us, I thank you. Let us build something extraordinary together.

That hopeful opening soon was spurned with a vengeance by the mainstream media, the advertising industry, enemy NGOs, liberal academia, and the Democratic Party. They rushed to judgment and meted out a swarm of criticism and disapproval.

Usually, media interest fades when a company goes private and its stock no longer trades and is no longer owned by thousands of pension funds and millions of 401(k) retirement plans. See Dell after Michael Dell took it private in 2013. Yet in covering Musk's takeover, the media acted as if they were chronicling the disastrous decline of the most important media company in the world. Many members of the media were attention whores on Twitter, preening on the platform to extend their reach far beyond what their own publications could draw.

The media covered Musk's staff cuts as cruel and draconian when, actually, they were necessary: he felt he was racing to save the company from disaster. Leadership by stoking self-created, imminent crisis to wake up the troops and weed out the unfaithful.

The media and Democrats were further outraged that Elon, right out of the gate, reopened the banned-for-life account of former president Trump (@realDonaldTrump) and restored the accounts of thousands of conservatives banished by the old management. Instantly, the press pack put two and two together to make five:

restoring conservative accounts will lead to a rise in hate speech and white supremacists on Twitter, and cutting staff means too few humans are around to stop this scourge from spreading. Albeit stopping it requires better algorithms rather than more humans.

This is so sad, and it is so telling about the media today. They could have celebrated the account restorations as a victory for free speech, instead of portraying them as a threat to the national conscience. Or to national security.

Two days after Elon's overture to advertisers, Montclair State University in New Jersey put out a press release on a new "study" saying hate speech had increased hours after Musk closed the deal. It said that before the Musk deal, the seven-day average of tweets with hate terms was never higher than 84 times per hour. But in the first twelve hours of Musk ownership, from October 28 at midnight to noon, hate speech terms were tweeted 4,778 times total, with a potential reach of three million views.

Musk's promise to reduce restrictions on content "represents an obvious danger to young people using the platform," the Montclair press release claimed. This, before Elon had imposed any changes in policy or algorithms. Plus, twelve hours is a ridiculously short time to conduct a study. The researchers lurched to headline-sparking conclusions while downplaying as "speculative" the clear possibility that wags were taunting Musk by posting trash, and testing the platform, and posting epithets just to provoke their enemies.

This "study" was poppycock. First off, tweets using hateful terms pose zero "danger" to anyone: Ignore them. Block them. Also, the study's citation of 4,778 hate-speech tweets in twelve hours works out to 398 bad tweets per hour. A pittance: X posts more than six thousand messages *every single second* of every minute of every hour, 24/7.

Moreover, this rise in hate speech in the first twelve hours post-Elon was fueled in part by pranksters on 4chan, a subversive "imageboard website" popular with young hackers. They urged followers to fill Twitter with a cascade of n-bombs and other epithets to make hate speech skyrocket. Just to mess with people. This angle went mostly unmentioned in hundreds of news stories sparked by the Montclair report. The media ran wild with an assumption they already held as true.

Bloomberg: "Musk's Twitter Roils with Hate Speech as Trolls Test New Limits." "Roils"? Similar stories ran on Reuters, ABC News, CBS News, NBC News, CNBC, CBC News, and Axios and in *Forbes*, *USA Today*, the *Los Angeles Times*, *Wired*, *Adweek*, and elsewhere. Also, on October 28, the *New York Times* reported that the Anti-Defamation League had found more than twelve hundred tweets and retweets with antisemitic words.

On December 2, the *Times* declared: "Hate Speech's Rise on Twitter Is Unprecedented, Researchers Find." Slurs against Blacks had jumped from an average of 1,282 a day pre-Musk to 3,876 a day after the takeover. Missing in all of this was context and perspective: four thousand racist tweets on a social media platform that posts more than five billion messages every single day falls short of qualifying as being worrisome, much less newsworthy.

Yet the media covered this with alacrity, and this further spooked advertisers. Half of Twitter's hundred largest sponsors stopped all spending on the platform. They were advised to do so by ad firms that, in turn, had been pressured by liberal NGOs with agendas of their own. This angle was also left out.

Among these organizations was the Center for Countering Digital Hate, the source for the *Times* story on December 2 regarding an "unprecedented" rise in hate speech on Twitter. This group was a prominent critic of the Musk takeover, and the House Judiciary Committee is investigating whether CCDH has assisted in widespread government efforts to censor conservative speech.

Other provocateurs: Media Matters for America, the Anti-Defamation League, Mediaite, and Meidas Touch. Their leaders served up a barrage of Elon-bashing. Many of these groups had received funding from the Open Society Foundations of liberal billionaire George Soros, a major target of Elon Musk's criticism. Musk has said Soros is part of a soft-on-crime "death cult" that supports no-bail policies.

This potential conflict of interest regarding the Musk-Soros feud was left out of the media coverage of the unfolding drama as well.

...

Elon likes to say that the most ironic outcome in life is often the most likely one. Twitter fits into this framework. He saw Twitter as having enormous potential as a safe harbor where millions or even billions of people could commune online and swap ideas and insights openly and frankly, without recrimination.

Yet upon buying control of Twitter, he found the very opposite thing. In December 2022, the Twitter Files exposé debuted on Twitter. It revealed that Twitter was a central, complicit player in the most egregious, rampant violation of First Amendment rights in the history of the United States of America.

And without Elon Musk, we might never have known this at all.

Government officials pressed Twitter, Facebook, and other outlets to ban, silence, restrain, and otherwise muzzle the accounts of thousands of Americans, most of them conservatives. This violated the First Amendment rights of untold thousands who wanted to be heard online—and millions of people online who had the right to hear those views.

In Silicon Valley, where 95 percent of workers' political contributions go to Democrats, the pink-haired radicals on staff were happy to cooperate. Especially at Old Twitter.

Assisted by the independent journalists Matt Taibbi, Michael Shellenberger, and Bari Weiss, Musk released thousands of internal documents detailing communications between supplicant, obeisant Twitter staff and demanding, scolding government overlords at the

FBI, CIA, National Security Agency, State Department, Homeland Security, and other agencies.

These government censors cloaked some of their efforts beneath a Stanford University–affiliated nonprofit called, without irony, the Election Integrity Partnership. The House Judiciary Committee has alleged that the organization has instead acted as a conduit for election interference, targeting the accounts of some of the most famous, and most ardent, conservative voices in America: President Trump, Fox News anchor Sean Hannity, former House Speaker Newt Gingrich, former Arkansas governor Mike Huckabee, U.S. senator Thom Tillis, Georgia congresswoman Marjorie Taylor Greene, Judicial Watch president Tom Fitton, *Federalist* editor in chief Mollie Hemingway. Plus Newsmax, where I am a frequent guest. And the *Babylon Bee*, whose banning reveals a total lack of any sense of humor.

Government spooks got Twitter and Facebook to censor the *New York Post* exposé of the Hunter Biden laptop scandal right before the 2020 election, bordering on election interference. And to mute "The Great Barrington Declaration," an open letter released in October 2020 and signed by three world-renowned epidemiologists, led by Dr. Jay Bhattacharya. It raised fair (and prescient) doubts about the Covid-19 pandemic and the questionable efficacy of using new vaccines and imposing lockdowns for all, instead of focusing only on the older population that was most at risk.

Twitter also muted comments that might have undermined confidence in new Covid-19 vaccines, and it even censored jokes made at the expense of de facto Covid czar Anthony Fauci. The FBI pushed the platform to tamp down even small accounts that reached only hundreds of followers, and it got Twitter to amplify the messages the FBI liked.

In my more than thirty years as a journalist, never have I seen anything close to the sweep and scale of this widespread government campaign to suppress free speech. It is stunning and historic, and this biggest threat to our freedoms continues to this day on every social media platform—except Elon Musk's X, fka Twitter.

Oddly, however, the mainstream media largely ignored the Twitter Files exposé. They sought to dismiss this story or bury it. In my writing for various outlets, I ended up producing more stories on the revelations of Twitter Files than the entire staffs of the *New York Times* and the *Washington Post*. Combined.

Their lack of outrage at the government's blatant and brazen assault on the First Amendment may owe to the fact that conservative voices, rather than liberal ones, were being silenced by government. Elon Musk would later say that Old Twitter suppressed ten conservative accounts for every one liberal account. The problem with the media's blasé take on silencing the Right is that, one day, conservatives may rise to overwhelming majority power in the government, and they could end up doing the same thing to liberals. And the media.

...

Elon Musk must feel like a storybook hero for his quixotic stand for free speech. This showed up in his inspirational Montoya moment on CNBC on May 16, 2023.

Musk sat down for a live, hour-long interview with David Faber of CNBC at the Tesla Gigafactory in Austin, following a shareholder meeting earlier the same day. Musk delayed the start of a board meeting to do the interview. Hours before, Musk had tweeted a disparaging comment about the liberal billionaire George Soros.

It was juvenile stuff: Musk said George Soros reminds him of Magneto, a supervillain from the X-Men comic books. Magneto, a holocaust survivor like Soros, is willing to sacrifice human life to ensure that the mutants of X-Men survive, just as Elon suspects that Soros would oppress humanity to enforce his super-liberal views. To the media, any criticism of Soros is antisemitic . . . because the media see one thing when they look at him: a Jew. Faber asks Musk how he decides when to tweet and when to hold back.

Faber: In terms of when you're going to engage. I mean, for example, even today, Elon, you tweeted this thing about George Soros. . . .

Musk: I said he reminds me of Magneto. This is like, you know, calm down, people. Let's not like make a metaphorical case out of it.

Faber: You also said, you said he wants to ruin the very fabric of civilization and Soros hates humanity. Like, when you do something like that, the—

Musk: Yeah, I think that's true. That's my opinion.

At this point, Elon is getting angry, resolute, ready for a fight. His jaw tightens. Faber keeps at it, telling him, "Okay, but why share it?"

Musk: I mean, there's freedom of speech. I'm allowed to say what I want to—

Faber: You absolutely are, but I'm trying to understand why you do, because you have to know it puts you in the middle of the partisan divide in the country. It makes you a lightning rod for criticism. I mean, do you like that?

This is when Elon Musk finally has tired of this exchange. He pauses, clearly thinking about what he wants to say on national television, and he tells Faber: "You know, I'm reminded of a scene in *The Princess Bride*. Great movie."

"Great movie," Faber concurs, and Elon goes on to invoke the swordsman Inigo Montoya, played by Mandy Patinkin.

Musk: Where he confronts the person who killed his father. And he says, "Offer me money. Offer me power. I don't care."

Faber: So, you just don't care. You want to share what you have to say?

Musk: I'll say what I want to say, and if the consequence of that is losing money, so be it. Nailed it.

As the year 2023 wore on, the media, as if acting in concert, started writing premature obituaries for Twitter. In February, a story on the website of Canada's CBC News noted, "Some predicted an imminent death for Twitter. It's still here. Can Elon Musk keep it alive?" In March, the *Financial Times* said the platform was "dying a slow and tedious death," and jeered, "Twitter is more like some kind of ghastly open-mic night than a 'digital town square.'" TechCrunch proclaimed: "Twitter is dying."

And there was this from *Business Insider* on July 12, 2023: "Welcome to 'Zombie Twitter' . . . Elon Musk was always going to destroy Twitter. The real surprise is how fast he was able to wreck it." That assault came from an old enemy: Linette Lopez, whom Musk had accused of paying a Tesla leaker in 2018.

Two days later came a strike from Bloomberg: "Twitter's Dying." Then from CNN.com (July 25): "Elon Musk has officially killed Twitter. The zombie platform lives on as X, a disfigured shell of its former self." And the *Los Angeles Times* (August 7), via a tech columnist: "A few sick days made it clear—Twitter is dying, and so is social media as we know it." Mark Twain might have relished this surfeit of premature and gleeful mourning.

Finally, a federal judge in July 2023 declared what the media refused to say: the Twitter Files had exposed the worst violation of our First Amendment rights in the history of our country.

The ruling came in *Missouri vs. Biden*, a lawsuit filed in May 2022 by the state attorneys general of Missouri and Louisiana against fifty-four defendants. Among them: President Biden, White House press secretary Karine Jean-Pierre, and thirteen federal agencies, including the FBI, State Department, Homeland Security, CDC, FDA, Census Bureau, and Health and Human Services.

By the time oral arguments were heard on May 26, 2023, the Twitter Files had exposed the shocking extent of government surveillance and censorship in social media. The presiding judge in the case, U.S. District Court judge Terry Doughty in Louisiana, issued a blistering ruling against the government and timed it for maximum impact: Independence Day, 2023. It spanned 155 pages and 721 footnotes. He opened with a famous quotation:

> *I may disapprove of what you say, but I would defend to the death your right to say it.*
> —EVELYN BEATRICE HILL, 1906, *THE FRIENDS OF VOLTAIRE*

His opening declaration: "This case is about the Free Speech Clause in the First Amendment to the United States Constitution. The explosion of social-media platforms has resulted in unique free speech issues—this is especially true in light of the COVID-19 pandemic. If the allegations made by Plaintiffs are true, the present case arguably involves the most massive attack against free speech in United States' history."

The Trump-appointed judge then let loose some great licks.

"If there is a bedrock principle underlying the First Amendment, it is that the government may not prohibit the expression of an idea simply because society finds the idea itself offensive or disagreeable."

"Although the censorship alleged in this case almost exclusively targeted conservative speech, the issues raised herein go beyond party lines. The right to free speech is not a member of any political party and does not hold any political ideology."

"Government action, aimed at the suppression of particular views on a subject that discriminates on the basis of viewpoint, is presumptively unconstitutional."

He closed with another quote, this one from President Harry S. Truman: "Once a government is committed to the principle of silencing the voice of opposition, it has only one place to go, and that is down the path of increasingly repressive measures, until it becomes a source of terror to all its citizens and creates a country where everyone lives in fear."

The judge issued a preliminary injunction banning contact with social media platforms by half a dozen federal agencies, including the FBI, Homeland Security, Health and Human Services, the Centers for Disease Control and Prevention, and the National Institute of Allergy and Infectious Diseases, as well as the U.S. surgeon general and the White House press secretary.

Further, Judge Doughty expressly banned ten activities and other contact with Twitter; Meta's Facebook, WhatsApp, and Instagram; Google and YouTube; WeChat; TikTok; and still others.

The Biden administration instantly appealed the decision, citing the approaching 2024 presidential election and how it needed to make sure election "disinformation" didn't get out of control. The Fifth Circuit Court of Appeals in New Orleans (one of nine circuit courts) weighed in on the Biden appeal on September 9, 2023, narrowing the injunction to cover the White House, FBI, CDC, and U.S. surgeon general. From there, the Biden administration appealed to the U.S. Supreme Court, which stayed the Fifth Circuit's injunction and issued a ruling on the case in mid-2024.

On June 26, the high court ruled 6–3 against the First Amendment plaintiffs who had sued the government and won the original injunction. It returned the case, now known as *Murthy v. Missouri*, to the Fifth Circuit for a lack of standing to sue—without ruling on the First Amendment at the heart of it. This brought a harsh dissent from Justice Samuel Alito, who wrote, "The Court's holding that the plaintiffs lack standing to challenge this scheme is, in my judgment, clearly wrong and very unfortunate." He called the

case "one of the most important free speech cases in many years."
An understatement.

As the X platform approached the one-year mark of Musk's tenure, the media churned out dozens of similarly designed stories on the anniversary and how much the old Twitter had deteriorated under Musk. This morass of negative coverage from so many rival outposts shared a striking sameness.

Rolling Stone was among the first to draw new blood. On October 4, 2023, it published a commentary headlined "Twitter Is at Death's Door, One Year After Elon Musk's Takeover," adding, "He's done everything he can to run it into the ground."

This prompted a Musk ally, @cb_doge, to counter that X now had one hundred billion impressions every day, half a billion new posts daily, 1.5 million new sign-ups each day (up 4 percent from the year before), plus a 14 percent increase in time spent on the platform and a 20 percent increase in video viewing. In fact, Twitter now had almost two hundred million monthly users among Gen Z, and it was the number one news app in various nations, and the fifth-most viewed website in the world, with almost eight billion visits the previous month.

The media left out the other half of the story. For the month of June 2024, X hosted 13.14 billion views, more than Facebook (12.44 billion) or Instagram (5.8 billion), and it boasted more than three billion unique visitors that month, triple the traffic at Facebook. This, according to statistics from Similarweb, which Elon Musk himself posted on July 31, 2024.

Beyond these numbers, and flying in the face of jealous and judgmental members of the media, X has grown into the most important news platform in the world, where almost everything breaks first. When President Joe Biden stepped down from the race for reelection, he announced his decision in a letter on X, rather than in a live televised address to the nation.

As well, X under Elon has emerged as the freest, most fearless media platform, standing alone against government censorship. X is banned in China, Iran, Russia, North Korea, Myanmar, Uzbekistan, and Turkmenistan. As the year 2024 wore on, Musk was in public face-offs with a chief judge in Brazil (which led to X's shutting down its local office there), a UK police official, and members of the European Commission.

In July 2024, Margrethe Vestager, the EC's commissioner for competition, posted a finger-wagging warning on X, accusing it of violating a new Digital Services Act "in key transparency areas. It misleads users, fails to provide adequate ad repository, and blocks access to data for researchers." Musk returned serve by tattling on the EC:

"The European Commission offered X an illegal secret deal: if we quietly censored speech without telling anyone, they would not fine us. The other platforms accepted that deal. X did not."

On Monday, August 12, at 12:25 p.m., eight hours or so before Elon was set to interview former president Trump on X, European commissioner Thierry Breton posted a one-page letter to Musk, teasing it with this: "With great audience comes greater responsibility. #DSA As there is a risk of amplification of potentially harmful content in connection with events with major audience around the world, I sent this letter to @elonmusk."

At 3:16 p.m., Musk reposted Breton's broadside and topped it with a meme borrowed from the cameo role of Tom Cruise in the film *Tropic Thunder*. Elon writing: "To be honest, I really wanted to respond with this Tropic Thunder meme, but I would NEVER do something so rude & irresponsible!" This, above a photo of Cruise in character and the headline:

Take a Big Step Back

AND LITERALLY, FUCK YOUR OWN FACE!

As the first year of Musk stewardship unfolded at the company, the media left out all that X fka Twitter was doing to muzzle hate speech. By July 2023, hate speech on the platform was down by one-third from before the Musk acquisition, X reported, based on data from tracking service Sprinklr. As a percentage of all content on X, hate speech "impressions" were down to an "average daily reach . . . of .003% between January and May 2023," the company reported. In other words, vastly less than 1 percent of the content on X is hate speech.

As X chief executive Linda Yaccarino tweeted on July 19, 2023, "More than 99% of content users and advertisers see on Twitter is healthy."

Under a policy called "Free Speech Not Reach," tweets deemed inappropriate were intentionally quelled to get 80 percent less reach than "healthy" messages. Moreover, under Elon Musk, the platform imposed a fivefold increase in account suspensions for child sexual exploitation compared with Old Twitter. Plus, 95 percent of these suspensions occurred before anyone filed a complaint, up from 75 percent before he took over.

The media gave X and Elon Musk basically zero credit for any of this. On Saturday, October 28, 2023, one year and a day after Elon Musk closed the acquisition of Twitter, the *New York Times* devoted the entire front page of the business section and two full, ad-free pages inside to an all-out hatchet job on his tenure.

Headline: "A Year of Musk: From Twitter's Town Square to a Spammy, Shrinking X." The top two-thirds of the section's front page was covered by an illustration of the new X logo impaling the partially shattered bluebird logo of Old Twitter. Poor little bluebird of unhappiness. Three stories served up attacks, unproven assertions, anecdotal cherry-picking, and questionable data from a battery of biased sources. The centerpiece article, "Swirl of Vitriol and False Posts," by three reporters, began:

"Now rebranded as X, the site has experienced a surge in racist, antisemitic and other hateful speech." Statistically, this is false, the company says, and the *Times* pretty much left that part out. The *Times* talked about "how much the platform [had] descended into the 'free-for-all hellscape' that [Musk] promised advertisers he wanted to avoid."

The *Times* left out the counterpoint: X data show that ads appear next to "healthy content" more than 99 percent of the time because of the steps taken by the Musk regime.

The *Times* featured thirteen prime examples of hate speech cited by a battery of organizations. Yet all of these groups are de facto members of what has become known as the Censorship Industrial Complex: left-wing, axe-grinding NGOs funded by liberal billionaire donors and contracted by government agencies to help silence supposed "misinformation" that, overwhelmingly, turns out to be conservative speech.

The *Times* relied on the Anti-Defamation League, which pressured advertisers to leave Twitter after Musk bought it, prompting Musk to threaten it with a lawsuit, and the *Times* left out these details of the conflict between Musk and the ADL. Another *Times* source, NewsGuard, is funded by the State Department, the Bill & Melinda Gates Foundation, and the Open Society Foundations of George Soros.

NewsGuard is working with European governments on censorship rules that would give them the power to unmask anonymous accounts and penalize platforms for the posts they publish and fail to remove on government demand. Less than two weeks before the *Times* stories ran, Musk tweeted: "What a scam! 'NewsGuard' should be disbanded immediately." The *Times* left this out, as well.

The Center for Countering Digital Hate, another *Times* source, was sued by Musk and X in August 2023 in the United States District Court for the Northern District of California. The lawsuit accuses CCDH of costing the platform millions of dollars in ad revenue with its claims about hate speech on Twitter. This also went undisclosed in the *Times* article.

(In March 2024, U.S. District Judge Charles Breyer, a Clinton appointee, dismissed the Musk lawsuit and said its sole purpose was to punish free speech, declaring: "Sometimes it is unclear what is driving a litigation, and only by reading between the lines of a complaint can one attempt to surmise a plaintiff's true purpose. Other times, a complaint is so unabashedly and vociferously about one thing that there can be no mistaking that purpose. This case represents the latter circumstance. This case is about punishing the Defendants for their speech.")

The *Times* also cited another source, the Institute for Strategic Dialogue, which has grants from the censorship-prone Department of Homeland Security and State Department, as well the United Nations and the European Union, Influence Watch reports. This, too, went unmentioned by the *Times*.

Instead of championing Elon Musk as a superhero fighting for free speech, the *Times* and most of the media portray him as a villain promoting supposedly "dangerous" content. Thus, the *Times* took umbrage when X filed a federal antitrust lawsuit against another de facto censorship group, the Global Alliance for Responsible Media (GARM), in August 2024.

X sued GARM and its overseer, the Word Federation of Advertisers, and major sponsors including CVS Health, Mars candy, and Unilever, in U.S. District Court for the Northern District of Texas. It charged the defendants with steering billions of dollars in ad orders away from X. Eighteen GARM members stopped advertising on X, and dozens of others reduced their spending by 70 percent or more, the lawsuit states.

The company based its case on a report by the House Judiciary Committee that found "evidence of an illegal boycott against many companies, including X," as X CEO Linda Yaccarino put it in a post in August 2024. As the report noted, "Evidence obtained by the Committee shows that GARM and its members directly organized boycotts and used other indirect tactics to target disfavored platforms, content creators, and news organizations in an effort to demonetize and, in effect, limit certain choices for consumers."

Musk himself reposted the Yaccarino note and added: "We tried peace 2 years, now it is war."

X filed the lawsuit on August 6, 2024. Just two days later, GARM closed down rather than fight. As the *New York Times* reported, the World Federation of Advertisers denied Musk's charges but said the nonprofit, GARM, lacked the funds to continue operating while it fights X in court. The case against WFA and the big advertisers continues.

In covering this spat, the *Times* said Musk had "declared war on advertisers," while other social media platforms have "been responsive to their concerns about offensive online content," adding that "Mr. Musk has also used the courts to stymie his competitors." The paper lamented that "the ripple effects of X's lawsuits against nonprofits have contributed to problems for researchers looking into extremism, disinformation and other malicious online content," and "helped to amplify a coordinated right-wing campaign to paint their work as a deep-state conspiracy to censor free speech."

The newspaper of record was thereby siding with those who want to muzzle some speech, rather than those who want more free speech.

Whatever happened to this once great newspaper?

A few days after the first anniversary of Elon Musk's takeover of Twitter, he visited Joe Rogan on Halloween night for another whiskey-lubricated podcast chat. It was their fourth, Rogan having made podcast history with the first one back in 2018. Rather than meet in Los Angeles, they met in Austin, Texas, where both men had moved a few years earlier. They huddled in Rogan's studio at his $14 million home. No billion-dollar doobie this time, at least not on camera; although there was the late-night delivery of a pizza designed by Rogan, with anchovies and pineapple. Yuck.

As they sat in Rogan's studio, late at night, Elon wore his customary black uniform. Joe wore a baseball jersey labeled "Puerto Rico" and sported a blond fright wig on his bald head. Twenty-five minutes into the interview, Rogan asks Elon: "What has it been like, you've owned X for a year now? Do you ever wake up in the middle of the night and have a dream that you didn't do it? And your life is infinitely easier?"

"Well," Elon allows, "it's certainly a recipe for trouble, I suppose, or contention."

Rogan asks, "What was it, ultimately, that led you to make the decision to do it?"

Elon pauses, gives a weary sigh, and says, "I mean, this is gonna sound somewhat melodramatic, but I was worried that it was having a corrosive effect on civilization. That it was just having a bad impact. And I think part of it is that it's where it was located, which is, you know, downtown San Francisco. . . . It's a zombie apocalypse. I mean, it's rough. . . . It's crazy."

Elon says Twitter had become "an information technology weapon to propagate what is, essentially, a mind virus to the rest of Earth. . . . It is the end of civilization."

Joe Rogan buys in: "And it's not just propagating the mind virus, but *suppressing* any opposing viewpoints."

Elon: "Yes. Well, in order for the virus to propagate, it must suppress opposing viewpoints." Later, he adds: "The First Amendment is only relevant if you allow people you don't like to say things you don't like. Because if you like it, you don't need a First Amendment. So, the whole point of free speech is that, frankly, even people you hate [can] say things you hate, because if people you hate can say things that you hate, that means that they can't stop you from saying what you want to say. Which is very, very important."

This then allows the best ideas to be heard and to compete for attention and adoption. This is especially important to Elon Musk, even though he views his ideas as being the best ones. His audience on X has more than doubled since he bought the platform: by September 2024, he was just shy of 200 million followers. Before he owned the company, Musk rarely tweeted more than 250 times a month. After, his output soared to a thousand or more messages a month in eight of the first eleven months. He also had X engineers rig a way to boost his impressions.

Rogan asks him whether the spying on social media platforms is ubiquitous, and Elon answers unflinchingly: "It's absolutely all the social media companies. In fact, right now, X, or formerly known as Twitter, is the only one that is not kowtowing to the government. It's the only one. There isn't—all the others just do exactly what the government wants."

Rogan: That is wild. What I was getting at, do you think that that's everywhere?

He mentions CNN, the *Times*, and the *Washington Post*.

Musk: I mean, it is weird, the degree to which the media is in lockstep. Like, why is the media in lockstep? And why doesn't the media question the government? They used to. . . . Seems weird. Something doesn't add up.

If there is a particular answer to this quandary, it has slim-to-no chance of ever being exposed by the media themselves. The answer, instead, will appear on X, offered up by citizen journalists and deep-dive experts, backed by the help of crowdsourcing among thousands of motivated onlookers. Thanks to Elon Musk.

ON THE MEDIA: TO HELL WITH THEM. THEY ARE SHAMELESS SHILLS.

**The BBC takedown. Why your PR
department is a waste of time.**

In April 2023, six months after Elon Musk completed his reluctant acquisition of Twitter, he sat down for a videotaped interview with a reporter for the BBC. In an open-office space at Twitter headquarters in San Francisco, Musk sat in profile on a folding chair on the left side of the screen, without any notes, entourage, or PR handlers. He was clad in his customary black jeans and black T-shirt, eschewing the black turtleneck of Steve Jobs fame.

Across from him, on the right side of the video screen and seated on a second folding chair, was Musk's interviewer: James Clayton, the British, Hollywood-stubbled technology correspondent for the BBC, wearing dark slacks and a suitably tweedy blazer. For Clayton, this meeting was entirely unexpected.

He said as much at the opening of their conversation, telling Musk this whole thing "came together by a very speculative email, which I didn't think would even be responded to. And you were, like, 'No, let's do it tonight.'"

"Sure," Musk responds.

Clayton: Anyway. All right. We're actually filming. Just so everyone knows, we're filming this for the BBC. So, we have three cameras and loads of lights. But this is also being listened to around the world.

Musk: Yeah. It's unique.

Clayton: Open and transparent. There we go.

Unbeknownst to Clayton and his camera crew beforehand, Musk had arranged for this star chamber to be broadcast live around the world on Twitter Spaces, in a real-time online call that three million users would be listening to live, plus millions more later on. He withheld notice of this from Clayton until just twenty minutes before the interview was to begin. This would run live, beyond the ability of the BBC to edit it and leave anything out; the public television network would post its shorter, carefully edited version hours later.

What ensued has to be one of the most devastating takedowns of the media that any CEO has ever conducted. Elon Musk is virulently anti-media, and he all but took an axe to the veddy British, self-serious, government-funded BBC, with its permanently furrowed brow. Millions of people around the world watched live on Twitter, plus millions more on replay. This clash was so stunning, so complete, that myriad media outlets covered the beatdown of one of their own.

The BBC reporter opens by saying people involved in "moderation" at Twitter argue "there's not enough people to police this stuff, particularly around hate speech, in the company." Elon asks him what hate speech he is referencing and whether the reporter, personally, has seen a rise in hate speech on the platform. The reporter answers yes, and Elon moves in for attack.

"Content you don't like, or hateful? Describe a hateful thing," he asks, and the BBC interviewer mentions "something that is slightly racist or slightly sexist. Those kinds of things."

Elon: "So you think if something is slightly sexist, it should be banned?"

Clayton: "No, I'm not saying anything. I'm saying—" and now Elon is on a roll. He prods the reporter repeatedly for specific examples of hate speech on the platform, and the reporter is unable to name a single one. And Elon declares: "Then I say, sir, that you don't know what you're talking about."

Stunned, the reporter asks, "Really?" This opens the way for another Elon assault. "Yes. Because you can't give me a single example of hateful content. Not even one tweet. And yet you claimed that the hateful content was high. That's false." The BBC scribe starts to object and gets cut off. Musk: "You just lied."

They go around and around on this point, the reporter unable to meet repeated calls for examples of hate speech he has seen, and finally he tells Elon, "This is not an interview about the BBC," and Elon retorts, "Oh, you thought it wasn't? . . . I'm interviewing you, too. You weren't expecting that." Game, set, match, Musk.

...

This was great television; riveting, real-life drama. Yet the BBC left it out entirely when it aired a truncated version of the interview hours later. Even though the BBC producers knew the rest of the world had already heard this live on Twitter Spaces. Unalloyed hubris.

Though the term *defining moment* is overused, Musk's BBC rout was that and then some. It well illustrates Elon's take-no-prisoners approach to the media: fuck 'em and feed 'em fish heads. This is an old saying I heard thirty-five years ago from an otherwise eloquent Cajun reporter who became a lifelong friend of mine. It applies especially well here.

Musk's testy, pugilistic stance vs. his BBC interlocutor offers instruction for any CEO or business owner or anyone who ends up having to contend with the garrulous, guileful, and anything-but-objective media outlets of today. Elon's media message: ignore them as much as you can—refuse to respond to their inquiries at all, if you are Elon Musk. (Though I do wish he would respond to mine.) This is why Musk views a PR department as a waste of time: rather than try to grapple with the media, he creates content without relying on it at all.

The press lives in its own gatekept world, and it resents Musk and his platform for supplanting it. Reporters will tell the stories they want to tell, so why waste time on them at all? When you must engage, step up first and preempt the press, rather than waiting for this bloodthirsty pack of hounds to come for you. Prepare ahead and punch back hard, rather than offering politeness to curry favor they won't afford you anyway. Interview your interviewer. And record it to keep them honest.

For a time after taking over Twitter and firing the PR department, Musk had an automated response go out to anyone who wrote to Twitter to ask for comment. It was a single "poop emoji," as the *New York Times*, the *Washington Post*, and the *Wall Street Journal*, among others, insisted on phrasing it to their readers. They hoped this would embarrass Musk into dropping this crudity, but they were wrong. Eventually, they stopped mentioning this.

Even for those of us who are spared the burden of having to deal with the media, Musk's antipathy offers sound advice for consumers of news: stop blindly believing what the media are reporting, start trusting them even less than you do now, and always question what they are leaving out. And search out the opposing views the media never want you to hear.

In many ways, the media have earned Musk's resentment and his damning view of their practitioners. They play a crucial role in fanning the rumors that short sellers use to bash Tesla stock. They take isolated accidents involving Tesla EVs and blow them up into major news events. When a SpaceX rocket explodes in a test flight, some journalists jeer.

Further, Musk says that because the Big Three makers of gas-burning cars, GM, Ford, and Stellantis (the former Chrysler), spend more than $6 billion a year on advertising, while Tesla has spent zero for most of its existence, the media are even more biased against him.

He ignores the old adage about avoiding a fight with a man who buys ink by the barrel, apocryphally attributed to Mark Twain. Elon Musk has an alacrity for messing with the media. He has called out the *New York Times*, Reuters, the *Guardian*, and CNN, among others. "What I find most surprising is that CNN still exists," he tweeted in April 2020.

Musk makes a plausible case for replacing them with citizen journalism on X. No wonder he has utter contempt for most of the media. It distresses me to say this because, for twenty-five glorious years, I was a proud, ink-stained wretch. First at the *Wall Street Journal* and then at *Forbes* magazine. Then I became an anchor at CNBC and Fox Business for more than six years.

I am unable to recognize the media today. What the hell happened to them?

Gone is any quaint, passé obligation to conduct a full examination of the truth and tell a fair and balanced account that attempts to reconcile conflicting versions of events. Gone is any interest in airing unpopular or unconventional views. Outlets on both the Left and the Right are guilty of this, as they chase online clicks and struggle mightily to draw attention to themselves.

The Four Horsemen of the liberal media—the *New York Times*, the *Washington Post*, CNN, and MSNBC—and their allies at the ABC, CBS, and NBC broadcast networks set the path for the rest of the pack. They march in lockstep, and most of them echo the same messages rather than seeking to speak with a unique voice.

In 1983, some fifty media companies competed, and since 2011 just half a dozen or so giants own 90 percent of news and media outlets in the United States. Comcast, Disney, Paramount Global (née Viacom), Warner Bros. Discovery, Fox News, and News Corp are the biggest. Meta and Google dominate the social media space.

One of Elon Musk's earliest clashes with media titans came in early 2013, when the *New York Times* ran a sarcastic, bitchy review by John M. Broder, a reporter who today is on the *Times* editorial board. Broder, an EV doubter, test-drove a $101,000 Tesla Model S from Washington to Boston. He made use of two new Tesla recharging stations along I-95 in Newark, Delaware, and Milford, Connecticut. They are two hundred miles apart from each other.

He made the journey in extreme cold, and the Tesla battery drained more quickly than expected. Ultimately, Broder reported, his Model S ran out of power and had to be placed on a flatbed truck and driven off to be recharged. The *Times* and Broder were merciless about it:

Stalled Out on Tesla's Electric Highway

This headline ran over a photo of the candy-apple-red Tesla being offloaded from the flatbed truck at the Tesla recharging station in Milford. Broder wrote: "The Model S has won multiple car-of-the-year awards and is, many reviews would have you believe, the coolest car on the planet. What fun, no? Well, no."

He told of anxiously fretting he might run out of power, and having to turn off the heat in freezing-cold weather and drive at only 54 miles per hour to use less charge. "If this is Tesla's vision of long-distance travel in America's future, I thought . . . it needs some work," Broder said.

Elon Musk struck back with fury and vengeance.

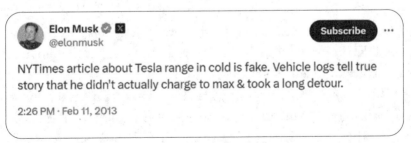

Elon Musk ✔ ✖
@elonmusk

Subscribe   ...

NYTimes article about Tesla range in cold is fake. Vehicle logs tell true story that he didn't actually charge to max & took a long detour.

2:26 PM · Feb 11, 2013

"Fake." Musk used this term to describe the media even before President Trump started dropping it like a bomb in his first presidential campaign in 2015. Musk cited fake news even before the BuzzFeed editor who claims to have coined the phrase in the fall of 2014. And the thing is, when you criticize one story by one reporter for one outlet, the rest of the media feel attacked, as well. Thus, John Schwartz, who has worked for the *Times* and the *Washington Post*, came to Broder's defense:

Note the scare quotes. A day later, tech journalist Kara Swisher tweeted that "it would be nice to see" Tesla data logs on how Broder's car actually performed. Every Tesla can track and report speed, charging record settings, and all other operational aspects. For customers, it does so only if they expressly grant permission allowing it. Musk had insisted, however, on activating this feature for every media test-drive, including Broder's.

This is because, a few years earlier, staffers for *Top Gear* magazine's TV show were accused of pretending that the Tesla they were testing had run out of charge and had to be pushed home. The vehicle log showed the car had fifty miles of power left. Musk, ever litigious, had Tesla file a lawsuit against *Top Gear* in the UK, and it was dismissed on the argument that the program was entertainment rather than information.

This would provide Musk with some vindication. At 4:30 p.m. on February 11, Musk did a phone interview with Maria Bartiromo on CNBC. Clearly upset about the reaction to the *Times* story published the day before, he set out to communicate a factual defense and impugn the reporter without challenging the institution. Separate the reporter from the publication: a classic PR technique. This was first used on me as a young reporter at the *Journal* in 1984.

Musk tells Maria, "We think the article is something of a setup. It's pretty unreasonable. I don't want to paint the whole *New York Times* as being problematic, but I do think that this writer and this particular article really is misleading." Bartiromo asks for details, and Musk cites vehicle logs showing that the *Times* reporter failed to fully charge the car, took "an extended detour through Manhattan" before driving to the next supercharger location, and drove ten miles over the speed limit, which would cause the battery to run down even more.

"And we explicitly warned him that you can't do these things," Musk tells her.

Then anchor Bill Griffith, a beloved CNBC veteran and one of the kindest people there when I worked alongside him, tells Musk, "I'm intrigued by the word 'setup' you used there in your first answer. . . . Is this a deliberate fabrication, in your view, of how this was portrayed?"

Elon: "You never know for sure in these things, but I would say that it's more likely than not. We explicitly said that to do this trip he needs to make sure he's fully charged when he starts up, that he doesn't take detours, and that he drives at a reasonable speed." He added, "So if somebody's explicitly asked to take reasonable actions in a test-drive and then blatantly doesn't, what conclusion is one supposed to reach?"

It is likely that Elon was working on soothing two audiences at once: Tesla investors and his employees. When your company is struggling, your people need to see leadership; they want to be told and shown that everything will be all right.

The next day, Musk revealed all, posting a 1,218-word blog on the Tesla website that utterly defenestrated the *Times*'s original 1,800-word attack. The blog was detailed, documented, and devastating for the *Times*. This is key to Elon's fuck-the-media strategy: instead of complaining that the media are biased, build your case, show it in facts and stats, and present it outside the media's own channels. In this case, on the Tesla blog, which then spreads on Twitter.

In his blog, Elon published five charts plotting Broder's "bizarre" and "irregular" moves. He showed that the car's cruise control was never set at only 54 mph as Broder claimed. "Broder in fact drove at speeds from 65 mph to 81 mph for a majority of the trip and at an average cabin temperature setting of 72 F. At the point in time that he claims to have turned the temperature down, he in fact turned the temperature up to 74 F."

While the reporter claimed he charged up for fifty-eight full minutes as cited in a *Times* graphic, in fact the recorded charge time was only forty-seven minutes. Had he spent the full fifty-eight, "it would have been virtually impossible to run out of energy for the remainder of his stated journey."

Broder also took a detour into downtown Manhattan. As the Tesla's display read, "0 miles remaining," Musk wrote, "instead of plugging in the car, he drove in circles for over half a mile in a tiny, 100-space parking lot. When the Model S valiantly refused to die, he eventually plugged it in. On the later legs, it is clear Broder was determined not to be foiled again."

In fact, the Model S battery "never ran out of energy at any time, including when Broder called the flatbed truck," Musk reported. The reporter stopped charging his car with only a thirty-two-mile range when he knew he had to drive sixty-one miles. On the final leg, Broder "drove right past a public charge station while the car repeatedly warned him that it was very low on range."

A devastating defenestration of Broder and the *Times*. In a final flourish, Musk shrewdly made the *Times* attack less about himself and more about hurting the cause of countering climate change with electric cars (however dubious that proposition). "We were played for a fool and as a result, [we] let down the cause of electric vehicles. For that, I am deeply sorry."

Noblesse oblige. Genius. Musk's blistering broadside made news everywhere, and the story's angle shifted to his pushback, "setting the Internet abuzz with a flurry of blog posts, Twitter messages and e-mail exchanges," as the *Times* reported. Broder himself wrote a follow-up denying many of Musk's countercharges, and another one after that. On February 18, the *Times*'s public editor published an extraordinary piece, all but siding against the *Times* and its author.

She wrote that, although she did not believe the *Times* reporter had hoped the drive would end badly, he had exercised questionable judgment and had left himself open to "valid criticism by taking casual and imprecise notes along the journey, unaware that his every move was being monitored. A little red notebook in the front seat is no match for digitally recorded driving logs, which Mr. Musk has used, in the most damaging (and sometimes quite misleading) ways possible, as he defended his vehicle's reputation." Again, game, set, match, Musk.

Elon would get bolder in his jousts with his media adversaries. And funnier. Five years on, in May 2018, nationwide media coverage focused on a single Tesla crash that resulted in a broken ankle. Near Salt Lake City, Utah, a twenty-eight-year-old woman driving her Tesla Model S at 60 miles per hour, in Autopilot mode, was staring at her phone screen when the car slammed into a fire department vehicle stopped at a red light.

She broke her ankle, and the accident was her fault: Tesla requires drivers to stay focused and keep their hands on the wheel in self-driving mode. At the same time, she may have been taking on faith the many times that Elon himself claimed that Autopilot was safer than human drivers and one day would be able to take over entirely. Either way, her crash was covered by the Associated Press, the *Washington Post*, ABC News, the Week, and other outlets.

On May 14, 2018, Elon let loose on Twitter, calling it "super messed up" that a crash that caused only a broken ankle made front-page news, "and the ~40,000 people who died in US auto accidents alone in past year get almost no coverage." He added that "what's actually amazing" is that usually a crash at 60 mph "results in severe injury or death."

The Musk Man has a point. Tesla cars are extraordinarily safe and durable. In January 2023, a crazed, paranoid man drove his Tesla off a 250-foot-high cliff near Devil's Slide, twenty miles south of San Francisco, with his wife and two small children onboard. Miraculously, all of them survived, with non-critical injuries. "We were very shocked," a battalion chief told reporters.

In fact, a few months prior to the broken-ankle crash back in May 2018, in another accident, a driver of a Model S in Culver City, California, was allegedly failing to pay attention and let the car smack into a parked fire truck at 65 mph—and the driver emerged uninjured, miraculously. Even the Culver City Fire Department was impressed, tweeting: "While working a freeway accident this morning, Engine 42 was struck by a #Tesla traveling at 65 mph. The driver reports the vehicle was on autopilot. Amazingly there were no injuries! Please stay alert while driving! #abc7eyewitness #ktla #CulverCity #distracteddriving."

Nine days later, at 2:25 p.m. eastern time on May 23, Musk set off a media firestorm with a series of tweets. Clearly irritated, he commented on a post by Electrek.co, a trade publication that flagged a new story saying Tesla stock could rally "as media negativity is 'increasingly immaterial.'" Musk responded: "The holier-than-thou hypocrisy of big media companies who lay claim to the truth, but publish only enough to sugarcoat the lie, is why the public no longer respects them."

To this, Andrew J. Hawkins, a reporter for the Verge with fewer than fifteen thousand followers of his account, @andyjayhawk, responded with transparent derision: "Musk continues his slow transformation into a media-baiting Trump figure screaming irrationally about fake news. Hope it works out for you dude!"

Musk struck back hard moments later: "Thought you'd say that. Anytime anyone criticizes the media, the media shrieks 'You're just like Trump!' Why do you think he got elected in the first place? Because no ones [*sic*] believes you any more [*sic*]. You lost your credibility a long time ago." To this, he added: "Problem is journos are under constant pressure to get max clicks & earn advertising dollars or get fired. Tricky situation, as Tesla doesn't advertise, but fossil fuel companies & gas/diesel car companies are among world's biggest advertisers."

At 3:41 p.m. the same day, Musk tweeted about creating a new website where the public can rate the media, publications, and individual reporters for accuracy and fairness. The mere mention of it sparked thousands of stories in response, as if he had proposed the arrest and incarceration of the media class. He started with a poll, and then he taunted his tormentors, drawing more than half a million votes in favor of his idea.

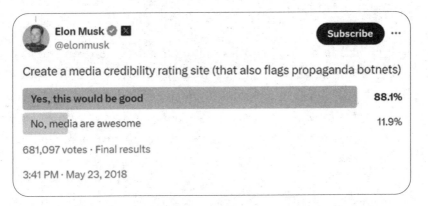

Some thirteen hours later, at 4:32 a.m. on May 24, Musk tweeted again, egging on the media:

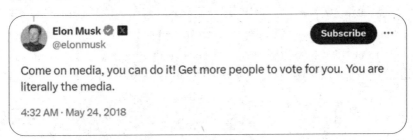

And again at 6:03 a.m.:

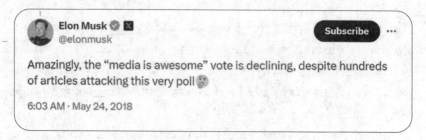

The next day, Elon tweeted news that he had acquired a new domain name for his would-be media criticism website.

His diatribe set off a million public conversations on the implications of this new ratings agency, as if it were well underway. It was just an idea. A "wouldn't-it-be-cool-if" idea. Yet all it took was a few simple, blunt tweets to generate waves of uproar and feigned pain among some the most powerful media outlets on Earth. They totally panicked.

A columnist in the *Washington Post* wrote: "Elon Musk wants to fix media mistrust with a dopey rating system. There's a better way." Reuters said, "Tesla's Musk bashes media, proposes credibility check," and *The Atlantic* tsk-tsked, "Elon Musk's Silly War with the Media." *Time* said he "Blasts Media 'Hypocrisy'" and used air quotes as if hypocrisy were a remote possibility. And Reporters Without Borders called him "a new threat to the American press" and said his "truth-rating system" would "undermine trust in the media."

Yet to this day, no website is up; no ratings service ever began.

Elon was all talk, and that alone was sufficient to getting the media to fret fiercely about it. They dance to his tune, even when they detest him.

While Musk was torching the media with his *Pravda* idea, a disgruntled worker at Tesla's Gigafactory in Nevada was laying plans to betray him. Short sellers were betting against Tesla's monumental struggle to rev up production to five thousand Model S vehicles per week. This was a milestone, and an unrealistically high expectation, set up by Elon Musk himself. This is a part of his leadership regimen: set goals that are beyond any you rightfully can expect to actually achieve, and find a way to get there. Even if you fall short, you end up much farther along than if you had been reasonable in your expectations.

Musk had spent his nights sleeping on the Gigafactory floor, in part to show leadership and prove to his workers that he was willing to do everything to help them hit the five-thousand-a-week mark. In three months, he had been away only one day. As he told Bloomberg in an interview weeks later, "I was wearing the same clothes for five days. Yeah, it was really intense. And everybody else was really intense, too."

Against this backdrop, the disgruntled Gigafactory worker sent out emails to a few reporters, offering internal secrets showing major production problems at the plant. News of this would embolden short sellers to bet even harder against Tesla stock. Linette Lopez, a columnist with *Business Insider*, took him up on the offer, relying on secret, purloined documents the worker had provided to her. On June 4, 2018, she published a story headlined "Internal Documents Reveal Tesla Is Blowing Through an Insane Amount of Raw Material and Cash to Make Model 3s, and Production Is Still a Nightmare."

The next day, Musk hosted Tesla's annual shareholder meeting, at which the story went unmentioned. And the day after that, on

June 6, Lopez posted a follow-up story also based on the factory worker's documents: "Tesla's New Gigafactory Robots That Are Supposed to Help It Ramp Up Model 3 Production Aren't Working Yet."

Furious, Musk launched an investigation, and the leaker was soon discovered: he was the one person among seven thousand workers at the Gigafactory who had downloaded the documents cited in Lopez's stories. His name was Martin Tripp, and he was frustrated by Tesla's inaction in addressing his complaints about the high amount of scrap on Gigafactory production lines.

The internal Tesla investigation, court records show, revealed that Tripp had tried to solicit other employees to leak to reporters. One worker, James Uelmen, who was Tripp's friend, contacted Musk and offered to be his mole. When Uelmen spoke to Tripp, "Tripp told Uelmen in a text message that Uelmen would get some money if he shared information with Lopez, and apparently told him the same thing in person," according to a later ruling in U.S. District Court.

Tripp texting: "Oh, if you are helpful you will get some money, I GUARANTEE you. There is stuff going on that I cannot tell anyone . . . it is GOOD though."

On July 5, 2018, at five o'clock in the morning, Musk went on the attack. Someone had posted a comment about the *Insider* columnist (@lopezlinette), and in response, Elon tweeted that she had published several "false articles about Tesla, including a doozy where she claimed Tesla scrapped more batteries than our total SX & 3 production number, which is physically impossible."

A follower suggested the reporter was linked to Musk's foe, the short seller James Chanos, and Musk branded this "very sketchy if true," and directly addressed Lopez: "Is it possible you're serving as an inside trading source for one of Tesla's biggest short-sellers?" A Twitter account with just 165 followers, @stetopinini, posted a snarky message aimed at the reporter for *Business Insider*, and

Elon surfed on it, asking Lopez if she'd promised to "compensate" Martin Tripp for inside information, and whether he had provided her with "exaggerated negative info" that was untrue.

Musk posted again at 2:13 p.m., and then once more at 2:42 p.m., asking Lopez whether she had ever provided Chanos with "material non-public information about Tesla." He chided her for calling Chanos "one of the greatest" and accused her of printing his views verbatim. "This is not journalism." Then came another post, this one on her "partying in Vegas with Chanos & Tepper with caption 'Love both these dudes'. Doesn't sound very objective."

Musk wanted to be sure Linette Lopez saw that one, because he purposely typed a "." before her @lopezlinette handle. He attached two screenshots of tweets she had posted four years earlier at an investment conference in Las Vegas, in which she bragged about having partied with two infamous short sellers: James Chanos and David Tepper. Lopez and *Business Insider* denied Musk's allegations.

Ultimately, Tesla sued the ex-worker for $167 million (the amount by which Tesla stock fell on the *Business Insider* scoop). A federal court judge threw out that claim (the stock had recovered within days) but otherwise sided overwhelmingly with Tesla and Elon Musk. In a later settlement with Telsa, Tripp admitted that he had violated several state laws and the Tesla confidentiality agreement, and he agreed to pay the company $400,000.

This Tesla victory was barely covered by the media, which focused, instead, on Musk's behavior in the whole episode. To them, Musk's messages were another sign of his manic instability. CNBC.com said, "Elon Musk lashes out at the media again," and the Associated Press reported that he had "become a bigger, more snarling presence on social media" and his tweets were up fourfold to four hundred per month since May. The *New Statesman* called him "a spoiled teenager trapped in the body of a billionaire," while *Vanity Fair* suggested, "Elon Musk Desperately Needs a Hobby."

In a Q and A with Bloomberg during this brouhaha, Musk is

asked about his use of Twitter to take on detractors, and he vows to reform his behavior:

"Generally, the view that I've had on Twitter is you're on Twitter, you're in like the meme—you're in meme war land. If you're on Twitter, you're in the arena. And so essentially if you attack me, it is therefore okay for me to attack back. Is there a place where you think I launched an attack on someone who has never attacked me?"

And says this: "I have made the mistaken assumption—and I will attempt to be better at this—of thinking that because somebody is on Twitter and is attacking me that it is open season. And that is my mistake. I will correct it."

Really nice intent, albeit Elon Musk has yet to make good on this vow. And if he had, his feed on the X platform would be a lot less interesting. And his enemies would be freed up to assail him without fear of reprisal. Never let your foes think you are too timid to fight back. Even a keyboard-courage bully wants to avoid a verbal punch in the face.

...

Elon Musk's relations with the media have gotten only more contentious since he acquired the former Twitter. They have bashed him and predicted the company's demise from the moment he took it over. They exaggerate claims of rising hate speech when user data show the opposite. And when he dares to push back, they howl in pain like a World Cup drama queen after getting jostled on the pitch, falling to the turf and squealing to fake an injury. Suddenly, some of the most powerful media platforms in the world are fragile and vulnerable, struggling under a merciless overlord.

To his credit, from the moment Musk took over Twitter, he took on the media and got in their collective, frowning face. They railed against him when, in one of Musk's first declarations, he restored the banned-for-life account of former president Trump and let Kanye West back on the platform (after the rapper was suspended for tweeting about Jewish control of the media).

The media maligned Musk when he dared to start charging $8 a month for the blue check mark that signals a verified account. This blue-check status previously was handed out by Twitter staff only to those it designated as being worthy of a blue check mark. Despite my more than thirty years at four of the best-known platforms in the world (the *WSJ*, *Forbes*, CNBC, Fox), I was turned down three times. Which was ridiculous and irksome.

The mainstream (read: liberal) media went into a massive meltdown in December 2022, when Elon Musk temporarily suspended the accounts of eight journalists for violating "terms of service" on Twitter. At 6:30 p.m. eastern time on Thursday, December 15, Twitter abruptly suspended the accounts of reporters for the *New York Times*, the *Washington Post*, CNN, the Intercept, and Mashable, and the liberal sports anchor Keith Olbermann. In most cases, they had reported on or retweeted posts of @elonjet, hosted by a college student, which tracked publicly available, real-time data on private jet whereabouts, including those of Elon Musk's.

The suspensions were set at seven days, and, oh, the humanity! Elon Musk responded petulantly on Twitter at 9:20 p.m. on December 15, 2022, saying, "Criticizing me all day long is totally fine, but doxxing my real-time location and endangering my family is not." And at 10:29 p.m.: "Accounts engaged in doxxing receive a temporary 7 day suspension."

Just before eleven that night, Musk posted a poll, and over half a million votes responded on whether to "unsuspend accounts who doxxed [his] exact location in real-time" immediately (43 percent), in more than than a week (38 percent), in one week (14 percent), or the next day (4.5 percent). Although he noted that if anyone had posted the real-time addresses of *Times* reporters, the FBI would descend, Congress would hold hearings, and "Biden would give speeches about the end of democracy."

Musk tweeted that the same rules apply to "journalists" as to everyone else—he sarcastically used scare quotes as if this term were stretching the truth. This struck said journalists as outrageous, given their utmost importance to society, in their view of themselves. Further, Musk likened publishing real-time locations to disclosing "assassination targets." A bit paranoid.

The next morning, thousands of stories around the world covered the mere temporary suspension of a few reporters. Never mind that these reporters continued to have access to their own publications and websites, and their accounts on Facebook, Instagram, TikTok, Snap, Rumble, Mastodon, Truth Social, and wherever else. Like I said, to attack one media outlet is to attack all of them, and all of them respond in kind.

Cue solemn, staged umbrage. The *Washington Post*'s top editor said the action "undermines Elon Musk's claim that he intends to run Twitter as a platform dedicated to free speech." CNN said, "Twitter's increasing instability and volatility should be of incredible concern for everyone who uses the platform." Yet nothing on Twitter need be of "incredible concern" to anyone. It is just words on a screen; you don't have to read them, and you don't have to abide by them or believe them. Turn the channel, as we used to say about old linear television.

Even the United fucking Nations weighed in with suitably harrumphy outrage. UN undersecretary-general Melissa Fleming said she was "deeply disturbed" and lectured, "Media freedom is not a toy. A free press is the cornerstone of democratic societies and a key tool in the fight against harmful disinformation."

Věra Jourová, vice president of the European Commission for Values and Transparency, issued a warning to Elon Musk: "There are red lines. And sanctions, soon."

In the U.S. House of Representatives, the New York glamour ham Alexandria Ocasio-Cortez accused Musk of "descending into abuse of power" and "erratically banning journalists." Totally escaping all three of these haughty government potentates: they posted their umbrage on Twitter. And no one stopped them, so what are they talking about?

A huge kerfuffle . . . over nothing. The next evening, Musk conducted a second poll, with almost 60 percent of responses advising him to lift the suspensions immediately (vs. 40 percent or so who advised waiting seven more days). So he did: "The people have spoken," he tweeted. Total time of the suspensions: twenty-seven hours. My account on Twitter was suspended for a full week on three separate occasions for offenses involving off-color jokes. These scribblers got off easy—and the scrap made them famous.

In the meantime, though, Elon Musk had exposed them for the precious, self-important hothouse orchids that so many of them are. Simply brilliant.

Musk envisions a day when the media will be replaced by citizen journalists on the X platform whose real-time reporting and expertise will be augmented by AI from xAI's Grok chatbot. As he put it in an onstage interview at Cannes Lions Festival in June 2024: "What we are doing on the X platform is, we are using AI to sum up the aggregated input from users who are at the scene and who are experts in the field and aggregate that into a real-time news feed which is far better than conventional journalism."

Musk, perhaps to illustrate his point, visited the U.S.-Mexico border at Eagle Pass, Texas, in September 2023. In just two days, some seventy-five hundred migrants, most of them fighting-age men, had blithely flooded the Texas town of twenty-eight thousand people. He used his own phone to go on X with live video to show what the media refused to show.

Elon made this plan on the spur of the moment, as he often does.

Just before two o'clock in the morning eastern time on September 26, 2023, a Tuesday, he tweeted to his more than 150 million followers, referring to his conversation with a Texas Republican congressman: "I spoke with Rep Tony Gonzales tonight—he confirmed that it is a serious issue. They are being overwhelmed by unprecedented numbers—just hit an all-time high and still growing!" He vowed to visit Eagle Pass later in the week "to see what's going on for myself."

His followers loved this; some said he seemed more presidential than President Biden. Two days later, Musk visited the congressman and, at 9:16 eastern time that night, on Thursday, September 28, 2023, he posted a fifteen-minute video to the X platform. Following the old rule of "when in Rome," he wore a black, ten-gallon cowboy hat, which some wags later said he was wearing backward.

Elon invited Representative Gonzalez, whose district includes more than eight hundred miles of Texas border, and a local sheriff to tell their story. He asked about illegal entrants at the border who sport tattoos on their faces. "They have the teardrop, uh, you know, tattoo . . . A teardrop is when you kill someone. And then you wear it out of pride. You're actually happy that you've killed someone, and you want people to know it," Elon observed.

Congressman Gonzalez went on to tell Musk of a recent arrival who had a teardrop tattoo and denied ever having been in prison. "And so the Border Patrol chief said, he goes, 'We do not have records from people from Venezuela. So we can't track them unless they were arrested in the United States. We really don't know who some of these actors are.' Many people you're seeing are fleeing poverty."

Musk: Sure, sure, sure.

Gonzalez: But there are others that are fleeing, you know, incarceration.

Musk: Yes. We are, basically, it seems like, the place where you can go to get away from the law.

With that, a surprised Musk spots a dozen or so illegals strolling across the border, unmolested. He turns his smartphone cam their way.

Musk's fifteen-minute interview at the border drew almost twenty-two million views in twenty-four hours and more than a hundred million views in less than a week. In one spontaneous moment, he had managed to let millions of Americans get a close-up look at some of the people struggling with the migrant influx. This is something the media, and President Biden, and congressional superstar Alexandria Ocasio-Cortez, and even Republicans in Washington had failed to do for three years.

Thereafter, Musk followed up with tweets saying the U.S. Border Patrol had just reported "the highest number of recorded illegal immigrants in history at over 260,000 this month," and that the full number may eclipse half a million, "the population of Wyoming." He called for a "greatly simplified process" requiring evidence for asylum beyond the current standard: "Just say the magic phrase, 'I seek asylum,' and you're in."

Musk's visit to the border, two hundred miles from his base at Tesla HQ near Austin, Texas, drew international attention (from the *Economic Times* in India, the *Australian*) and lots of coverage in the UK (in the *Daily Mail*, the *Independent*, the *Daily Mirror*, Reuters), as well as generating headlines in conservative staples of the U.S. media: Fox News and the *Wall Street Journal* (both controlled by the Murdoch family). But the Four Horsemen of the liberal media covered none of it. The *New York Times* ignored the Musk visit entirely, a search of the *Times* website shows. So did the *Washington Post*, and CNN, and MSNBC. As if this wasn't newsworthy. So shamelessly slanted.

After making his sobering visit to Eagle Pass, which the media assiduously avoided covering, for the most part, Musk summed up his media cynicism in another tweet, this one at 4:49 p.m. on September 29, 2023: "I don't read the legacy media propaganda much anymore. It's a waste of time and a sadness generator. Just get my news from X—much more immediate, has actual world-class subject matter experts and tons of humor. Sooo much better!"

One week later, news broke that the Biden administration had reversed its major policy stance against President Trump's border wall to stop illegal immigration. After the final year of Trump, when fewer than half a million illegal border crossings were counted, more than six million illegal entrants had streamed over the Mexico border in just three years.

Belatedly, the Department of Homeland Security announced that it was waiving twenty-six federal laws, including the Endangered Species Act and the Clean Water Act, to begin emergency construction of a new barrier in Starr County, Texas, immediately.

Eagle Pass will be left out of this, oddly enough. Yet Elon Musk's visit there, and the video he posted, which drew more than a hundred million views in a week, likely played a role in this stunning policy change by the Biden administration. Musk was able to shine a light on a real crisis the media had ignored, beating them at their own game.

DREAM *HUGE!* AND BE WILLING TO SPEND DECADES IN PURSUIT.

Twenty years ago, Elon Musk wanted to go to Mars. He still does.

It happened more than twenty years ago, yet James Cantrell still recalls, vividly, the first time he heard from an internet multimillionaire who introduced himself as Ian Musk. At least, that was the name Cantrell thought he had heard; this was back when cell service was spottier and scratchier than it is today.

The date, coincidentally, was Friday the thirteenth, July 2001, and Cantrell had left work early from the Space Dynamics Laboratory at Utah State University in Logan, nestled in the Rocky Mountains near the northern border of Utah. The setting felt like the definition of God's country, with its high mountain valley and two-mile-high peaks, especially in the summers, with placid 80-degree days even in July.

So, at one o'clock in the afternoon, Cantrell had the top down on his convertible, a 1998 Chrysler Sebring, painted gold. He was bathed in sunlight and enjoying a cool breeze as he drove past patches of alfalfa fields on the way to his home. Then he heard the ringing of his state-of-the-art Motorola StarTAC 2000 flip phone. He was almost as proud of that phone as he was of the Chrysler he was driving.

Since childhood, Cantrell had been an enthusiastic early adopter of each new tech wave. He had built a stereo amplifier from scratch at age twelve. It took him four tries. He attended high school in Palo Alto, in the heart of Silicon Valley.

By the time of Elon's call, Cantrell had been a space cowboy for fifteen years. While still an undergrad at Utah State, he had worked on the Mars Explorer and Mars Balloon missions for NASA's Jet Propulsion Laboratory in Pasadena, which is featured in the Matt Damon film *The Martian*. Then came a couple of years at the French Space Agency, consulting to the French-Soviet Mars program, and then a return to Space Dynamics.

There, Cantrell led spacecraft engineering for classified satellite contracts for the U.S. Department of Defense. He also prospected for new contracts and traveled to Moscow at various times to take a role in joint U.S.-Russia defense missile projects. Which sounds strange now that Russia has re-emerged as a threat to U.S. security and global leadership.

The unlikely (or ill-advised) cooperation with Russia was a diversionary strategy for the United States after the breakup of the Soviet Union a decade earlier. The U.S. wanted to divert Russia's vaunted missile-making prowess from producing ICBMs to making rockets for launching satellites, and it was willing to put up federal contracts for Russian work.

Russia's willingness, for decades, to throw massive resources into guns instead of butter had led to its economic rather than military collapse near the end of the Reagan administration. Yet a lasting benefit was that Russia had the best homegrown rocket designers in the world. Their rockets were better, faster, and, especially, cheaper, selling at $2 million apiece vs. $60 million at the chief U.S. rival, the old McDonnell-Douglas.

The newly emerging market for Russian rockets to ferry satellites into orbit had started to interest U.S. investors. Jim Cantrell was building his Russian connections into a new consulting business, squiring investors to Russia to meet with some of his rocket sources and show them the circus, as he put it. Six months earlier, he had escorted Bill Gross, the founder of Idealab and the progenitor of more than a hundred startups, and his brother, Lawrence, to Moscow to visit a few government-controlled rocket makers.

When Cantrell's StarTAC chirped that afternoon, he saw the 650 area code—for Palo Alto, where he had grown up—on the LCD screen and picked up the call, expecting someone he knew. Instead, it was a strange voice in a strange accent, speaking rapidly and excitedly:

"Is this Jim Cantrell?" Yes. And then the voice launched into a nonstop stream of consciousness: he was an internet millionaire who had funded PayPal, and he wanted to do something meaningful with his life. Something that would involve going to Mars and making humanity a multiplanetary species. He also wanted to get humanity off of fossil fuels. He even put in a plug for freedom of speech.

All of this in just a few minutes, Cantrell is thinking. *This guy is just jamming it in, but it sounds like it could be interesting.* So, he tells the caller he will be at home in ten minutes and will call him back. Done.

Cantrell gets home, says hi to his two kids, retreats to his home office, and dials the number on the StarTAC, but he reaches only the screechy, high-pitched wail of a 1980s fax machine. Jim's thinking: *An internet millionaire with a twenty-year-old fax machine. Sounds dubious.*

He'd never heard of PayPal, and he didn't yet use Google. Cantrell gets on his desktop computer, uses the dial-up modem, and endures still more screeching to hook up to the net. He goes on the Altavista search engine and looks up "Ian Musk" and PayPal. This leads him to "Elon Musk" and more searching.

He comes across a long profile of Elon and his car collection, and now Cantrell is impressed, because Cantrell is a car guy and a race car driver. Sports cars and drag race cars. He notices that Musk's collection includes a rare, beautiful, black Jaguar E-type roadster, and a McLaren. Nice.

Twenty minutes later, his StarTAC rings again: now this guy is angry at Cantrell for failing to call him back. When Cantrell explains he had reached a fax machine and couldn't leave a message amid all that screeching, suddenly the caller retreats and apologizes.

"I'm sorry. This is, yeah, I use this fax number so people don't have my cell phone number, but this is my mobile number." This was the first of many times that Elon Musk would get enraged at something Cantrell said or did or neglected to do over the next year.

It also was the first and last time Musk ever apologized to him for it, as Cantrell views it.

Apology accepted, the guy launches right back into his going-to-Mars spiel, without skipping a beat. Cantrell had heard from a number of tech investors keen on space, but this young man, who had turned thirty years old only two weeks earlier, instantly displayed a rare intensity. Musk told him a mutual friend had said Cantrell could help him "get Russian rockets" for what he wanted to do "on Mars." He wants to meet, and he asks whether Cantrell lives near an airport. Cantrell tells Musk he can see Logan Airport from his front porch, and Elon responds that he has a private jet and says, "Great. I'll be there tomorrow." Saturday.

Cantrell hesitates: he doesn't know this man. In his past dealings with the Russians, he had grown wary of their tactics and connections. This Musk guy could be some whack job or a Russian hit man; it is premature to bring him home to his wife and their kids. So, he concocts a quick lie and tells Elon he has to fly commercial out of Salt Lake City to Oregon on Sunday, suggesting that they meet past security in the Delta Air Lines conference room.

This way, this new stranger—accent on the "strange"—would be less likely to be carrying a weapon, as Cantrell calculated the situation. Plus, cops would be walking the premises.

Musk agrees, and two days later they set up in a rented airport conference room in Salt Lake and talked in a torrent of details about Musk's ambitions for a mission to Mars. For three hours. They were joined by Bob Zubrin, a Brooklyn-born, onetime cab-driver who made himself into a space engineer and nuclear physicist for Martin Marietta's rocket program.

Zubrin was the mutual friend who had referred Musk to Jim Cantrell, and his presence made Cantrell feel a good deal more at ease. If Zubrin was willing to show up in person, the risk of being here with this Elon Musk guy must be negligible. Good to know.

In 1990, Bob Zubrin and a colleague had authored a research paper on supercheap innovations that could power a Mars trip by using the Mars atmosphere to produce water, oxygen, and ingredients for rocket fuel to enable a return trip to Earth. Thereafter, people could colonize the place. In 1998, frustrated with the lack of progress that NASA was making in planning a manned mission to Mars, Bob founded the Mars Society.

The first thing Cantrell noticed, as soon as they sat down, was Musk's outsized intellect: Elon was supersmart, connected the dots extremely fast. And then there was his vision. Elon Musk thought really big. So big, Cantrell realized later, that the scale of it took his breath away.

A manned mission to Mars was impossible for most minds to contemplate, let alone plan on executing. The most breathtaking element of all was that Musk wanted to do this on his own, with private funding, rather than under the stifling, micromanaging control of government. In 2001, this notion of privately financing a mission to Mars was unthinkable. Space exploration was mostly a nation-state pursuit, affordable only to the biggest governments and the richest, most powerful corporate behemoths.

And now this newcomer, a skinny internet whiz kid with already-thinning hair, who showed up in a white T-shirt as if he were ready for phys ed class, was telling Cantrell and Zubrin, "Hey, we're gonna go to Mars, right?" Crazier still, Musk was willing to invest $100 million of his own funds in this impossible dream.

It was audacious as hell, and Jim Cantrell had to love it. Fuck it, let's go for it.

To this Sinatra construct, Musk added two supporting pillars: unending patience to achieve intentionally grandiose dreams, even over decades; and an endemic, preternatural inability to see or contemplate any possibility of failure. Even though he was pursuing the impossible.

This blindness to failure was another key that Cantrell spotted during his first meeting with Musk at the Salt Lake City airport. The three men ended up leaving the Delta conference room to head downtown to have dinner at Cantrell's favorite spot, the Market Street Grill. Three more hours of conversation, and never once did Elon Musk break into social niceties to get to know one another. He was untrained and unpracticed in the protocol of it, and he was uninterested in it, as Cantrell could see.

Instead, their conversation focused on one topic: How could they make this happen?

In the Ethos of Elon, dreaming the impossible dream—and then pursuing it doggedly and relentlessly for many years to come—is the engine of innovation. It provides the motivation for reaching and stretching farther than you ever might try, otherwise; thereby, you end up making more progress than everyone else has made, even if you fall short of your most ambitious goals.

Dreaming big, really big, also fuels the abiding and audacious self-confidence to believe you can achieve what no one else before you dared even try. As if to dream it means you are already capable of doing it. To dream it is to *do it*. At the same time, pursuing huge dreams can offer solace in setbacks: these obstacles become expected steps on the path to attaining impossibly great outcomes. Of *course* setbacks happen: this stuff is supposed to be really hard.

The impossible goals Musk pursues are even more ambitious than they appear. At SpaceX, the company that emerged from his first meetings with Jim Cantrell, Bob Zubrin, and a handful of other space pioneers and entrepreneurs, his aim goes far beyond making it to Mars. Elon wants to build a city there. He hopes that a million people could inhabit the red planet in twenty years, which sounds like a huge overreach. Always overpromise.

Even that ambition, moreover, is part of a bigger whole: After settling on Mars, we could also settle, say, a moon of Jupiter, and from there, perhaps, we could expand to the asteroid belt, as he mentioned in August 2024 in his podcast chat with Lex Fridman.

Similarly, Musk's Neuralink is experimenting with paralyzed patients—but, eventually, he envisions speeding up human brains to communicate faster with computers and AI, and even with other chip-equipped humans. Elon also sees a human-microchip meld as a way to ensure safer AI: Keep your friends close and your enemies closer, as he tells his pal, Fridman:

"The long-term aspiration of Neuralink is to improve the AI-human symbiosis by increasing the bandwidth of communication. In the most benign scenario of AI, you have to consider that the AI is simply going to get bored waiting for you to spit out a few words. If the AI can communicate at terabits per second, and your communication is at bits per second, it's like [AI is] talking to a tree."

Musk continues: "We could better align collective human will with AI if the [human] output rate was dramatically increased. And I think there's potential to increase the output rate by, I don't know, three, maybe six, maybe more orders of magnitude." Then Fridman asks him, "Do you think there'll be a world in the next couple of decades where it's hundreds of millions of people [that] have Neuralinks?"

Elon: "Yeah I do." Once the technology is "extremely safe, and you can have superhuman abilities, and let's say you can upload your memories, so you wouldn't lose memories, then I think probably a lot of people would choose to have it. It would supersede the cell phone."

His dreams are just as grandiose for Optimus, the humanoid robot that Tesla is developing to deploy by the hundreds on factory production lines. At Tesla's annual shareholder meeting in June 2024, Elon declared that one day millions and even billions of robots will be in operation. "I think everyone in the world is gonna want one." He even predicted that the robots could lift Tesla's value someday to $25 trillion—over half the recent value of the five hundred largest companies combined. This forecast may never come true, but Elon dreams huge.

On the Lex Fridman podcast, Musk predicted the demand for robots one day will lead to producing a billion units annually. Every single new robot will be a new, additional data source for transmitting real-time, real-world data based on what it sees.

At some point in the future, Elon's seemingly different pursuits will come together in a beneficial synergy. Grok, the AI engine of Musk's xAI company, will glean insights from millions of Optimus robots that transmit data on what they see, and from millions of Tesla cars, and from the posts of hundreds of millions of users on the X platform. An Optimus robot arm might be able to be attached to an amputee or a paralyzed patient and operated by the patient's embedded Neuralink brain chip.

Elon Musk has shown these traits again and again in his career, in particular at SpaceX, the company that emerged from his first meetings with Jim Cantrell, Bob Zubrin, and a handful of other space pioneers and entrepreneurs.

Many of us, by contrast, are too timid, too rational and sensible, to dream huge dreams. We are too afraid of failure and fallout, too daunted by the risk of loss and looking silly or naive or arrogant in our ambitions. Too reluctant to let down our loved ones and colleagues and investors. Or too beaten down to realize that we can achieve something far greater than we know.

And, so, we settle. We settle for the safe and the normal expectation of outcomes and returns. Instead of reaching for the highest heights we can imagine achieving, we settle for lesser goals to avoid disappointment in trying to achieve bigger ones. We forget an adage that drove the past three decades of innovation in Silicon Valley, the most innovative place on the planet:

If you haven't failed, you haven't learned. Onward.

Today some people, especially Millennials and Gen-Zers, are so afraid of failing that they avoid the risk of even trying. TikTok is filled with meme videos of twenty-one-year-olds daunted by the prospect of working full-time for the rest of their lives with a few weeks of vacation in between. They feel oppressed by having to commute to the office, and they whine about their lack of sway in the world. Instead of doing something about it.

Dreaming bigger dreams would help these pups by giving them something to strive toward and commit to for years to come, making them realize that all of this hard work is for something better, a better future for themselves and for the people they love.

Dream bigger dreams. How to apply this Elon lesson to our own lives and careers? We operate on a much smaller scale, with lesser financial stakes and lower risk, and we toil in jobs that afford less latitude and less freedom to improvise. Yet there must be ways we, too, can dream bigger dreams and set ourselves to the years it will take to achieve them. Even if only in our mindset, and in the way we view the things that happen in our world and how we process them and react to them.

And it is okay if we dream huge and don't quite make it: we end up farther along toward that dream, anyway, if we worked hard enough for long enough to attain it. This can propel our next dream.

Possible applications: every one of us today can be dreaming of starting our own business on the side, leveraging the skills, contacts, contracts, and connections from our main line of work to provide a related service that is missing elsewhere. Taking the steps to set up this business can make us more transportable, resalable, and flexible if our current job leaves us, even if we never end up starting that new business.

If you are in a job you despise, start dreaming of the job you really want, and start plotting how to get there, in terms of education, training, next job, and connections. By taking these steps forward and doing something tangible, you will brighten your attitude and outlook, because you are taking action to improve your own state. It feels empowering. Instead of just sitting there and bitching about your situation, a popular pursuit for many people nowadays, you are taking action, moving forward.

Likewise, if you are thriving in a job, ask for a bigger raise than you have ever sought before. Look for new ways to bring in more revenue or cut operating costs. Apply for a promotion that seems out of reach to your bosses.

Early in my career at the *Wall Street Journal* in New York, I raised my hand for one of the most coveted jobs in journalism: Page One editor. My bosses kindly considered me, though I wasn't yet ready for the post; this made them see me in a new and more serious way. At bottom, my yearning for the Page One editor job owed to my real, underlying dream, which was to run my own show, to have as few layers as possible between the stories I wanted to tell and the reader. Whether at the *Journal*, or at the top of a magazine, or with my own TV show someday.

A few years later, the Page One job was coming open again, just as I got an offer from *Forbes* at a 50 percent raise. When I was told that, at best, I was one of three candidates for the Page One job, I accepted the offer from *Forbes*, and it was a beneficial leap in my pay and career. Still, I took the second-in-command job of managing editor, without real control of the magazine, so I wasn't yet running my own show.

All along, I knew I wanted to be on television someday and host my own show and tell the stories I wanted to tell. After nine years at *Forbes*, and doing weekly hits every Saturday on *Forbes on Fox* on Fox News, I leapt into TV, joining CNBC. Sure enough, eighteen months in, I snagged the dream: I became the solo anchor of a prime-time show on CNBC in April 2009, in the aftermath of the Great Meltdown. It was exhilarating. Five months later, my show was canceled. A hard blow, but oh man, what a magnificent ride.

Today I host my own podcast, *What's Bugging Me*, on the Ricochet platform, and I have almost absolute control over the show's content and messaging, with the help and occasional second-guessing of a talented producer. Sometimes our dreams work out in unexpected ways.

Dreaming huge can work in our personal lives, too. Say your dream is to retire to Florida, which charges no personal income tax, and buy a lakeside home where you can walk out on your dock and fish every morning. Working toward this dream can help you feel more motivated and in pursuit of something bigger.

Start planning the saving, investing, and fundraising that will put you on that trajectory. Search for extra sources of income, take a second job, start a business on the side.

Or perhaps you have been through a rough divorce, and your dream is to find the true love of your life in a world of shallow hookups. The dream drives the steps you take as you plot how to turn this into a reality; and planning for this helps manifest a better mood that lifts you out of the bitterness of what you just endured.

Each one of us has the right to start dreaming again. Especially today, in a world that is cursed by so many people for its problems and injustices, where cynicism and criticism and shopping for umbrage have turned into a blood sport. Where panic trumps hope.

The one prerequisite to dreaming the biggest dreams possible: you have to be willing to hold on to them and pursue them almost forever. For years and even decades to come. If you are chasing after something that can be attained in a few years, you are failing to dream big enough.

Elon Musk set his sights on Mars over two decades ago, and he still is 140 million miles away from the Red Planet. That is equivalent to almost five hundred missions to the moon. At the same time, however, after more than twenty years of toil, he now is closer than ever.

At dinner with Jim Cantrell and Bob Zubin in downtown Salt Lake City, Musk held forth and talked about first principles: breaking down a given problem or challenge to its most fundamental parts, and figuring out the most basic truth of something, and then building from there, issue by issue. To this day, it's one of his favorite topics.

Cantrell was nodding and looking at Bob Zubrin and thinking: *Yeah, this is what we engineers do, by definition.* Then again, Cantrell could see that this approach freed up Musk's mind. He was emphatic and wedded to the facts, and where other people got distracted by details, Elon managed to stay focused on the things that mattered. And this arose out of Musk's ability to break down a problem and identify its most basic essence.

By the end of the meal, the three men had agreed that they would study the mission, define it, and then figure out which rockets would best fit the mission's parameters, and find a way to procure them. This was the start of the project they named Mars Oasis. Russia had landed the first craft on Mars in 1971; the Mars 3 lasted 117 seconds and sent back one grainy, gray image before going kaput. Only the United States had been to Mars since then, with the Viking 1 and 2 in 1976 and the Pathfinder in 1997.

Immediately, because Elon Musk was always in a hurry, Jim Cantrell started building a team and roughing out projected costs.

When he came up with $100 million, Musk told him that sum was, indeed, how much he had to spend on this effort. Cantrell tapped his contacts at Jet Propulsion Laboratory who had worked on the Mars rover missions. Chris Thompson signed on, and he would become, after Elon himself, the second employee at SpaceX. Years later he would team up with Cantrell at Phantom Space, a startup that aims to launch satellites at only one-third the cost of SpaceX.

Then Michael D. Griffin got involved. He had designed missile-defense satellites at Johns Hopkins University's Applied Physics Laboratory, and had been the CEO of a launch startup, Orbital Sciences. Later in his career he would serve as a NASA administrator (2005–2009) and U.S. under secretary of defense (2018–2020).

The film director James Cameron dropped in to lend advice. He was a helicopter pilot by hobby, and he had a surprisingly sophisticated understanding of engineering, Cantrell observed. Cameron advised the group on how to communicate the best message to the public. Another advisor was a space superstar, Tony Spear. He had joined JPL in 1962 and put in thirty-six years there, ultimately running the Mars Pathfinder mission from conception to landing on July 4, 1997, and retiring a year later. Spear had accompanied Cantrell and the Gross brothers on their recent trip to Moscow to see the circus.

The Pathfinder had landed on Mars by using parachutes to slow its descent to the planet's surface, the craft protected inside a bubble-wrap-like padded suit of air bags known as a balloon. The capsule landed and tumbled end over end until coming to a standstill. The bubble gradually deflated, and the rover emerged from the tangle and began its surveillance mission.

A real mission to Mars would aim at landing a full spaceship on the surface, using rocket burn to slow its landing, and, presumably, being able to create fuel to mount a launch and return to Earth. Otherwise, it would be a one-way trip, and you'd die on Mars, however long you might live. Cantrell viewed mission Mars Oasis as entirely doable, plausible. He was of the belief that anything is possible, you just have to break it down into the core elements, as Elon was doing here. Nothing in life was about getting close; it was about doing it or not doing it.

These odysseys we find ourselves pursuing, to accomplish the most difficult things, end up being fueled by this belief that, ultimately, we *will* make it happen. No matter how long it takes—and great achievements *should* take a long time to emerge. This, Cantrell felt, was a critical mindset for all entrepreneurs to possess. Some people called it faith, others called it gumption, but either way, it was this inner drive that just kept you going.

He recognized that this was Elon's strength. Early in their efforts, a life-or-death debate erupted. Elon wanted to send a nest of mice on the Mars trip to inspire the imagination of millions of fans on Earth. Most members of the team told Cantrell this idea was crazy, and it fell on Cantrell to communicate their concerns to Musk. He asked Elon to consider the downside, something Elon rarely does: What if millions of people back home started following the mice's journey and gave them names and devoted webcams to them? And then they died?

Suddenly, a bunch of rodents that we use in medical experiments or kill in traps in our kitchens would become idealized symbols of humans bound for Mars, and you'd have a humanitarian disaster unfolding nightly on television. Plus, Cantrell pointed out, this could turn into a pornographic mission to Mars if the camera captured the mice breeding all night long.

So, he told Elon they had to scrap the mouse-tronaut idea, and then Bob Zubrin was pissed off at Cantrell, because this had been his idea from the start. His priority had been getting humans to Mars, and the DNA of mice and men share an 85 percent overlap, so this could have been a cool way to show that Mars can support life.

That idea was shelved, and the group turned to a plan to send a patch of greenery up to the Red Planet, whose rusty iron-ore makeup gives the surface and the atmosphere the fiery rose tint we see from Earth. A "plant growth chamber," gently landed on Mars, could use the Martian atmosphere's carbon dioxide to grow weeds from Earth, which would produce oxygen. It was another way of showing the promise that we can live on Mars, one day. If a few racks of growing plants could survive on Mars, someday millions of acres of vegetation might create a survivable atmosphere for humans.

No government-run space mission would ever be allowed to pull off a stunt like this one, for fear of contaminating another planet and risking unforeseen consequences. This contamination is prohibited by various international space treaties signed by every government space organization on Earth. Elon Musk was utterly free to ignore these treaties, if he chose, because his Mars mission would be a privately financed pursuit.

The finite funding source of this effort necessarily led to Russia as the supplier of the rockets, given the cost advantage. Musk was paying $100 an hour to Cantrell and other consultants on Mars Oasis, and he often dickered over rates and pushed for discounts, as Cantrell recalls it. Early on, however, he hired a Russian consultant for a fee of $10,000.

The consultant was a senior executive at Lavochkin Research, the Russian company that had made every Mars lander for the Russian space program, as well as assorted surface-to-air missiles, ICBMs, and aircraft. One option for the Musk group was to out-source the entire project to Lavochkin, simply pay it to build the lander and the delivery vehicle and handle the launch. The $10,000 fee was for an initial study of the proposed mission. Earnest money.

But the fee had to be paid in cash. Russia wasn't part of the Swift banking system. The Lavochkin exec was coming to Pasadena to attend a space conference in August, just weeks after Mars Oasis had taken form. Cantrell would have to meet him there and hand over the Benjamins. This led to an urgent search for $10K by three men: Cantrell, who lacked the cash himself, and two internet multi-millionaires. Elon Musk had made his early fortune on Zip2 and PayPal, and with him was his college pal from Penn, Adeo Ressi. By this time, Ressi had started a local-news website and sold it to AOL, and then sold a website firm for $88 million.

So, Cantrell climbs in the back seat of Adeo's rented late '90s Camaro convertible (its top down), Elon takes the passenger seat up front, and Adeo takes the wheel, and they start traversing the freeways dissecting the sprawl of Los Angles to tap friends and ATMs for the funds. Ultimately, though Cantrell is vague on de-tails, some PayPal friends of Musk's stepped up, and a hundred $100 bills were put into a pouch and prepared for the handover.

When they met the Lavochkin leader at the space conference and handed him the pouch, he started removing stacks of C-notes and tucking them into the various pockets of his boxy, poorly tailored suit. To Cantrell, it felt like they had just pulled off a drug deal.

In the meantime, Musk began cramming, borrowing books on aviation, rocketry, and space flight from Cantrell, including his propulsion elements book, and a book Mike Griffin had written on rocket propulsion. Cantrell and the design team knew a launch to Mars could take place only once every two years, when Earth was closest to Mars and the distance traveled would be the shortest. The right array of rocket engines would traverse the required 140 million miles in perhaps nine months; to go faster would test the physics limiting how much energy you could put into the trajectory.

Making a return trip to Earth would require carrying enough fuel on the way to Mars (too heavy) or creating the fuel on Mars. Mars Oasis would be a one-way affair, landing the craft on the planet, letting loose the plant chamber, and staying behind forever-more. It was a start, and it was what Elon Musk could afford to do.

In August 2001, Jim Cantrell squires Musk and Adeo Ressi on a first fact-finding trip to the UK and Russia. They get a lukewarm reception from engineers at the University of Surrey, which had bought Russian rocket engines at $2 million apiece. Then they fly to Moscow for introductory meetings with various suppliers to the Russian government's space program, wanting to test their interest in Mars Oasis. Their visit to the staff at Lavochkin, the premiere rocket maker, was a necessary warm-up, more of a museum tour than a business meeting.

Literally: Cantrell and his cohorts get a tour of Lavochkin's museum, filled with artifacts from its many missile successes of past decades.

One night in Moscow, Elon and Adeo ask Jim Cantrell about the Ugly Duck, which they wanted to visit. Cantrell asks them: Do you know what it really is? Elon tells him a cousin in South Africa told him about it, and it sounds kind of interesting. Cantrell, in his days working on the French-Soviet space program in the 1990s, had U.S. national security clearance, and he was ordered to stay out of the Ugly Duck and places like it: wild nightclubs where almost anything goes. A quick tryst on the bar, even, and other compromising activities that could be used to blackmail someone in a sensitive position.

He offers to take them to the Ugly Duck and drop them off, because no way is Cantrell going in there, and they can take a taxi back to the hotel. Cantrell warns Elon and Adeo to bring their passports. In Russia, you had to have it with you at all times, especially as a foreigner.

Cut to the next morning, 9:30. They have a bus arriving at 10:00 to take them to visit more companies. Cantrell is already downstairs at breakfast in the hotel, coffee'd up and waiting, when Adeo appears, hungover and looking miserable. A few minutes later Elon shows up, looking even worse. They wince and sip at hot coffee, and Elon looks at Adeo and says: "Do you want to tell him? Do you want me to tell him?"

Adeo Ressi takes up the baton and tells Cantrell their story: "Yeah, well, remember those passports you told us about? We didn't take 'em." At two o'clock in the morning, they were riding in a cab back to their hotel with a new friend they had met at the Ugly Duck, a Russian woman (presumably a *femme fatale*, given the Duck's infamous reputation).

Suddenly, Moscow police, standing at a corner of Red Square, stopped their cab and demanded to see their documents. Cantrell tells them: "Yes, it was a shakedown, and how much did it cost you?" They admitted to $800 apiece, all the cash they had, as Cantrell tells the tale many years later. Then they asked him if he could loan them some cash.

They found little interest in the Mars project on that trip. They flew from Moscow to Paris, visiting engineers connected to the Ariane rocket program, who basically waved them off. Cantrell got the feeling that the French were thinking: *This silly boy.* They flew home from Paris to New York, and a few weeks later, on September 11, 2001, the 9/11 attacks took down the World Trade Center towers in Manhattan. Their next trip to Moscow, that October, took place in a newly dangerous and paranoid world.

Cantrell thought of canceling that trip, but Musk was in too much of a hurry. They visited more suppliers and met with the Lavochkin executive to review the viability report that had cost Musk $10,000 in cash.

Musk and Cantrell made a third and final trip to Moscow in November. At the time, the Russians were dominating the satellite launch business, as various European governments and aerospace companies lined up, as well as the U.S. government. It looked as though Russia was going to wipe out the Americans in the newly emerging industry.

Thus, on Musk's third visit to pitch his mission to some of the finest rocket designers in the world, the room was bathed in Russian arrogance and skepticism. Elon, Jim Cantrell, and Mike Griffin were to meet with the chief designer of one of the most important missile projects at Lavochkin. Chief designers back then were like rock stars in Russia, granted wide latitude over big budgets to pull off missile miracles.

This one oversaw the effort to convert the Dnepr, the largest Russian rocket, made by the international space company Kosmotros. It was an ICBM capable of mustering 211 tons of mass liftoff and carrying a payload of almost 4 tons, and measuring 112 feet tall and 10 feet in diameter. The Dnepr had the muscle to make it to Mars.

Cantrell will always remember the scene, and, as an aspiring novelist today, he tells the story well. The three men and their Russian driver approach a site protected by an intimidating level of security. An argument in Russian breaks out at the first guard post, and Cantrell can understand most of it because of his work with Soviet space cadets in the '90s.

"We can't let Americans in here," the guard tells the driver, but the driver declares that they have an appointment to see the *chief designer*, and they are allowed to enter the compound. They approach thirty-foot-high walls topped by razor wire, and wait for a large, iron door, powered by a ten-horsepower motor, to slide open, slowly, and then they drive into a snowy courtyard. Cantrell is thinking it looks like every movie scene of Moscow in winter, circa World War II.

That, or a scene from *Young Frankenstein*. They approach a massive steel front door; the driver swings an old door knocker, hard; and they wait outside for five minutes in the cold. Mike Griffin, looking at the scene around him, whispers to Cantrell: "Get me the fuck out of here." He wanted to be elsewhere. "Let's get in the car. Let's *go!*"

But then they hear a procession of dead bolts clacking and locks sliding, and the door swings open to reveal a Russian engineer in a black, furry ushanka and a heavy, Michelin Man coat. It is as frigid inside the building as it is outside. They can see their breath. He leads them down a long hallway lit by only three bare lightbulbs, past office doorways covered in thick, padded vinyl, a sign of importance and rank. *It feels like a fucking insane asylum*, Cantrell is saying to himself.

At the end of the hallway, they enter a large conference room. Elon Musk, flanked by Jim and Mike, is greeted by two dozen Russians. It is just before lunch, and the men dine on finger sandwiches—cucumber, assorted mystery meats—and make innocuous conversation. Socialize first, then get down to business, the European way.

For some reason, no one has taken a seat at the conference table, and everyone continues to stand as the real meeting begins. Jim Cantrell is in a dress shirt, tie, and jacket, business attire for a serious business meeting. Mike is dressed likewise, but Elon Musk is wearing black slacks and a white T-shirt—an undershirt, really.

And brown shoes, and Cantrell hates brown shoes—they were ugly; why did anybody ever make them, much less buy them? Plus, it looked as if Elon had skipped running a comb through his hair that morning. He was the Hollywood cliché of an absentminded professor.

Damn it. Cantrell had explained to the thirty-year-old phenom that the Russians saw how you dressed as a sign of respect. Or disrespect. They were old-school in this way; they wore neckties with their old Soviet suits, which were poorly made and ill fitting. If Musk had heard the fashion tips, he had chosen to disregard them.

At long last, the chief designer begins the meeting by asking, "Well, how can I help you? Why are you here?" Musk launches into his spiel about making humanity a multiplanetary species, getting humanity off fossil fuels, and stopping tyrants from controlling free speech. Failing to read the room with that last point, perhaps.

Cantrell can see the chief designer's eyes rolling back in his head as he fidgets and grows impatient. In Russia, if you had gold fillings, you were doing well and might even have an "in" with the KGB, but this rocket man was missing teeth, and his bad, boxy suit overwhelmed his skinny frame. This man had an angry air.

Elon noticed none of this; he just kept on with his fantastical filibuster about his mission to Mars, and how he wanted to make use of Lavochkin's Dnepr, and on and on, dismounting with, "And we'd like to buy several rockets."

A long pause ensues, and the chief designer starts to speak in Russian, expecting the company's interpreter to translate his words into English. Unbeknownst to them, Cantrell didn't actually need the interpreter because he could comprehend all of it. "Well, please understand," the chief designer begins, "this is a serious machine. It's a weapon of war. It's not some toy." The translator is stopping short of translating any of this to English, and the designer continues in Russian:

"These are serious machines for serious people. You are not a serious person. Take your bullshit internet money and go back to America." And then he spits on Elon's *brown* shoes—he may have deserved it just for wearing brown shoes, in Cantrell's view—and on Cantrell's appropriate black shoes, too.

It was a little saliva just for show, to convey contempt. Finally, Elon got it, telling Cantrell: "I think he just spit on us." Cantrell, deadpan: "Yeah, I think that's a sign of disrespect." This scene is depicted in a few pages of Walter Isaacson's 688-page Musk opus.

The interpreter for Lavochkin then finally spoke up, politely and tactfully, saying, "The chief designer thanks you for your time. I don't think we'll be able to make our rockets work for your mission." Mike Griffin turns to Cantrell and his original hunch: "Let's get the fuck out of here," and Cantrell tells their host they are disappointed but thanks him for his time.

He debriefs Elon on the drive back to their hotel, and if the events have fazed Musk in any way, he hides any sign of this. The next morning, before taking an afternoon flight back to New York, they check out of the hotel and tote their luggage with them to a city house in the middle of Moscow for a meeting with Kosmotros, the maker of the Dnepr.

Kosmotros had thrived with the help of U.S. contracts aimed at stopping it from selling old SSTs to other countries after the breakup of the U.S.S.R., turning former nukes into satellite launchers. Swords into plowshares. It had developed a Western sales style to appeal to clients in the United States and Europe.

Four Russians—three Kosmotros engineers and a fourth man whom Cantrell remembers as the Blue-Eyed Colonel, who seemed to be running this show—sit down and take in Elon Musk's pitch. They speak English. Elon culminates with an offer of $5 million for two rockets, a premium compared to the $2 million-apiece price another bidder had recently paid.

The four Komostros men start speaking Russian to each other, unaware that Cantrell can understand what they are saying, and Cantrell hears the phrase "malinky malchik," little boy. Then they returned to English: they would be willing to sell rockets, but at $8 million. Each.

They go back and forth in a long discussion, Elon arguing with the Russians about marginal costs and revealing that he knew they had just sold the rockets to someone else—the University of Surrey—for $2 million a pop, and them telling him maybe so, but not now, and not to you. By noon, this impasse is impregnable, and the three men—Elon Musk, future global industrialist; Mike Griffin, future NASA chief and U.S. under secretary of defense; and Jim Cantrell, future founder of the startup Phantom Space— drag their bags out into the snow and hail a cab for the airport.

Cantrell is feeling totally defeated at this point. He was hired to procure Russian rockets for this mission, and he has failed, and Cantrell *hates* to fail at anything. The men share a very quiet ride to the airport, no one speaking, and then go through layers and layers of security at the airport. Why was it always so much harder to leave Moscow than to enter the city?

They board a mostly empty flight back to New York, riding in coach with Cantrell and Griffin sitting together some rows back from Elon. Once you took off from the airport, it felt like you were free again, and Cantrell and Griffin toasted with whiskey while Elon clacked on his laptop. He was already making plans for the next steps.

Mike, aiming to tease Elon, nudges Cantrell and announces, "What the fuck do you think that idiot savant up there is doing?" Cantrell invokes a sci-fi cult classic, "Plan 9 to save humanity, I'm guessing," and Elon turns around in his seat and tells them, "Hey guys, I think we can build the rocket ourselves."

Mike tells Elon that he will have to walk over a whole army of dead bodies to get there, that others have tried this and failed, and Musk tells him: "But I have a spreadsheet."

Cantrell, sarcastically: "Wow, we've never had a spreadsheet of a rocket before."

"Oh, fuck you both," Elon says, and he turns back to his laptop and punches up the spreadsheet and invites them to have a look. The other two men are rolling their eyes, but they inspect what Elon has laid down and are surprised to see that it is pretty good. First principles: each component required and the likely cost, what to make vs. what to buy, the size of the engines and basic size of the rocket.

Mike asks Elon, "Where did you get this stuff?" Cantrell offers that Musk has been studying Cantrell's propulsion books, but Mike says, "Bullshit. Something more is going on here. Elon got this stuff from somebody." And it turns out Mike Griffin is right.

Elon had been spending weekends with Chris Thompson and rocket makers. One guy had been building a ten-thousand-pound liquid rocket engine in his garage, and he and his pals were spending their beer money on building thirty-foot-tall rockets and launching them in the desert. Smaller-scale test launches, really.

It was there, watching these rockets lift up into the sky, that Musk had a sort of religious moment, he now tells Jim and Mike, and this was when he decided they should build the rocket from the bottom up. And this, basically, is how SpaceX started, Elon telling them they would form a company and build this rocket themselves, and he wanted them both to be part of it.

Both men would end up declining Musk's offer. To Cantrell, it was another form of insanity, a decision made only hours after getting rejected in Moscow, although now he realized that Elon, in reality, must have decided this even before making the trip. In Russia, he was just making sure his instincts were right. No one else was going to be as reliable and as devoted to this pursuit as Musk himself, and, thus, he would launch one of the largest, most expensive DIY projects in world history.

Jim Cantrell would spend the next few months helping assemble a new team of rocket designers and builders, including Chris Thompson. Cantrell left later in 2002, doubting that Musk would be successful at what he wanted to do: mass-produce huge, outsize rockets to make it all the way to Mars at a cost of $100 million per. He didn't see how Musk would ever be able to raise the capital. Plus, Cantrell had tired of Musk's bad temper. The last time Elon yelled at him, it was over Cantrell's estimate for how much it would cost for the fuel tanks on a self-made rocket. Musk called him and told him he would eat his ball cap if Cantrell was right—and Cantrell turned out to be right, as he tells the story later.

He earned maybe $18,000 overall from Musk, and he bought an old Maserati and later sold it for $25,000. Musk went on to build SpaceX into a company with almost $9 billion a year in revenue and a total value of perhaps $200 billion.

Two decades onward, SpaceX continues to pursue its founding mission of flying to Mars. It pays the bills by dominating the commercial space launch industry. It ferries satellites into space and taxis astronauts to the International Space Station, billing the U.S. government hundreds of millions of dollars per year. It also sells launch services to foreign governments and multinational corporations.

Along the way, SpaceX has placed more than six thousand of its own satellites in the Starlink constellation, each one about the size of a sofa, with a goal of twelve thousand by 2027 and forty-two thousand birds, eventually. This network already can cover almost the entire planet with navigation, visibility, surveillance, high-speed wireless internet, and other services.

Today, Starlink has grown into a mission-critical, global network, economically, strategically, and militarily. It serves two million customers in sixty countries on all seven continents. SpaceX's more than 6,000 birds aloft compare with just 1,619 for NASA and 3,203 for China. Musk's company owns more than half of all the satellites hovering in low orbit, 340 miles above the surface of Earth.

Yet none of this would have happened without Elon Musk's huge dream of making it to Mars. And all of it did happen, even though, twenty-some years later, he has yet to turn the ultimate goal into reality. If this is base reality.

SpaceX at $200 billion in valuation makes Elon's 42 percent stake worth $83 billion. Starlink is pegged at 40 percent of that value, or $80 billion, and Musk in a few years may issue publicly traded stock in Starlink itself. Even though he views shareholders as a million little dictators, as he once told Cantrell. But when your net worth spans twelve digits, who cares? Musk is motivated by a lot more than money.

When Musk visited the chief designer at Lavochkin and others in Russia back in 2001, Cantrell realizes now, they had no idea that this nerdy, poorly dressed young slacker in a T-shirt was bearing the seeds of their own destruction. Musk was a monster of their own making. SpaceX crushed the Russians, and the French, and everyone else in the private space business that grew up in the next two decades.

The biggest dreams require an inexhaustible supply of hope, and Jim Cantrell sometimes talks about an experiment conducted in the 1950s that addressed this. A bunch of rats were released into a vat of water, and they were unable to cling to any side walls for a chance to escape. After twenty minutes, exhausted, they drowned.

Then a second bunch of rats were put into the same vat of water, and just before they were about to drown, they were pulled out and rescued. And when these same rats were placed back in the water later, they would tread water and slip against the slick walls, again and again, for hours, expecting to be rescued. Hope is a powerful motivator. Persistence is key to survival.

Elon Musk should be an inspiration to us all, Cantrell argues, showing us that no dream is too big. The problem is that most people give up too early. The surest way to lose the race is to quit the race, Cantrell likes to say. In the race to Mars, Elon Musk remains in it to win it.

ALWAYS BET ON YOURSELF, AND DOUBLE DOWN.

Early days. Zip2, PayPal, SpaceX.

Three years into the biggest jump of my career—after twenty-five years as a journalist for the *Wall Street Journal* and then *Forbes* to television as an anchor on CNBC—I faced a decision fraught with implications that were both financial and personal. My first-ever contract was coming up for renewal, and it was unclear whether the network was going to keep me on.

Admittedly, my transition had been rocky, entailing on-air fights with other talent, complaints from guests for the questions I asked, and a feud with jeering bloggers that drew headlines. I also had hosted a nightly prime-time show that was canceled after five months. As well, if CNBC decided to send me packing, it had the right to keep me sidelined and unable to sign a new deal anywhere else for six months afterward. Which would be damaging to both my resale value and my income.

Just as I was assessing my chances of re-signing, I came across a beautiful two-bedroom apartment in Brooklyn that I wanted to buy. In the eight years since my divorce up to this time, I had been spending $40,000 a year on rent, moving to three different apartments. A waste of more than $300,000 that could have gone into a home that I could own.

Now I was able to put down a 20 percent payment on a million-dollar apartment, if I really stretched and exhausted all my savings to get the deal done. But what if CNBC cut me? I might lose the apartment and my down payment because of events that were entirely foreseeable. So, as my contract was waning, I broached the subject with the CEO of CNBC, Mark Hoffman, one day when he made a rare descent down the curved main stairs and into the newsroom. He stood six feet five inches tall and used this to his benefit. I told him about my situation and the apartment for sale and asked whether if he were in my shoes, he would buy it.

"You should always bet on yourself," Hoffman responded.

Easy for him to say: he had already made it, and he's six foot five. And this was his only point: always bet on yourself. He offered no assurances that my contract would be renewed. So, instead of taking the risk and buying the apartment, I continued renting. The TV business was just too unpredictable, too unreliable.

A month later, CNBC offered to renew my contract, but at a 30 percent pay cut. I was able to jump to Fox Business Network at no pay cut, thanks to my agent, and I felt vindicated. More than a decade later, I now realize that my choice to keep on renting was the worst investment decision I have ever made. Real estate prices in New York are a good deal higher now, and I am still a renter. I have plowed another half a million dollars into rent that I will never get back. All because I was unwilling to bet on myself—and to really go all in.

A lesson lies therein, yes? Elon Musk learned it long ago. Always bet on yourself. And go all in, because you know you can deliver. Musk has done this again and again, at breathtaking scale, and he did it long before he had built up a war chest of untold billions of dollars in wealth. Musk did this from the very start of his career, like a well-comped whale at the $2,000 poker table at the Bellagio in Las Vegas, who keeps winning stacks of chips and letting half of them ride. Musk kept going all in, even as the stakes and risks grew ever larger.

Where does he get the moxie? Unflinching self-confidence is a prerequisite to always betting on yourself. Is this a product of nature or nurture, encoded in his DNA or instilled in him by his kick-ass mother? Or unlocked in him as an angry answer to a father he regarded as a bad dad?

My own mother, who raised my brother and me on her own from the time we were ages twelve and thirteen years old, tried to build our self-confidence while also bracing us for disappointment. When I told her of my plans to run for student council in middle school, she said, *Gee, great, but don't get your hopes up.* This became a recurrent refrain. Only many years later did it occur to me to ask, *Why not?* Always betting on yourself may seem out of reach to many of us. At least, we may think of it that way, to our own detriment.

Only the cream of the crop rises to the very top; the rest of us are down here in the dregs with everybody else. And we know it. Or maybe the problem is that we accept this when a better option might exist. It is safer to hold on to what you have than to keep letting your winners ride, as Elon Musk does. We are trained to expect less, to settle for less, rather than encouraged to expect more and demand more. The Bible, the first parts of which were laid down twenty-seven hundred years ago, says that God comforts the humble, and that pride precedes a fall from grace.

You get what you get, and you don't get upset: my daughter was taught this lesson at age six at her school in Brooklyn (never mind that it was a private school charging $40,000 a year in tuition). We are reined in by our parents and teachers and taught to be modest, and later we are suppressed by our peers and our employers and perhaps by human nature itself.

And so, stripped of this abiding faith in ourselves, we end up achieving less, and earning less, and maybe even living less. Living lives of quiet desperation, as Henry David Thoreau put it in *Walden*, published in 1854. Rather than living large and out loud.

Elon Musk plays it entirely the opposite way. And the key thing is, this buoyant, abiding self-confidence more likely was a *precursor* to his success rather than the result of it. Elon believed in himself and his destiny long before he had accomplished anything at all. So, he bet on his own capabilities before they were proven, and, thus, he put self-imposed pressure on himself to deliver. To live up to the risk he was taking, with the specter of failure being so devastating that he refused to consider it at all.

By now, we can see how it is that Elon could be so willing to bet on himself, given the mental and social construct he has designed for his own life. In some ways, this started when Elon Musk, at age seventeen, left his home country of South Africa to start seeking a better life in the United States, stopping first in Canada, where his mother, Maye Musk, had been born. Elon has tweeted (in 2018) that he arrived with $2,000 to his name, a backpack, and a "suitcase full of books."

He enrolled at Queen's University at Kingston, in Ontario, and two years later, he transferred to the University of Pennsylvania on a scholarship. At Penn he earned bachelor's degrees in economics and physics, a prescient combo for founding SpaceX a decade later.

In 1995, Musk moved to Stanford University near Palo Alto, California, the soul of Silicon Valley. Saddled with $110,000 in student debt, he was there to pursue a PhD in physics, but two days in, he quit and bet on himself again. Musk wanted to surf the dot-com wave, so he teamed up with his younger brother, Kimbal, and a friend, Gregory Kouri, to form a startup called Global Link Information Network in 1995. (Kouri would go on to invest with Musk in PayPal and Tesla, before dying of a heart attack at age fifty-one in 2012.)

Global Link was less than miraculous in its conception. Musk bought a digital disk of city addresses and borrowed mapping software from an outfit named Navteq, lashing the two together to fashion a city guide to restaurants and stores, three years before the advent of Google.

It turns out Elon's father had put up the $28,000 that Elon borrowed to get started. To conserve cash, Elon and his brother lived in the startup's rented office, despite its lack of a shower. Imbued with abundant confidence in his own so-so programming skills, Musk wrote the original code himself.

In 1996, Musk raised $3 million from the venture capital firm Mohr Davidow Ventures for a majority stake, and the firm was renamed Zip2. As in zip code. A new staff of professional programmers arrived and rewrote Musk's code from scratch, describing it later as a "hair ball" for its mass of messy complications.

The new owners insisted that Musk give up most of his stake in Zip2 and step aside as CEO in favor of a more experienced executive: Richard Sorkin, a Stanford MBA who had worked at Apple, Steve Jobs's NeXT, and a string of startups. Elon stayed on as chief technology officer and proceeded to spend his nights rewriting the code produced by Zip2 programmers, which they took as a "diss."

Musk had conceived of Zip2 as a consumer service letting you order a pizza online and use a map to go pick it up. Sorkin, by contrast, positioned Zip2 as a vendor to newspapers looking to avoid getting crushed by the internet wave. Hundreds signed up, led by the *New York Times*. In 1998, Sorkin tried to merge Zip2 with rival CitySearch, and Elon Musk staged a mutiny on the board. Sorkin stepped aside as CEO (and stayed on as chairman) and was replaced by Derek Proudian.

A year later, near the height of the internet bubble, Zip2 sold itself to Compaq Computer for $307 million in cash. Musk netted $22 million personally on the sale. Age twenty-eight at the time, he took the first $1 million and bought a McClaren sports car, an ill-advised purchase: no car, anywhere, ever, is worth spending $1 million to buy; and it loses 30 percent of its value as soon as you drive it away from the dealership.

Although the windfall was enough to last the rest of his life, months later, Musk formed X.com, pursuing the "everything app" and funding it with $12 million of his Zip2 largesse. This defied protocol in Silicon Valley, where most startup dreams are funded by Other People's Money. Using your own money on this scale borders on craziness.

The old saying attributed to Abraham Lincoln comes to mind: a defendant who represents himself in court has a fool for a client. Likewise, an entrepreneur who finances his own startup, on Elon's scale, may have a fool for a funder. Yet this is a fundamental way of doing business in the Ethos of Elon.

As Elon told a CNN reporter in an interview in 1999, shortly after starting the new company, "It's all like a series of poker games, and now I've gone to a higher-stake poker game and carry those chips with me. I've spent almost all of those chips back in the new game."

X.com became one of the first federally insured online banks, and it signed up two hundred thousand customers rather quickly. But it faced cutthroat competition from another startup, Confinity, which had been created by Peter Thiel and Max Levchin. They lacked the abundant funding that X enjoyed, thanks to Musk's own financing.

A year later, in March 2000, Thiel and Musk met in person to discuss a possible merger, and Elon picked up Thiel in his McLaren. A power move. This is when, as famously recounted in the book *The Founders*, Thiel asked Musk, "So, what can this thing do?" Musk replied, "Watch this," and gunned it. The million-dollar car spun out, went skyborne, and crashed, totaling the vehicle.

It was a miracle—inside the simulation, perhaps—that they survived, and more so that they were unscathed, walking away from the carnage and hitchhiking to their next meeting. Reportedly, the McClaren was uninsured. Sometimes betting on your abilities can go too far.

Undaunted by this bizarre turn, or maybe bonded by it, they did the merger the same month and named the combined company after Confinity's product, PayPal. Musk took over as CEO, and they first aimed at handling online payments for users of the PalmPilot. A narrow and ill-fated market, as it would turn out.

Once again, Elon clashed with his board. He wanted PayPal to become a banking and investing platform for all users, while Thiel and Levchin wanted to confine the focus to an online payment scheme. In 2000, the board fired Musk and replaced him with Peter Thiel—while Musk was in mid-flight to Sydney with his first bride, Justine, to start their honeymoon.

As soon as they landed, Musk boarded a flight back to the U.S. so he could confront the firing in person in Palo Alto. He must have been thinking: *Show one moment of humanity, and they will fuck you for it.*

So, Elon Musk bet on himself once again, on an even larger scale. He quit PayPal to go out on his own, leaving behind his beloved X.com domain name. Then came the PayPal public stock offering in early 2002, which doubled Musk's wealth to $60 million in a single day, and weeks later he founded SpaceX. Musk's stake in PayPal then tripled to almost $180 million when it got acquired by eBay the following October, freeing up Elon to fund the rocket ship startup with $100 million of his own money.

Even when Musk arrives late to a venture rather than creating it, he bets on his abilities to unlock the superior performance that has eluded it in the past. His bet on Tesla started at $6.5 million in 2004 and grew to $70 million over the next four years, before he took over as CEO. Assuming control was an even bigger gamble on his own abilities.

Many years later, at its peak in late 2021, when Tesla stock was at $250 a share, Musk's stake (17 percent stake of the company at the time) was worth $135 billion. This marked an astounding return of more than nineteen-hundred-fold in fifteen years on his $70 million investment, an average annual return of 13 percent per year for fifteen years straight—30 percent better than the annual return on the S&P 500 stock index in the same time.

Two years after investing in Tesla, Musk allied with his cousins, Lyndon and Peter Rive, to form SolarCity, a solar panel startup in 2006. Musk this time was betting on his cousins rather than himself, and he put upwards of $30 million into the company and held a 22 percent stake in it. Compared with his stellar track record, SolarCity was a flop—though Musk's $30 million investment had grown to more $500 million by the time Tesla bought Solar City for $2.6 billion in 2016. This was paid to Musk and other Solar-City investors in Tesla stock.

Shareholder lawsuits later alleged this was a sweetheart deal on inappropriately generous terms for SolarCity, which was teetering on the brink of bankruptcy when Tesla bought it. The other members of the Tesla board agreed to settle the litigation for $60 million, but Musk chose to go in the opposite direction. He fought the lawsuit, insisting the deal had come at a fair price, based on independent appraisals and reached in arms-length negotiations.

A trial judge in a Delaware court agreed, the plaintiffs appealed, and the state's highest court sided with Elon on all key points. Game, set, match, Musk.

In 2014, Musk hinted at more of his futuristic ideas in his on-stage chat with his future official biographer, Walter Isaacson, at the *Vanity Fair* conference in San Francisco. In the Q and A at the end, Elon starts talking about the simulation theory, and this opens up an outpouring of observations that would presage new businesses in the next few years.

One questioner comes up to the microphone and says her name is Danielle and she is an architect working with students at Stanford School of Business. They are devising innovative ways to solve big problems in cities. "We've identified Detroit as our prime target," she tells him, then asks: "What do you see as citywide innovation?"

Suddenly, Elon riffs on the idea of layers of underground high-speed tunnels beneath cities. (The Boring Company, which he would create three years later, is the start of this longshot dream.)

Elon: This may sound trite, but I honestly think tunnels should be given a lot more consideration. So, I mean if you look at a city, you have all these apartment buildings and office buildings and they're on many levels. Like, there are an average of, in Manhattan, I don't know what it is, an average of like thirty stories or something like that, but then you've got a street, which is one story. This is an obvious issue. Like, you have a thirty-to-one ratio of, you know—

Walter: So, we should have multilayered highways, underground, stacked up.

Elon: Yeah. You can have tunnels, too. The tunnels don't have to follow the buildings. They can be, they can go diagonally. Yeah. [*Seeing this in his mind now.*] And you can have as many levels as you want. So, it's really just the cost of building the tunnels. But really, a tunnel's a hole in the ground. Like, how hard can it really be? [*Audience laughter*] So, it seems like if some entrepreneurs put their effort into building tunnels, you know, that effectively will be transformative to cities around the world.

Isaacson prompts him for more ideas, and Elon goes on a stream-of-consciousness tour of sci-fi plausibility.

Elon: It's sort of tunnels. Tunnels and tubes. And for long-distance travel, I really think that the vertical takeoff [and] landing electric supersonic aircraft is the way to go. And I think it's very doable.

So, that would be the way to go for long-distance transportation, like if you're going more than like five hundred miles, because then you have any-to-any, you solve the any-to-any problem over long distances. For shorter distances, because you have a time to climb and a time to descend penalty below five hundred miles, aircraft are not as good. So, that's why I think, sort of use, some sort of evacuated tube is a better way to travel.

Walter: What is an evacuated tube?

Elon: Well, you know, just something where you reduce the air density so the drag is dramatically reduced, then it's like it's as though you got teleported to altitude. And you can go much faster and not have to have the climb-and-descend issues.

This idea for a "hyperloop" helped several startups raise hundreds of millions of dollars from other investors to pursue it. A few answers later, Walter Isaacson asks Musk about PayPal, the company Elon left in 2000 after the board rejected his vision of the "everything app." eBay now was spinning off PayPal as a separate public company, and Isaacson asks him, "Are you somewhat disappointed with the way PayPal then proceeded?"

Elon: "Yeah, PayPal has definitely, I mean, it hasn't moved much since from when, when it was sort of bought by eBay. The long-term vision that I had for PayPal or, sort of, in sort of finance, was to, to—well, it sounds a bit strange—like, to convert the financial system from a series of heterogeneous, insecure databases to one database, or, well, not one database, so maybe there'd be like a few more."

He continues: "Money is just a number in a database. That's what it is. And it's primarily an information mechanism for labor allocation. And the current databases are not very efficient. Like, they're, you know, they're these old legacy mainframes that don't talk to each other very well, have poor security, and only do their batch processing once a day." He then says spinning off PayPal is the right move.

"I think I'd convert it into more of a full-service financial institution. So, you just want to do all the things that are consuming. You want to have, like, all the financial services that somebody needs in one place, seamlessly integrated together and easy to use. And I really, really care about the consumer. I think a lot of banks don't seem to care that much about the customer. So, I think there's an opportunity to be, like, a really good bank, effectively, but much more than what people think."

Walter Isaacson takes a final question from a Reuters reporter, who asks about a just-unveiled effort by the Indian government to send a space probe to Mars—for just $75 million, one-eighth the cost of a similar NASA effort. Musk calls it "a very impressive mission, given that it was executed by a government entity," and turns to another futuristic dream of his: Mars.

"Ultimately, we have to be able to do missions to Mars for much less than that. Otherwise it'll be impossible to establish a self-sustaining civilization on Mars. Because we'll have to transport millions of tons of cargo, millions of people, and the cost of moving to Mars has to be affordable. Otherwise, people won't be able to go. So, it has to ultimately come down by a couple of orders of magnitude from that level. . . . I would say well below a million."

Much of this was a clue to future plans to come. A year later, in 2015, Musk helped start OpenAI, wanting it to grow into a counterbalance to Google and Microsoft, which had locked up roughly two-thirds of the world's AI scientists. But in 2016 he parted ways with the OpenAI board. He wanted OpenAI to be nonprofit and open-source—"free" software that anyone could copy, use, and update with improvements. The board was keener on the for-profit potential. Rather than bend to the will of other board members, Musk packed up and quit. He would circle back around; once he has fixed his mind on something, he always comes back to it.

Musk founded Neuralink the same year to explore embedding computer chips into human brains. Only eight years later did he win federal approval to embed the first test chip into the brain of a young quadriplegic male patient named Noland Arbaugh, who underwent surgery in January 2024. Video of Arbaugh using only his brain to move a cursor on a computer screen riveted the media. Later, the patient bragged to Joe Rogan that the chip would give him an unfair advantage in videogames, letting him pull the trigger before even thinking it.

This was followed by Musk's forming still another outfit: the Boring Company, for digging underground tunnels for traffic diversion. These were long-term bets, decades-long, on Musk's personal vision for where technology is headed and where it might be deployed to maximum benefit. He was funding ideas that seemed too outlandish for others to pursue, and this grew out of the confidence he held in his own hunches.

In 2017, at long last, Elon Musk reacquired the X.com domain name that he had left behind at PayPal way back in the year 2000. He paid PayPal $1 million for it. As Musk tweeted on July 10, 2017: "Thanks PayPal for allowing me to buy back X.com! No plans right now, but it has great sentimental value to me." Sandbagger. He had plans all along.

Meanwhile, OpenAI went on to take a $1 billion investment from Microsoft in 2019, followed by a $10 billion infusion from the software giant in January 2023 in exchange for a 49 percent stake. Thereby wedding one of the two behemoths that Musk had hoped to counter.

So, Musk bet on himself once again. In March 2023, he registered the corporate name xAI, and in July he unveiled the new company to the world. By year-end, he had taken the wraps off of Grok, a new AI chatbot aimed at one-upping ChatGPT. It has a "fun mode" that is sarcastic à la *The Hitchhiker's Guide to the Galaxy* by Douglas Adams.

By this time, Elon had already placed the largest bet on himself that he has ever made, acquiring Twitter for $44 billion. Then he relaunched the platform as X.com in July 2023, using the domain name he had bought back from PayPal in 2017. Thus, he resumed pursuit of the strategy he had wanted to execute back in 2000, while targeting a core business of PayPal.

Musk personally invested a massive $30 billion to take control of

Twitter. He had started buying the stock on January 31, 2022, and had spent $3 billion acquiring a 9.2 percent stake by April. To buy the whole shebang, he put up $27 billion more in cash. A very large bet indeed. To raise the funding, Musk sold $15.5 billion in Tesla shares and borrowed $12.8 billion from Morgan Stanley and other titans, using Tesla stock as collateral. He also cobbled together $7.1 billion from eighteen other investors, including Fidelity, Sequoia, the Andreessen-Horowitz VC fund, and his pal Oracle founder Larry Ellison.

Saudi prince Alwaleed bin Talal also invested, as did the sovereign wealth fund of Qatar. This may yet draw federal scrutiny of the Twitter deal, given that Elon is the highest nail. Thus, the Twitter deal illustrates a leadership axiom of the bet-on-yourself strategy: when you lead the way by betting on yourself, others are more willing to follow you. Your self-bet stokes their willingness to bet alongside you. Because you have "skin in the game."

X is a long-term play, and one year is insufficient to measure its success or failure. Albeit one year in, Elon Musk's investor group was down over $4 billion, with Fidelity marking down its $316 million investment by 65 percent, and star tech investor Cathie Wood of ARK Investment Management shaving 47 percent off the stated value of her Twitter stake. Meanwhile, Morgan Stanley and the other lenders were down $2 billion on the resale value of their $12.8 billion in Twitter loans. Ouch.

But their losses on paper pale by comparison with those of Musk himself: his $30 billion stake was down by $19 billion a year after buying Twitter. Then again, he is protected by a much larger margin for error in making bad bets, now that his net worth at times exceeds $200 billion. The rows of zeroes are staggering on his scale, and Musk's ability to bet on himself would seem to lack any parallel to the life lived by the rest of us. Yet the same principles are at play, whether you are worth gazillions of dollars or less than $1 million.

Either way, you still have to choose whether to bet bigger on yourself, whether to step up and assume the greater risk and the harder tumble if things go bad. You still have to outwork everyone else to make good on your bet. At either level, you still must contend with rivals and enemies and detractors and follow your own narrative instead of theirs.

And regardless of whether you are building a billion-dollar fortune or a $1 million retirement fund, the task requires relentless pursuit and persistence, and diligent devotion and intense focus. And years of commitment to continue working on it. We must be able to endure setback upon setback and keep moving forward. We must be steeled by self-knowledge that we possess the stamina and the abilities to make our bet on ourselves pay off better than ever before.

Self-confidence can pay for itself, if we stick to it and get smart about it. We must be willing to go for it. To bet on ourselves, always, and work like hell for years to come to deliver.

IT IS BETTER TO LAUNCH AND BURN THAN NEVER TO LAUNCH AT ALL.

Progress and setbacks at SpaceX

In the full year of 2023, SpaceX staged a record-high total of ninety-six successful rocket launches. Each spacecraft ferried satellites into space, with the first-stage section returning on its own power to land vertically and, quite remarkably, back where it started or even on a floating drone platform in the middle of the sea.

Among the more noteworthy feats that SpaceX achieved in the year:

It racked up ninety-one launches of the Falcon 9, plus five launches of the bigger Falcon Heavy, up from only sixty-one missions the year before. This works out to a new launch every four days. SpaceX launched the Falcon 9 more times in one year than it had in the first full decade after the Falcon's arrival; one craft has now been flown nineteen times, a record. The company also logged its 250th landing of an orbital rocket booster, and it managed to launch two rockets just three hours apart, something never seen since 1966.

In late December, a Falcon Heavy rocket lifted off from Kennedy Space Center in Cape Canaveral, Florida, to send into orbit a top-secret payload: the U.S. Space Force's X-37B spaceplane. The unmanned aircraft, a thirty-foot-long mini-shuttle that lands like a plane, stayed in orbit more than nine hundred days in its previous mission. It conducts automated experiments on solar energy, the effects of radiation, and other phenomena.

This impressive litany, however, largely failed to captivate the media. Instead, they zoomed up on two huge, spectacular failures.

Cut to April 20, 2023, 4/20, an especially appropriate date given the jokes that Elon Musk makes about marijuana and "420," slang for same. Starship, the next-generation rocket that one day will get us to Mars, is standing tall on the launchpad in Boca Chica, Texas. Starship is about to undergo its first full test flight as a fully stacked, towering monster: the first-stage Super Heavy booster, topped by the second-stage Starship vehicle. This, after five years of prototypes, static fire tests, and various liftoffs and landings that ended in explosions.

If all goes as planned, the rocket ship will take off from Boca Chica and fire its first stage, which will fall back down to Earth for a "hard splashdown" in the Gulf of Mexico seven minutes in. Then the upper-stage Starship craft will orbit the planet for half a lap or so before touching down in the Pacific Ocean off Hawaii. Again, if all goes as planned.

The thought of attempting to launch this massive craft into space seems all but impossible. Starship is the largest, most powerful rocket ever made. It is a monster of magnificent proportions, so big and so tall and looming that it is almost scary to see it in person.

Elon himself seems almost in awe of the sheer heft and scale of Starship. As he told an interviewer for the *Full Send* podcast in August 2022:

> Starship is gigantic compared to anything that's ever been done before. This is not like a tiny little thing [that] lands on the moon. This is a giant-ass spaceship [that] lands on the moon. It's capable of putting one hundred tons of payload on the moon, so a lot. You could build a moon base with Starship. So, we can go way beyond what was done with the Apollo program, where they just had a small lander and they sort of were on the surface of the moon for some number of hours, and then they got back

in and took off. The Apollo program was not capable of building a moon base. But the Starship system is capable of building a moon base. I mean, it's designed to be capable of building a city on the moon or Mars. That's what the system is designed to be able to do.

This spaceship is just 3 feet shy of 400 feet tall or forty stories high (compared with 305 feet high for the Statue of Liberty and its pedestal). And 30 feet in diameter, with a weight of five thousand tons or eleven million pounds all fueled up.

That is 72 percent taller than the Falcon 9 (at 230 feet high), and more than twice the Falcon's diameter of 12 feet—and more than nine times the Falcon's total weight of 1.2 million pounds. In spite of its lightweight, stainless-steel hull. If size matters—and it does—then Starship matters a lot.

And thrust matters, too. The Falcon 9 is powered by nine Merlin engines, each one ten feet long, three feet in diameter, with a weight of almost 1,400 pounds, and a thrust of 190,000 pounds of force. By contrast, Starship's Super Heavy booster will be powered by thirty-three engines in the new Raptor class. On top of that, literally, the Starship space vehicle has six more Raptors.

SpaceX designs and produces both Merlin and Raptor entirely in the USA. A rarity. Each ten-foot-tall Raptor engine is 40 percent wider in diameter than the Merlin and weighs almost three times as much (3,500 pounds), with two and a half-times as much thrust (507,000 pounds). This compares with 63,000 pounds of thrust for a Boeing 767 jetliner.

The Raptor has a thrust-to-weight ratio of 143.8, meaning the rocket engine can lift aloft an object that weighs 143.8 times as much as its own weight. This is a lot. The force of thirty-three Raptors all firing together would be so powerful that Elon Musk himself, in a live Twitter Spaces call on April 16, 2023, likened it to a box of grenades. "You know, really big grenades." He worried whether the launchpad could survive it, adding that it could take several months to rebuild it if they melted it.

"I would consider anything that does not result in the destruction of the launch mount itself . . . to be a win," Musk told his subscribers on the Twitter Spaces call. "If we get far enough away from the launchpad before something goes wrong, I would consider that to be a success. Just don't blow up the launchpad." A telling metric.

By this time, for Elon, failure was a constant co-pilot at SpaceX. The path to this first full flight test of Starship on 4/20 was filled with frequent mishaps and multiple setbacks. This mother of all rockets consumed the years 2012 to 2018 to develop it, followed by five years of building and testing. SpaceX innovated and iterated continuously in small, incremental steps, fast and furiously, mass-producing prototypes and burning through them with brazen nonchalance.

This towering Starship ready for launch was Ship 24, the twenty-sixth model that SpaceX had designed and built in five years. Fifteen of them were scrapped before testing. Eight others before this one ended up exploding at one point or another. Try, try again, and fly, fly again. SpaceX and its thirteen thousand employees are undaunted by failure and stimulated by setbacks, thanks to the leadership and unrelenting optimism of their CEO, who has been in Boca Chica for every launch of Starship. And every explosion.

By now, these SpaceX cadets are conditioned by another of the Eleven Lessons of Elon: it is better to launch and burn than never to launch at all. In Elon's world, failure to launch is one of the worst sins you can commit, right up there with procrastination, which he hates, especially in the people who work for him. Those two traits are inextricably interrelated.

In our own lives and careers, we dread the idea of failure because we see it as a final outcome and an ending. As irretrievable. So, wanting to avoid that ill fate, many of us refuse to go for it, we shy away from demanding the best and most of ourselves. We make excuses for refusing to take the bigger risk that might lead to huge returns if we ventured forth. And, once again, we settle for something less than what we can achieve, and the rewards in our lives and careers are lesser as a consequence of this timidity. If you are aware of this, the feeling gets even worse: you know you are underachieving. Giving up.

Whereas Elon Musk has reframed failure: it is simply a temporary, short-term result and a required part of the process. Failure can be a beneficial factor, one that reveals where the weaknesses are in a given business, system, or technological innovation. It offers rewards of its own, if we look at it right and respond to it well. And, most of all, if we learn from it.

The same goes for Starship, which began as a gleam in the eye of Elon Musk in 2005, three years before SpaceX had staged the very first launch of its first rocket, the Falcon 1. He conjured up a vision of a BFR—a Big Fucking Rocket, which he later politely dubbed the Big Falcon Rocket, before getting all Trekkie about it and renaming it Starship.

In his mind, it would be powerful enough to lift one hundred tons of payload into low Earth orbit, almost 350 miles above Earth. This would be four times the twenty-five-ton (fifty-thousand-pound) payload carried by the Falcon 9 today. A ship with this power and mass could take astronauts to the moon, almost a quarter-million miles away from Earth. NASA plans to use Starship for a manned Artemis III mission to the moon in 2025, if it can prove itself flightworthy and safe enough to carry human cargo.

Starship could make it all the way to Mars, though this will require a trek of 140 *million* miles, consuming nine months. This lofty goal is Starship's ultimate mission.

The first prototype, Starhopper, underwent static-fire tests on the ground in 2018 and two low-altitude test flights a year later (coasting airborne, without a launch). Then came two non-flying prototypes, one of which was destroyed in a pressure stress test in 2019; the other was disassembled in 2020. Two more models followed and collapsed in pressure testing, and another prototype exploded during the fifth live firing test of the engine.

And then, on August 5, 2020, the first major prototype to undergo a high-altitude test managed to make a timid climb to five hundred feet before successfully landing on its own on an adjacent launchpad in Boca Chica. In the annals of private space exploration, this is akin to the maiden flight by the Wright brothers at Kitty Hawk, North Carolina, on December 17, 1903.

The second high-altitude rocket fared similarly well one month later. Then came Starship SN8, the eighth model and the first upper-stage prototype. It flew almost eight miles high on December 9, 2020, coasting back to Earth and then malfunctioning and damaging itself in a hard landing. This brought an investigation by the Federal Aviation Administration, which subsequently demanded various fixes and cleared the way for the next test flight.

Weeks later, on February 2, 2021, a ninth Starship prototype crash-landed when one engine failed to ignite to help slow the descent. Undaunted, on March 10, Elon Musk and SpaceX mounted the launch of Starship SN10. It followed its predecessor's flight path and landed so hard that its landing legs collapsed, and it leaned like the Tower of Pisa for ten minutes . . . before exploding.

Boom! Just twenty days later, on March 30, Starship SN11 took off and flew on the same flight path as SN9 and SN10 had flown—and blew up upon descent. Engine trouble. Three more prototypes were thrown out before assembly was finished, and then on May 5, 2021, SN15, the sixteen-story-tall top half of the Starship rocket, launched from Boca Chica. And landed safely!

It flew six miles high and returned to where it had started, landing on an adjacent pad and becoming the first craft to survive, after four earlier high-altitude rockets had exploded in one way or another. More important, as Elon Musk told reporters at the time,

SN15 contained hundreds of improvements gleaned from the four flops that had preceded this launch.

NASA officials, watching all of this closely, had to admire the doggedness SpaceX displayed in launching prototype after prototype, undaunted and undeterred by failure after failure and explosion after explosion. The space agency rewarded this by handing SpaceX a $2.9 billion contract for the first two missions to the moon, snubbing Jeff Bezos's Blue Origin, despite its alliance with NASA contractor Lockheed Martin and other incumbents.

And so on April 20, 2023, after almost two years of development and static fire testing of both the top half, the dark-colored Starship vehicle, and its booster, the bright-white Super Heavy, the two-stage rocket was stacked, in place, and ready to rock.

At 8:33 a.m. local time, at SpaceX's Starbase launch site in Boca Chica, the combined forty-story-tall rocket began to shudder as Super Heavy's Raptor engines ignited and it struggled to lift itself off the launchpad. On-site, hundreds of employees roared with delight as this behemoth cleared the tower.

Thirty seconds in, it had climbed one kilometer (six-tenths of a mile) up in the sky, and at one hundred seconds, Starship was fifteen kilometers (nine miles) high and still rising. It now was roaring up at twice the speed of most rocket launches. At two minutes forty seconds, and twenty-six kilometers (sixteen miles) high, the bottom Super Heavy booster stage's rockets started a planned shutdown as it prepared to separate from the Starship top half and fall back to Earth, headed for the Gulf of Mexico. The rocket started to make the pre-programmed required flip to make this separation, and something went wrong.

Three of the thirty-three Raptor engines on Starship Heavy (the bottom half) had failed to ignite on takeoff, and by this time a total of eight engines now had failed. The two-part rocket ship started to circle in on itself, Super Heavy unable to separate from the top-half

Starship flier. It became clear that Starship would fall far short of the mission's stated goal—to take a half lap in orbit around Earth and splash down in the Pacific.

On the live-stream voiceover from SpaceX, you can hear the worries of John Insprucker, the company's principal engineer, and Kate Tice, engineering manager.

Insprucker: Right now, it looks like we saw the start of the flip, but obviously, we're seeing from the ground cameras the entire Starship stack continuing to rotate. We should have had separation by now. Obviously, this does not appear to be a nominal [normal] situation.

Tice: Yeah, it does appear to be spinning, but I do want to remind everyone that everything after clearing the tower was icing on the cake.

At that very moment, four minutes after liftoff and now twenty-nine kilometers (eighteen miles) high, Starship exploded into a million pieces. Flight engineers, sensing that the craft was spiraling out of control, had pushed the kill button to activate the "flight determination system," but it was unresponsive for forty tense seconds before finally blowing up in a plume of smoke.

The crowd at SpaceX's Starbase roared in elation, an odd reaction. These people were almost relieved and surprised, it seems, that Starship had gotten airborne at all. Moments after Starship blew up, Insprucker and Tice hosted a live debriefing on the live-stream for a few minutes. Kate Tice telling viewers, "As we said before, obviously we wanted to make it all the way through, but to get this far, honestly, is amazing."

John Insprucker: If you're just joining us, Starship just experienced what we call a Rapid Unscheduled Disassembly, or a RUD [pronounced "rudd"], during ascent. [Which is a funny euphemism for "explosion"; it sounds like a joke Elon would make.] But, now, this was a development test, this was the first test flight for Starship, and the goal is to gather the data and, as we said, clear the pad and get ready to go again.

He adds: "So, you never know exactly what's gonna happen, but, as we promised, excitement is guaranteed! Starship gave us a rather spectacular end to what was truly an incredible test thus far." His reference to a RUD would unleash a torrent of taunts on Twitter, where wags' hopes were high that the craft's new owner, Elon Musk, would see their taunts and perhaps even take a swipe at one of them.

As one account with almost half a million followers jeered: "SpaceX is calling it 'a rapid unscheduled disassembly.' In my day, we called it an explosion." This drew 1.2 million views. Another sniper tweeted, "Elon Musk's day: 'rapid unscheduled disassembly' of Starship in the morning, 'rapid scheduled disassembly' of Twitter in the afternoon." Dictionary.com chimed in: "We're pretty good with synonyms, but 'rapid unscheduled disassembly' is a new one, even for us."

The mainstream media, likewise, were less than generous. The *Washington Post*: "SpaceX's Starship lifts off successfully, but explodes in first flight." The *Financial Times*: "SpaceX Rocket Explodes Before Reaching Orbit." CNN.com: "SpaceX's Starship Rocket Lifts Off for Inaugural Test Flight but Explodes Midair."

Reuters got personal about it: "Elon Musk's Starship Explodes Minutes After First Test Flight's Liftoff." The *New York Times* headline sounded almost sarcastic: "SpaceX's Starship 'Learning Experience' Ends in Explosion." But the former newspaper of record did manage to note this: "SpaceX has a history of learning from mistakes. The company's mantra is essentially, 'Fail fast, but learn faster.'" Bingo, baby.

The Raptor engines had caused catastrophic damage to the

launch platform on takeoff, blowing apart the entire surface and sending concrete chunks flying as far as half a mile away. Some pieces were jettisoned into the sea. Only a giant crater was left behind where the launchpad had been moments before. The launch also sparked a fire over almost four acres.

Thus, by Elon's own measure, stated days before the launch on 4/20, when he said avoiding destruction of the launchpad would be a win, this was an abject failure. Wasn't it?

Instead of splashing down safely into the Gulf of Mexico and the Pacific Ocean, the two rocket sections of Starship shattered into bits. SpaceX originally had told the Federal Aviation Administration that any debris in a catastrophe would likely fall within a radius of seven hundred acres or so, about one square mile.

In actuality, the launch and explosion unleashed sand-like, pebble-sized "particulate matter" that rained down on residents and their property in South Padre Island, four miles north of Boca Chica (as the crow flies; it is a forty-two-mile trek to drive there), and in Port Isabel, six and a half miles northwest of the launchpad.

This enraged officials at the U.S. Fish and Wildlife Service, which mounted an investigation.

It was learned, however, that the "particulate matter" was harmless, basically beach sand, dirt, and dust kicked up in the first ignition. Ultimately, the agency issued no fines or penalties and said it would continue working with SpaceX on future flights.

The FAA, meanwhile, grounded the Super Heavy program and launched a "mishap investigation" of its own. In September 2023, the agency closed its review and demanded sixty-three improvements, including rocket redesigns to prevent leaks and fires, a better fire-suppression system on the Super Heavy, a reinforced launchpad with a new flame deflector, and additional review, analysis, and testing of safety systems.

And although Elon Musk had no assurance as to when the FAA would decree that Starship could fly again, by this time he had already moved the next rocket into place. Waiting. And hoping. After the test flight on April 20, Musk had said Starship could be ready to fly in six to eight weeks, but the FAA took seven months to grant a license, doing so on November 15, 2023.

The FAA fixes and hundreds of other incremental tweaks cleared the way for a second flight of the combined two-stage Starship 25 on November 18. At 7:03 a.m. in Boca Chica, taking off from a newly rebuilt and reinforced launchpad, Starship's Super Heavy booster ignited and the rocket successfully cleared the tower—without destroying the pad this time. Even though all thirty-three Raptor engines lit up, up from twenty-two and eleven failures in April. The booster then cleared a second major hurdle by successfully separating from the top Starship section to start falling back to Earth.

Then something went wrong, again. The Super Heavy booster was leaking propellant, which cut off the communications to the flight computer. The command center at Starbase lost contact with Super Heavy, and the craft, instead of firing its engines again to turn itself vertical for splashing down in the Gulf of Mexico, suddenly exploded.

Super Heavy had responded to the comms loss by triggering its own self-destruction.

The upper-stage Starship, meanwhile, started to head east for a lap around the planet to end up afloat in the Pacific, a few miles off the coast of Hawaii. A full eight minutes after launch, however, the Starship space vehicle blew apart in a second huge explosion.

Like the booster it had just discarded, Starship blew itself up by its own command, rather nobly so, after making it all the way up to outer space, which starts at sixty-two miles. Ship 25 rose up ninety-one miles (146 kilometers, or 480,000 feet). This was a vast improvement over the eighteen-mile ascent (29 kilometers, or 95,000 feet) of its predecessor, Ship 24, seven months earlier.

Then again, it fell short of the mission's goal of having Starship reach 150 miles (240 kilometers) above Earth. But so what?

Instantly, conditioned by Elon's coaching, the SpaceX faithful put the best reframe on a stunning disappointment. John Insprucker telling the launch viewers, "The real topping on the cake today, that successful liftoff." Kate Tice emphasizing the next flight: "We got so much data, and that will all help us to improve for our next flight."

This time around, the media were a bit more forgiving of failure. CNN.com was all but mournful: "The Most Powerful Rocket Ever Built Just Went Farther Than It Had Ever Gone, Then Was Lost." The *New York Times* reported, "SpaceX Makes Progress in 2nd Launch of Giant Moon and Mars Rocket." The *FT* proclaimed: "Elon Musk's Starship Rocket Reaches Space for the First Time." Reuters quoted NASA chief Bill Nelson, who called the launch an "opportunity to learn—then fly again."

The next day, Elon Musk posted on X, already looking forward to the next flight:

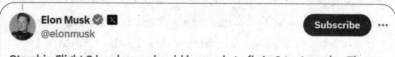

Elon Musk ✔ ✖
@elonmusk

Subscribe

Starship Flight 3 hardware should be ready to fly in 3 to 4 weeks. There are three ships in final production in the high bay (as can be seen from the highway).

9:07 PM · Nov.19, 2023 · **2.3M** Views

And on December 18, just one month after Ship 25 separated into two parts and ended in two separate explosions, SpaceX posted a tweet with three gorgeous sunset photos of the next Super Heavy and its Starship mate, assuring followers, "Flight 3 vehicles on the pad at Starbase for testing ahead of Starship's next launch." Two days later, the company announced a successful "static" (stationary) fire test of the next Starship, ship number 28, and its six engines, which all lit up as planned for a few seconds. The next version was ready and waiting.

It was a long wait. Starship Flight 3 finally was cleared for liftoff on March 14, 2024, after which it flew for almost fifty minutes and reached orbital velocity, a first, and then it broke up upon re-entering the atmosphere. Three months later, on June 6, Flight 4 blasted off from Boca Chica—and both parts returned safely to Earth. Another first.

On August 8, SpaceX announced on Musk's X platform that Flight 5 was ready to rock: "Flight 5 Starship and Super Heavy are ready to fly, pending regulatory approval." A polite nudge, perhaps, aimed at NASA and the FAA. But on September 11, 2024, the FAA publicly declared, via a statement to Space.com: "SpaceX must meet all safety, environmental and other licensing requirements prior to FAA launch authorization. . . . A final license determination for Starship Flight 5 is not expected before late November 2024."

This was two months later than the FAA had first planned, and this clearly irked Elon, who always is in a hurry. He already was miffed, most likely, by the FAA's action the week prior in proposing a fine of $633,009—how precise!—against SpaceX for launching without a license two months earlier. Now this.

On September 24, FAA administrator Michael G. Whitaker was grilled about the delay in a congressional hearing by Rep. Kevin Kiley, a Republican from California. The congressman demanded to know whether it was for reasons of safety—or paperwork. He concluded safety had little, if anything, to do with it. Later the same day, he posted on X to say the FAA head "struggled to justify the 2-month delay his agency has imposed on the launch. Holding back progress for non-safety reasons is against the national interest."

Elon reposted this and added the "100" emoji to express his 100 percent support for it. At 2:41 in the morning two days later, September 26, he pumped up the volume on X:

America is being smothered by ever larger mountains of irrational regulations from ever more new agencies that serve no purpose apart from the aggrandizement of bureaucrats.

Humanity, and life as we know it, are doomed to extinction without significant regulatory reform. We need to become a multiplanet civilization and a spacefaring species! This is my absolute showstopper for why Kamala and the giant government machine that is her legion of puppetmasters cannot win. Trump or doom. This is the fork in the road of destiny.

And at 2:54 a.m., he switched back to extolling just how awesome Starship truly is. He reposted a SpaceX message, showing a photo of a giant launch tower equipped with two huge mechanical arms that are designed to grab onto Super Heavy as the ship descends onto a launchpad. This will be tested in Flight 5—when the FAA finally approves it. Elon wrote: "The largest flying object ever made will be caught in mid air with giant Mechazilla arms." This, over the company statement:

SpaceX engineers have spent years preparing and months testing for the booster catch attempt on Flight 5, with technicians pouring tens of thousands of hours into building the infrastructure to maximize our chances for success.

Indeed. On October 13, 2024, SpaceX launched Flight 5 and was able to return the 250-ton empty Super Heavy to its launchpad, where it was embraced by the two huge mechanical arms. One of the most incredible achievements in the history of space flight.

···

It is unclear whether Elon Musk will be able to make good on the $2.9 billion contract he signed with NASA for SpaceX to handle a key part of the Artemis III mission to the moon in 2025. A NASA rocket, the SLS (Space Launch System), is supposed to lift the astronauts into orbit, where a waiting Starship would dock with it and ferry them to a moon landing.

In the next Starship test in early 2024, SpaceX was planning to stage a demonstration of refueling capability in space with this moon mission in mind.

None of this would have been possible without the long litany of failures followed by fixes that is the way of life at SpaceX. Elon Musk is imbued with the ability to look past each passing failure to unlock more secrets to the successes that are coming up next. Surfing on top of failure requires repetition and continuous iteration. SpaceX people learned this in the flurry of trial and error in the effort to perfect the Falcon 9.

In the first flight, which took off from Cape Canaveral on June 4, 2010, the first-stage booster was supposed to parachute down to the ocean, but the chutes never deployed, and the booster burned up on reentry. In the second flight, on December 8, the same thing happened again.

Then came two flights in 2012, three in 2013, and six in 2014, including four in nine weeks (July to September). None of these tried landing after takeoff, an unheard-of feat.

Seven more test flights of the Falcon 9 followed in 2015, including the first successful landing on a pad at Cape Canaveral on December 22, on the very first time that SpaceX tried to make it happen. Hurray!

One month later, a new catastrophic failure. On January 17, 2016, a Falcon rocket landed gently enough on a drone ship, puckishly named *Of Course I Still Love You*. It was waiting in the Pacific Ocean off the coast of Southern California, near the Vandenberg Space Force Base, where the rocket had started its mission.

But a landing leg on the rocket failed to latch into place properly, and the Falcon teetered over on its side and exploded. Unfazed and dispassionate, Musk posted video of this on Instagram.

From eight flights in 2016, SpaceX jumped to eighteen launches in 2017, including five reused boosters. This was starting to turn into a real business. Then twenty-one launches in 2018, including the first launch of Falcon Heavy, and seven successful drone ship landings and only one failure, plus four successful ground landings and one mishap. Traffic declined to just thirteen launches in 2019, although *Of Course I Still Love You* successfully received six good landings and only one failure. Then a 100 percent jump to twenty-six Falcon launches in 2020, the Year of Covid, the busiest year ever for SpaceX.

The year started with two good landings on a drone ship, but then two tries went awry. They would be the last bad landings of the year. SpaceX recovered nicely and mounted nineteen successful landings on *Of Course I Still Love You*, a miraculous feat of engineering.

In 2021, Elon Musk targeted forty-eight launches because he always aims too high—or overpromises and falls short, as his critics would carp. SpaceX managed to pull off "only" thirty-one successful launches, including flawless landings on the ocean platform twenty-nine times with only one failure. And in 2022, a big jump to sixty-one flights at SpaceX, and then ninety-six Falcon launches in 2023, all of them successful.

In 2024, SpaceX set even more ambitious objectives for the year ahead: a total of 144 launches in twelve months, most of them of the Falcon 9 workhorse. A dozen per month, one launch every three days or so. This pace would mark a 50 percent increase in launches in just one year.

Elon Musk and the staff of SpaceX have this business to themselves. The ninety-six launches of Falcon 9 and Super Heavy in 2023 were more than the sixty-seven launches staged by the entire nation of China in the same period; Russia pulled off only a dozen launches.

Consistency, reliability, and reusability are of paramount importance. In the first six months of 2024, SpaceX launched sixty-seven

Falcon missions and delivered almost nine hundred metric tons into orbit.

SpaceX has proved itself to be vastly more efficient than bigger, older rivals. As one post on X noted, accurately, in August 2024: "In 2014, NASA awarded contracts to two companies to build spacecraft capable of bringing astronauts and cargo to the International Space Station. SpaceX received $2.6 billion, launched first mission in 2020 and has done 13 crew missions with 49 astronauts so far. Boeing received $4.2 billion," and didn't mount its first manned flight of the Starliner until June 6, 2024, carrying just two astronauts.

That first mission to the ISS was planned to last for eight days, but things went awry. Boeing's Starliner suffered thruster malfunctions and leaks in its propulsion system, and NASA concluded it was unsafe for the two astronauts to ride the craft back home. These two persons, Butch Wilmore and Suni Williams, were stranded at the station for months on end. In an awkward embarrassment for Boeing, NASA in August elected to have SpaceX pick up the astronauts and return them home in February 2025, eight months later than first planned.

Starlink satellites comprised 65 percent of the SpaceX launches in 2023, and many of the missions in 2024 were set to add to this. Starlink has more than six thousand birds in low Earth orbit, with SpaceX having won approval to put double that number into the constellation so far. It aims to expand that approval to more than forty thousand craft in the skies.

As more satellites are added, Starlink's coverage of the world will expand and its costs will decline. It now provides service to more than two million customers in sixty nations. The federal government, meanwhile, set up a $42.5 billion program for broadband access in 2021—and three years later still had yet to start providing service. As Brendan Carr, a Republican member of the Federal Communications Commission, noted on X in June 2024, "In 2021, the

Biden Administration got $42.45 billion from Congress to deploy high-speed Internet to millions of Americans. Years later, it has not connected even 1 person with those funds. In fact, it now says that no construction projects will even start until 2025 at earliest."

As one account on X (@kane) noted at the time, for that same $42.5 billion "you could send 10 Starlink terminals at full retail price ($500) to every family below the poverty line in the USA (7.4M) and still have $5.5B leftover for San Francisco to spend on corrupt nonprofits." Which is largely accurate, give or take.

Scaling up in volume reduces the cost per launch, as does making both of Starship's two stages reusable rather than just the bottom booster. A satellite launch on Falcon 9 now costs $67 million, vastly less than the $400 million charged by Boeing and Lockheed. At some point, Starship aims to launch satellites at a price of only $10 million. Creative destruction writ large.

THE MOST LIKELY OUTCOME IS OFTEN THE MOST IRONIC ONE.

How to anticipate the flukes, surprises, and setbacks of life

"This one goes to eleven," as guitarist Nigel Tufnel (Christopher Guest) pointed out forty years ago in the mockumentary *This Is Spinal Tap*. In this eleventh and final chapter of *The Leadership Genius of Elon Musk*, we draw Lesson 11 directly from the mouth of the man himself—or, better yet, from his keyboard.

As the X platform's Grok AI engine puts it: "Elon Musk's earliest known quote or tweet about the most ironic outcome being the most likely one or vice versa is from a 2018 interview with Kara Swisher on the *Recode Decode* podcast. During the interview, Elon Musk said: 'The most ironic outcome is the one that nobody expects. And I think that there's some truth to that. And then, also, I think sometimes the most entertaining outcome is the most likely.'"

Ask Grok to dig a little deeper, and you learn that Musk started doubling down on this in mid-2023. In June, he said it in regard to the future of SpaceX; and in July about Tesla; and in September on the future of EVs; and in December, when he said, "Fate loves irony," about the future of space exploration; and in January 2024 on the odds of AI eclipsing human intelligence.

So, the most ironic outcome (the opposite of what you expected to happen) is the most likely one, in Elon's view. And sometimes the most *entertaining* outcome ends up being the most likely outcome, he posits. A syllogism is at work here: many times, the most ironic outcome also is the most entertaining, entirely because it is the opposite of what was supposed to happen.

Therein, the Eleventh Lesson of Elon may share an underlying foundation with Lesson 1 regarding the overwhelming likelihood (in Musk's mind) that we are living inside a simulation run by someone else, somewhere else, perhaps a million years from now.

In that, if this is all just one mass-illusion videogame, the most entertaining outcomes would be part of the package. Why muster the massive computing power of, say, all the computers combined on forty-five or fifty planet Earths to run a simulation that would produce *boring* outcomes?

As we explore how Elon came to this lesson and how it can inform our lives and shape our expectations, we should get one thing clear from the start: the real meaning of the words *irony*, *ironic*, and *ironically*. Many of us use these terms wrongly—we say "ironically" when, really, we mean "coincidentally," "surprisingly," or even "tragically." The singer Alanis Morissette committed this common malapropism in her 1995 chart-topping song "Ironic," in which every instance she cites is something other than ironic.

Irony is evident when someone says or does one thing and, beneath the surface and between the lines, actually means or intends the exact opposite. Something is ironic when it is the opposite of what was stated, intended, or expected. If Donald Trump were to say, "Joe Biden was a great president," he would be saying this ironically, because, in truth, he believes Biden to have been a terrible president.

Likewise, situational irony occurs when, say, a hospital constructs a new cancer-treatment wing and names it after the donor, who is CEO of a tobacco company. Or when you pursue a particular goal, and the outcome is the opposite of what you had intended—as a direct result of your efforts to the contrary. This is part of any tragic hero, and Elon Musk has had various entanglements with this bittersweet version of irony. He speaks from experience.

Though Elon Musk was already famous from his exploits and achievements at Tesla and SpaceX, buying Twitter elevated his profile higher than ever before—exposing him to praise, surely, but more so to condemnation, criticism, and damnation from any and every direction. He wanted to arrive at Twitter as a conquering hero and champion of free speech when he bought the platform in late 2022. He vowed to make it the freest platform in the world.

But Musk instead ended up being criticized for *cracking down* on free speech in some countries—the opposite of his intentions. He was decried as a villain and accused of unleashing a new level of hate speech, though this was largely false. Further, his acquisition of Twitter put governments on guard, and, if anything, their efforts to censor online posts intensified as a result of this change in control.

As one writer for *El País*, Spain's national newspaper, noted in May 2023: "Although the billionaire owner of SpaceX and Tesla presents himself as a free speech absolutist, the social network he controls has bowed to hundreds of government orders during his first six months at the helm, according to data provided by the company to a public audit that tracks pressure from governments or judges on online platforms."

The X platform surrendered to the Modi government in India and removed references to a BBC documentary that criticized the country's prime minister, Narendra Modi, in early 2023. It also censored posts criticizing the Indian government's response to farmer protests.

Further, in Australia, X took down video of a terrorist stabbing a priest, as local law required. And the social media outlet agreed to muzzle accounts specified by the Turkish government. In Germany, the company has provided information on user identities to the government to let it investigate violations of laws that criminalize statements denying the Holocaust, inciting hatred of minorities, or slandering elected politicians.

Also, instead of helping spread free speech in Pakistan, X got itself banned entirely in the region in April 2024, in the wake of unrest following national elections. This, the government said, was a matter of "national security, maintaining public order, and preserving the integrity of our nation." Supporters of former Pakistani prime minister Imran Khan were using X to promote claims that Khan had been unjustly removed from office in 2022.

In these instances, X was following the laws in the nations where it was operating, as every company must do. As Musk publicly explained matters in the India flap: "The rules in India for what can appear on social media are quite strict, and we can't go beyond the laws of the country. . . . If we have a choice of either our people go to prison or we comply with the laws, we will comply with the laws."

The Intercept, a liberal investigative website, further lampooned Elon for preaching free speech and doing the opposite. In March 2023, it reported that he was promoting a decade-old Twitter lawsuit aimed at combatting government surveillance of social media—while also selling X user data to a data-mining company (literally called Dataminr). That company then provided the data to the Secret Service for law-enforcement purposes.

The website notes that the ironies abound. "X's Musk-era warnings of government surveillance abuses are contradictory to the company's continued sale of user data for the purpose of government surveillance. . . . It's the kind of ideological contradiction typical of X's owner. Musk has managed to sell himself as a heterodox critic of U.S. foreign policy and big government while simultaneously enriching himself by selling the state expensive military hardware through his rocket company SpaceX."

Another ironic outcome in the Twitter deal: Musk himself ended up using Twitter to restrain some speech of his critics, while hyper-promoting his own messaging. At one point, Elon shut down the accounts of eight reporters affiliated with the likes of the *New York Times*, the *Washington Post*, and CNN, liberal mouthpieces all of them. For all of twenty-seven hours, as it turned out. Also, given that X tells advertisers that more than 99 percent of its ads run alongside "healthy" content, this means it is banning "inappropriate" speech from possibly millions of accounts.

Plus, X algorithms continue to restrain the expressions of some users, sparking new complaints that Elon Musk is violating their free speech rights. As one perturbed user put it under the account @The1Parzival: "Hey .@elonmusk & @lindayaX [CEO Linda Yaccarino] if you don't remove all the censorship features affecting my account, I'm going to tie this place up with so much litigation that your grandchildren are going to need lawyers."

Never mind, for a moment, that the First Amendment prohibits *government* from messing with free speech: a private platform has every right to do so. For Elon Musk, however, this contradicts the Musk mystique of being a free speech hero.

That Musk deigned to buy Twitter at all was another ironic outcome. The liberal censors running the company were eagerly cooperating with the requests of U.S. government agencies, made in violation of the First Amendment of the United States Constitution, to muzzle the accounts of thousands of conservatives.

Their complicity in stifling protected speech riled the First Amendment sensibilities of this obstinate, recalcitrant billionaire and Twitter fan—who then turned around and delivered the opposite outcome, freeing up speech on Twitter more than ever before. Especially in the United States, where free speech is paramount.

In the first two years after buying Twitter, Musk would encounter myriad more ironies, large and small. In September 2023, he announced that he had fired the "Election Integrity Team" at the platform. As Elon put it in a tweet: "Oh, you mean the 'Election Integrity' Team that was undermining election integrity? Yeah, they're gone." Created to ensure election integrity and then functioning to undermine same: situational irony.

In a similarly ironic vein, Musk's enemies, led by the Anti-Defamation League and Media Matters for America, rallied on X to label Elon an antisemite in the weeks after the October 7, 2023, Hamas terrorist attacks in which twelve hundred Israeli civilians were slaughtered. The outlets' efforts boomeranged to spur the opposite effect: they turned him into one of the most ardent, most powerful supporters of Israel and the Jewish people.

The allegations of antisemitism erupted after Musk reposted a tweet from a small account in the wake of the attacks. It made the point that liberal Jewish voters had supported the Left's loose immigration policies, thereby letting in thousands of antisemites who now were marching in favor of Hamas.

The mainstream media ran wild in accusing Elon of antisemitism for this small, supposed offense. It said Musk was endorsing a right-wing conspiracy known as the "great replacement theory," when nothing of the sort was either mentioned or invoked. Nor endorsed. The media made that leap. CNBC ran segment after segment exploring the accusations against Musk and quoting some of his enemies.

The torrent of criticism clearly caught Elon Musk by surprise; he considered himself, if anything, a passionate supporter of Israel. Having hosted Prime Minister Benjamin Netanyahu even before the October 7 attacks, Musk went on to visit Bibi in Israel weeks afterward. While there, he watched devastating video of the savage attacks by Hamas. He visited a kibbutz ravaged by the terrorists, and the Auschwitz memorial. He endorsed what he said was the "necessary" annihilation of Hamas, and he placed a chain of dog tags around his neck for the hostages.

An antisemite would have a hard time convincingly faking this to this extent.

Elon's reach on X, at 200 million followers as of September 2024, rattles politicians. So much so that a strong stance he takes on one side of an issue may have an opposite effect, as in Eagle Pass, Texas. He visited the Texas border to focus public attention on the crisis in illegal immigration. His interviews with local law enforcement, which he shot himself on his smartphone, drew millions of views. Even as the rest of the media and most politicians avoided visiting there, lest they be contaminated by the fallout of a true national emergency.

This may have backfired. When the Biden administration moved to unlock spending to resume construction on some segments of the Trump border wall, it left out Eagle Pass. This may have been done out of pure spite against Elon for visiting there.

Musk has watched other ironic outcomes play out at publicly held Tesla. When he tweeted the infamous "$420" post on August 7, 2018, saying, "Funding secured," and joking about taking the company private, Musk was jousting with short sellers who were betting billions of dollars against the company's stock. He had called on the Securities and Exchange Commission to investigate the shorts, to no avail. Instead, the SEC investigated Elon Musk, and it ended up imposing a $20 million fine against him personally for violating disclosure rules.

Likewise for Musk's prideful promotion of the advanced technological prowess of the Tesla Autopilot driving system and its fancier, $99-a-month version, Full Self-Driving Capability. His aim was to build support for AI and self-driving software as the future of the auto industry, safer for Tesla drivers and likewise safer for other drivers nearby. And to stimulate development at other car companies, as well.

Instead, Musk's enthusiasm and the ensuing media coverage may have roused more scrutiny from federal regulators and ended up hampering the adoption of computerized driving. The National Highway Transportation Safety Administration started investigating Tesla for the Autopilot system in August 2021, prompted by just 11 reported accidents. It later expanded the probe to cover 36 Tesla crashes, and then 736. Out of almost two million Teslas sold since 2015.

Since then, the regulatory skepticism has spread to other makers. The NHTSA "appears to be getting more aggressive in regulating the devices," the Associated Press said in May 2024, reporting that the agency had announced four separate investigations of self-driving systems: the Waymo self-driving taxi company, Amazon's Zoox self-driving cars, a new review of a Tesla recall, and Ford's BlueCruise. General Motors' Cruise auto-driving also came under review.

In each instance, regulators intervened in response to only a minuscule number of accidents involving auto-driving software: twenty-two at Waymo; just two at Zoox, involving rear-end fender benders; and only two at Ford, in which a Mustang Mach-E smashed into a stationary vehicle. This, in a nation of forty thousand traffic accidents every year. Self-driving is the least of the factors contributing to accidents, yet it is getting lots of attention. This will delay the advent, adoption, and proliferation of hands-free driving.

Precisely the opposite of what Elon Musk has been advocating.

Musk also advocates stock-based compensation for executives, rather than a high salary, large bonuses, and lavish perks. He and others see this as the best way to align management interests with those of shareholders. It also helps hold down the levels of cash compensation, especially in a startup where cash is scarce. The executives benefit only when the shareholders benefit.

In 2018, Musk agreed to a compensation package at Tesla that would pay him zero in salary and bonuses for the next ten years. His stock options would kick in only after a robust rise in the price of Tesla shares. And, once again, his efforts triggered the opposite outcome: worldwide media coverage and criticism of one of the richest CEO payoffs of all time.

As in: $56 billion!

Elon Musk, once again, was in the middle of the storm. When he signed the deal, the conventional thinking was that it never would pay off. Elon was on a fool's crusade. Seventy-three percent of shareholders approved the contract, happy to have him work free of charge for the next decade. His stock-based rewards were notched to attaining a series of up to twelve key targets for rising market value, revenue, and cash flow.

For each $50 billion rise in Tesla's total market capitalization, Musk would receive stock options for an extra 1 percent stake in the company. This would be equivalent to creating an entire Ford Motor Company, which ranks nineteenth on the Fortune 500 and has a market cap of $50 billion.

Tesla stunned Wall Street and cleared every one of the hurdles. Its market cap, at $53 billion when Musk signed this deal, soared more than twentyfold to a peak of $1.2 trillion in 2021. That is around the time that I bought it, frankly, jumping on this bandwagon very late. Then the stock returned to Earth and a total value of more than half a trillion dollars by early 2024. This was still up more than tenfold, and, at the stock's peak, Musk's estimated $56 billion windfall led to the creation of upwards of $1 trillion in new wealth held by other investors. By late September 2024, the market value of Tesla was back above the $800 billion mark.

The sums are so astounding that, of course, some small-time shareholder sued. A Delaware chancery judge (the same one who ruled that Elon Musk must go ahead with his Twitter purchase) threw out the Musk package as so obscenely rich it was illegal. "Unfathomable," she called it. This ruling, utterly the opposite of any reasonable legal expectation, came in response to a Tesla shareholder who held only nine shares. Wobbly legal standing, at best. The ruling seemed likely to be overturned on appeal, unless another ironic outcome loomed.

And then came another ironic twist: the lawyers who sued Musk for getting paid too much asked the court for legal fees of an astounding $6 billion—outrageous compensation for lawyers filing a lawsuit about outrageous compensation. The request came from three firms: New York's Bernstein Litowitz Berger & Frossman and Friedman Oster & Tejtel and one in Delaware, Andrews & Springer. These fees would have to come from Tesla itself, whose shareholders these attorneys purport to represent.

The balls on these guys.

Elon Musk decried the ruling. Thereafter, he asked Tesla shareholders to move the company's legal base out of Delaware and switch to Texas; he also moved the incorporations of Space X and Neuralink from Delaware to Texas. He has encouraged other companies to do the same, arguing that Delaware no longer can be trusted as a legal harbor for incorporation.

By June 2024, the very same Musk pay package went before another vote of Tesla shareholders, seeking their approval once again. They also voted on his proposed move of the company's base to Texas. Glass Lewis, an advisory firm to pension funds and other institutional investors, recommended that shareholders vote against Elon's pay package and against the reincorporation in Texas, just as the firm had advised against the Musk pay setup back in 2018.

But the investors, to their credit, ignored Glass Lewis and voted with Elon: Tesla would move its corporate base to the Lone Star State, and Elon Musk would get the stock-based compensation a judge had tried to deny him. By this time, it was worth roughly $48 billion. I made sure to vote my Tesla shares in favor of Elon's contract and in favor of the move to Texas.

That outcome was the opposite of what the judge had intended it to be. Score one for Elon.

Ironic outcomes are evident at SpaceX, as well. Although Musk enjoys thumbing his nose at authority, he is eager for approval from the same authorities. When late one night in October 2022,

Ukraine military commanders asked him to turn on Starlink satellite coverage over Crimea so they could dispatch armed underwater drones to attack a Russian ship, he refused. The main reason was that U.S. law blocked Starlink from serving Crimea because it was a Russia-controlled territory, blacked out by U.S. sanctions against Russia.

But Musk also seems to have wanted praise for averting what he viewed as a possible spark for a World War III, as he later told his authorized biographer, Walter Isaacson. The author portrayed Musk's decision heroically, but when word of this broke, instead of winning kudos from U.S. politicians, Musk caught a beating from critics who accused him of meddling in U.S. foreign policy. Senator Elizabeth Warren called for an investigation by both the Senate and the Department of Defense.

And when Starlink landed a federal contract for almost $900 million in 2020 to provide internet service to 640,000 unwired homes in thirty-five states across rural America, the aim was to bring them into the internet age. The outcome was all too ironic. In December 2023, the Federal Communications Commission rescinded the contract amid the Biden administration's not-so-secret war on Elon Musk. This will thwart the goal of serving rural customers for years to come.

Musk projects his view on ironic outcomes onto the rest of the world. He has decried the DEI (diversity, equity, and inclusion) movement for rendering the opposite of its intentions. As Elon noted in a post on X in January 2024: "DEI is just another word for racism. Shame on anyone who uses it." And a month later, in response to a report on DEI problems in hospitals, he wrote: "DEI puts the lives of your loved ones at risk."

Musk was referring to corporate moves by the likes of, say, Boeing, which in 2022 revised its executive compensation parameters, previously based solely on safety and quality, to add diversity and climate change to bonus criteria. After the death of the Black career criminal George Floyd under the knee of a white police officer, the hundred largest companies filled some 325,000 new jobs—and 94 percent of them went to people of color, Bloomberg reported. This, even though whites comprise 58 percent of the U.S. population. Of 4 million jobs filled by employers from 2020 to 2023, white jobholders had a net *decrease* of more than 900,000 jobs, meaning *all* of the 4 million new jobs were filled by non-whites.

This is *exclusion* of whites, the very opposite of inclusion.

Elon's pals get this concept, too. On February 4, 2024, David Sacks, who worked alongside Musk at PayPal and invested in his takeover of Twitter, put out this tweet: "The Inflation Reduction Act was actually a trillion-dollar spending bill. The border security bill is actually a mass amnesty. Just assume bills do the opposite of what they say."

This is both funny and true. An "Inflation Reduction Act" should slash government spending, because inflation is caused by a massive increase in the government-created supply of money that chases after the same old amount of goods. But this law, passed in August 2022, included new spending of $370 billion on "energy security and climate change," plus $64 billion in new Obamacare subsidies. This was part of a $2 trillion package that included $550 billion in new spending in just five years, and $1.2 trillion over ten years, for "infrastructure." Plus $280 billion over ten years for R&D for next-generation chip technology.

The Inflation Reduction Act is likely to *increase* inflation rather than reduce it.

Similarly ironic results were likely to accompany the border security bill, which was proposed in February 2024. When David Sacks took a shot at the bill on X, Elon Musk reposted the broadside and topped it with this: "The long-term goal of the so-called 'Border Security' bill is enabling illegals to vote! It will do the total opposite of securing the border."

The bill's official title: "Emergency National Security Supplemental Appropriations Act, 2024." Division B of the bill was titled "Border Security and Combating Fentanyl Supplemental Appropriations Act, 2024." Backdrop: in the first Trump term, illegal encounters at the southern border ran an average of just shy of half a million per year. In the first three years of Biden's administration, this quadrupled to almost 2.2 million illegal crossings per year.

Yet this "border security" bill would have allowed five thousand illegal entrants into the United States at the southern border *every single day* before triggering emergency powers to shut down the border. This amounts to almost two million illegal entrants per year as a starting point. On top of an additional one million *legal* entrants per year. No limits were to be imposed on illegal migrants from countries outside the Americas, including our enemies: China (the fastest-growing group, up past thirty thousand in 2023 from just fifteen hundred a year previously), Russia, Iran, North Korea, and Syria.

And of $118 billion in new spending set by this supposed emergency act, only $20 billion was aimed at fixing the border. So, this bill offered no border security at all, really. It died in the Senate in May 2024, and a month later, President Biden announced new emergency measures to avert a border crisis that, until this point, he had insisted wasn't a crisis. America's patience, he told the nation, was "wearing thin." Plus, he was by this time trailing in most polls in half a dozen swing states that would determine the 2024 election.

This new presidential order was a half measure: emergency provisions could be imposed when more than twenty-five hundred illegal aliens cross the southern border in a single day. Meaning almost a million illegal entrants per year is otherwise okay, the United States having given up on zero.

Even that presidential order was itself an ironic outcome to Biden's original intentions. When he assumed the office in January

2021, President Biden instantly rescinded sixty-four executive orders imposed by President Trump, which were aimed at tightening border security. Cracking down now, at the risk of alienating the liberal alliance he needed to have any hope of winning reelection, was the opposite of what Biden wanted to do. Forced by his own actions.

The mainstream media reported it otherwise, conveying Biden's assertion that Trump and the Republicans were to blame for the border crisis. As Elon Musk himself had posted on Leap Day a few months earlier, "People who get their news from legacy TV live in a fake alternate reality. Those so-called 'toughest reforms' would have made invasion-level migration permanent. That diabolical 'Border Bill' deserved to die and shame on those who supported it."

Years ago, as it happens, Elon had joined his PayPal friend David Sacks as an investor in and executive producer of the 2005 comic film *Thank You for Smoking*. It is based on the wry and satirical 1994 novel by Christopher Buckley (a friend of mine in my days at *Forbes*). It is pertinent here because, in the story, Washington lobbyists for cigarettes, alcohol, and guns form a drinking clique they call the MOD Squad, for Merchants of Death. They work for (fictional) industry groups: the Academy of Tobacco Studies, which debunks tobacco's risks; the Moderation Council, which seeks to block restrictions on alcohol; and the Second Amendment Foundation for Education and Training, which fights gun laws. Ironically named, every one.

For Elon Musk, the deepest dive into situational irony came in the story of OpenAI, one of the world's most advanced labs for artificial intelligence. OpenAI created ChatGPT, a Large Language Model AI engine, after Elon provided most of the funding to start it. He was driven by his own fears about the prospects for AI's advancing beyond the ability of humans to rein it in; and he fretted that Google and Microsoft would dominate the field.

Yet his efforts may have instead increased the odds of these things coming true.

We know this story because Elon Musk's lawyers laid it out in detail in a lawsuit filed on February 29, 2024, against Open AI and its leaders in California Superior Court in San Francisco. Then OpenAI responded on March 5 by posting a blog that revealed private emails between Elon and OpenAI executives. It also filed a blistering response in court on March 11.

The picture that emerges shows that the sheer will and resoluteness of Elon Musk played a role in producing the ironic outcome of OpenAI's becoming a vassal of the dreaded dreadnought Microsoft. With Elon nowhere in sight to rein things in.

Cut to 2012, and a meeting at the SpaceX factory in Hawthorne, California, between Musk and Demis Hassabis, co-founder of an AI startup called DeepMind. The two men discussed the great threats facing society, and Elon came away newly alarmed about what he had learned from Hassabis about "the potential of AI to become super-intelligent, surpass human intelligence, and threaten humanity," as described in the Musk suit.

Another investor in DeepMind was so rattled by the AI startup's potential that he is reported to have said the best thing he could have done for the human race was "shoot Mr. Hassabis then and there." A joke right out of *Terminator 2: Judgment Day*, released in 1991.

In 2013, Musk was discussing the risks of AI and DeepMind with others, including Larry Page, co-founder of Google and CEO at the time. A particularly "passionate" exchange—read: an argument—with Larry ensued at one point. The Musk lawsuit says this encounter happened in 2013, although a report in the *New York Times* quotes witnesses who said it occurred in June 2015 during Musk's three-day party for his forty-fourth birthday. Both may be true.

When Musk said he was worried that AI might replace humans, Larry Page responded that this would "be the next stage of evolution"—and then he branded Elon Musk a "specist" who favored humans over intelligent machines. Elon responding: "Well, yes, I am pro-human."

Funny stuff. Later in 2013, Musk's fears grew more urgent when he learned that Google was about to acquire DeepMind, putting it in the hands of Larry Page—"Someone who viewed it and its power so cavalierly, and could hide its design and capabilities behind closed doors," as Musk's attorneys described it later in his lawsuit.

Musk tried uniting with a fellow co-founder of PayPal, Luke Nosek, to make a rival bid for DeepMind, but Hassabis sold to Google. Musk began hosting a series of dinner conversations with tech leaders on ways to counter Google in AI and promote AI safety, including a meeting with then president Barack Obama.

Musk worried that Google and Microsoft were already becoming the dominant players in the next wave, AI, and that they were too rapacious and profit-driven to be trusted as a safeguard to stop AI from growing out of control.

In March 2015, he was contacted by Sam Altman, then a month shy of his thirtieth birthday, who was CEO of the Y Combinator startup incubator. Altman asked Musk to co-author a letter to the U.S. government about the risks of AI. Upside for Altman: this also was a slick way of sliding into Musk's orbit and getting access to his wealth.

In May of that year, Altman emailed Musk, proposing a new company structured "so that the tech belongs to the world via some sort of nonprofit but the people working on it get startup-like compensation if it works. Obviously we'd comply with/aggressively support all regulation."

Musk responded to him with brevity: "Probably worth a conversation."

Their open letter on AI was published on October 28, 2015, signed by Elon, Sam Altman, the famed astrophysicist Stephen Hawking, Apple co-founder Steve Wozniak, and upwards of a thousand other scientists. A month later, Musk committed to funding the new AI lab, a nonprofit whose fiduciary obligations would be to humanity rather than to any private shareholder.

Elon himself coined the new entity's name: Open AI Institute, or OpenAI for short. The company incorporated in Delaware on December 8, 2015, stating:

"The specific purpose of this corporation is to provide funding for research, development and distribution of technology related to artificial intelligence. The resulting technology will benefit the public and the corporation will seek to open source technology for the public benefit when applicable. The corporation is not organized for the private gain of any person."

When the company's formation was announced three days later, with Musk and Altman as co-chairmen, the public statement said OpenAI was designed to "benefit humanity," and that its research would be "free from financial obligation."

From the start, however, Elon began making arguments that helped push OpenAI into Microsoft's arms. In 2015, he started urging OpenAI staff to announce a $1 billion fundraising effort, writing in an email: "We need to go with a much bigger number than $100M to avoid sounding hopeless," and offering to cover any shortfall.

Elon plunged into recruiting world-class AI talent for OpenAI, pumping $16 million of his own funds into the startup in the ensuing year (2016), and leasing space in San Francisco to the firm and covering the monthly rent. In 2017, Altman and Gregory Brockman, OpenAI's chief technology officer, suggested switching OpenAI Inc. from a nonprofit to a for-profit company.

Musk balked, and he was putting up most of the funding. Yet he owned zero equity in this enterprise. He told them to spin out on their own if they wanted to go for-profit, declaring bluntly: "I will no longer fund OpenAI until you have made a firm commitment to stay or I'm just being a fool who is essentially providing free funding to a startup. Discussions are over."

This observation would prove to be prescient. Altman assured Elon, "I remain enthusiastic about the nonprofit structure!" This would turn out to be less than the full, unvarnished truth. That exclamation point should have been a tell.

In early 2018, according to private emails publicized indiscreetly by OpenAI in the blog it posted after Musk sued the company, he warned OpenAI staff: "Even raising several hundred million won't be enough. This needs billions per year immediately or forget it."

Then Musk suggested that OpenAI should "attach to Tesla as its cash cow . . . Tesla is the only path that could even hope to hold a candle to Google." He is said to have wanted majority equity control, board control, and the title of CEO. Spurned, he stepped down as co-chairman in February, even as he continued funding the startup. Another $3.5 million, now up to a total $40 million or so he had contributed by this time.

Elon's exhortations about raising funding may have imbued OpenAI's Altman with an urgency to find a sugar daddy. One year later, in March 2019, OpenAI did indeed create the for-profit subsidiary that Musk had opposed: OpenAI LP. The "important warning" at the top of the summary term sheet for the new unit told investors that it "exists to advance OpenAI Inc.'s mission of ensuring that safe artificial general intelligence is developed and benefits all of humanity." This would "take precedence over any obligation to generate a profit."

Therefore, the term sheet advised, "It would be wise to view any investment in OpenAI in the spirit of a donation." Musk was concerned but stayed in, donating another $3.48 million to the nonprofit arm of OpenAI that year (2019).

Then in September 2020, a shocker: OpenAI announced a deal

to license its chatbot technology *exclusively* to Microsoft, which had committed an opening investment of $1 billion in the fledgling firm. This ultimately grew to a total $13 billion in Microsoft funds for a 49 percent stake in the OpenAI for-profit business, and today the combined concern is valued at $150 billion.

Altman, apparently, had heeded Musk's warnings about the need for lots of cash at OpenAI. Soon after, OpenAI began to operate in a way that contradicted the priorities that Elon Musk and Sam Altman had set out at the start. At first, OpenAI open-sourced the workings of GPT versions 1, 2, and 3, letting rival developers access the code directly. But with ChatGPT-4, suddenly OpenAI stopped providing open-source details, withholding them as proprietary—the opposite of its mission statement.

In November 2023, the OpenAI board stunned Silicon Valley by firing CEO Sam Altman, and said he had been less than fully transparent about his doings, presumably involving the for-profit alliance with Microsoft. Altman's number two, Gregory Brockman, instantly quit in protest, and Altman, in an extraordinary *and ironic* outcome, engineered his own comeback at the company. He then replaced the board with his own picks.

Three months later, Elon Musk struck back. On February 29, Leap Day 2024, Musk filed his lawsuit against OpenAI and Sam Altman and Gregory Brockman in superior court in San Francisco, seeking a jury trial on charges of breach of contract, breach of fiduciary duty, and unfair competition.

Filed as case number CGC-24-612746, the thirty-five-page complaint, plus exhibits, lays out a litany of opposite outcomes from what Musk had originally intended to achieve. The lawsuit notes that OpenAI's board has the authority to determine when the company has achieved the utmost, all-knowing level of AI, called artificial general intelligence. Under the original terms of its founding, AGI must be distributed freely to the world rather than handed only to Microsoft.

But Musk doubts the board will be willing to declare that AGI has arrived, because this would go against the interest of Microsoft, with its 49 percent stake in the for-profit half of the business. His lawsuit states:

"Given Microsoft's enormous financial interest in keeping the gate closed to the public, OpenAI, Inc.'s new captured, conflicted and compliant Board will have every reason to delay ever making a finding that OpenAI has attained AGI. To the contrary, OpenAI's attainment of AGI, like 'Tomorrow' in Annie, will always be a day away, ensuring that Microsoft will be licensed to OpenAI's latest technology and the public will be shut out, *precisely the opposite* of the Founding Agreement." (Italics added.)

The legal complaint continues: "GPT-4 is hence *the opposite of* 'open AI.' [Italics added, again.] And it is closed for propriety commercial reasons: Microsoft stands to make a fortune selling GPT-4 to the public . . . Contrary to the Founding Agreement, Defendants have chosen to use GPT-4 not for the benefit of humanity, but as proprietary technology to maximize profits for literally the largest company in the world." And isn't it ironic, don't ya think?

Two weeks later OpenAI struck back. It hired a high-powered law firm that had fought Elon Musk before, Wachtell, Lipton, Rosen & Katz. Wachtell had represented the Old Twitter board in the Delaware court case the company filed to force Musk to proceed with his takeover. Musk later sued the firm for $90 million for the stiff bill it charged Twitter to sue him. That case was sent to arbitration in October 2023, and it still was undecided almost a year later.

Given that bitter history, Wachtell's response to the Musk lawsuit against OpenAI was understandably bitchy, calling it "frivolous" and worse: "Musk's claims rest on convoluted—often incoherent—factual premises." The OpenAI response said that Musk cites a Founding Agreement, but no such contract exists, and "any actual agreement is conspicuously missing from the pleading."

Right, so, Elon Musk handed these guys upwards of $45 million of his own money with no hard-copy agreement. It is like the line from the very old, and still very funny, film *Animal House*, when frat pledge Flounder (Stephen Furst) is upset that his brother's car got trashed, and Otter (Tim Matheson) tells him, "You fucked up, you trusted us!"

Musk's lawyers got the original judge to recuse himself from the case in early May 2024. They argued that Judge Ethan Schulman of San Francisco was "prejudiced against Plaintiff [Musk], his attorneys, and/or the interests of Plaintiff or his attorneys, such that Plaintiff cannot have a fair and impartial trial or hearing." The judge granted the request without holding a hearing or making a ruling.

On June 11, 2024, however, Musk withdrew the lawsuit without citing a reason. On August 4, he launched a new case, broadening the scope and claims and filing this time in federal court in San Francisco, where it is pending.

Musk provided the first $45 million of OpenAI's startup capital, and Altman and his team raised $90 million from other investors. This means that Musk, if he had insisted on holding an ownership stake in the upstart, could have laid claim to, say, a 33 percent stake in OpenAI. This would be worth $50 billion, based at OpenAI's $150 billion price tag in the fall of 2024. Instead, he walked away with nothing but even worse fears about AI's future.

His lawsuit against Sam Altman and OpenAI continues to grind its way, slowly, through California's overburdened, clogged court system, with any outcome uncertain by the time this book went to press. Musk is litigious to a fault—most times it is wiser to settle than to fight—but even he would rather take his chances in the marketplace than in the courtroom.

And so, on July 12, 2023, Musk announced the formation of xAI. It was late to the market and starting from behind, but it had a formidable ally: Twitter, now X. Large Language Models learn by scanning millions and millions of words in articles, books, posts, and other online forms. Musk's new engine has unfettered access to X, which posts six thousand messages every single second. This provides a superfast learning curve, and it also cuts costs as media companies begin charging AI companies for ingesting their huge caches of digital content—and suing, in some cases.

In September 2023, the Authors Guild, led by novelist John Grisham, *Game of Thrones* author George R. R. Martin, and fifteen other fiction writers, filed a lawsuit against OpenAI in federal court in New York. It called ChatGPT a "massive commercial enterprise" committing "systematic theft on a mass scale." In December, a group of nonfiction authors sued OpenAI and Microsoft, and the New York Times Company filed a similar suit as well, both of them in U.S. District Court in New York.

And in May 2024, OpenAI signed a deal to pay a quarter of a billion dollars to the *Wall Street Journal* for five years of access to its articles. Meanwhile, the actress Scarlett Johansson threatened to sue OpenAI the same month, after it introduced (then withdrew) a new voice for ChatGPT, Sky, which sounded like Johansson herself. Sam Altman had wooed Scarlett personally but was unable to persuade her to contribute her voice to his chatbot. For him, getting sued by her would be the opposite of the outcome he was hoping to create.

Altman would have one more ironic twist waiting for Elon, his former benefactor. On September 25, 2024, OpenAI scrapped all pretense of acting as a nonprofit "to benefit humanity as a whole." It announced plans to convert itself from a nonprofit to a for-profit company. Altman himself would receive a 7 percent stake in the company, which had just been valued at $150 billion, making this award worth $10 billion.

This was the very opposite of what Sam Altman had promised when he and Elon Musk started the company in 2015.

Later that night, at 9:54 Eastern, Elon posted his view of Altman's move: "This is deeply wrong," he wrote, posting atop an item that sarcastically noted, "How to make $10 billion dollars: -Raise $50 million from Elon Musk to start a nonprofit—Tell everyone you are doing this for the sake of humanity and raise billions—Convert from nonprofit to for-profit and grant yourself equity."

At 2:15 a.m., Musk fired another shot: "You can't just convert a nonprofit into a for-profit. That is illegal." This got "community noted" to point out that the law allows this conversion, with three links offering backup. Et tu, Elon followers?

For the rest of us, knowing the Eleventh Lesson of Elon can help us plot strategy and anticipate how our best efforts might, instead, trigger counterproductive effects. Once we know this, we can plan for it, perhaps preempt it. Surely this recognition would, at the least, help us laugh instead of cry when things go awry. The unexpected becomes expected: of course it worked out this way; it was the most entertaining outcome.

In these eleven Lessons of Elon, an underlying theme is that reality may be less a matter of what everything appears to be and more a matter of how we choose to see it, what we choose to emphasize, and how we process this. If Elon Musk wanted to feel oppressed and maligned by all the attacks and criticisms coming his way from government, politicians, the media, virtue-signaling activists, and an unending procession of other detractors, he could do so. And give up. Woe is he.

But this would be counterproductive, and it might drain energy from Musk's pursuits, producing a profound and damaging loss for him and for us. Instead, Elon sees himself as the superhero of his own virtual-reality simulation, indistinguishable from base reality and every bit as real.

In this super-realistic simulation, Elon Musk makes his own

rules, he plots to pull off the impossible, he reaches for the stars, and he overcomes all who would try to stop him. They are reduced to supporting characters in Elon's videogame, dramatic props placed there to help make him even better. And even more determined to overcome their opposition and succeed at things no one before him has achieved.

Elon's lessons can inspire that sense of mission and achievement in the rest of us. Instead of caving in to adversity, giving up in the face of fierce opposition to something we want to get done, we can choose to look at all of this static in a new way: it is all part of the game, part of making our lives more entertaining. For ourselves, and, maybe, for whoever is running this whole thing.

CONCLUSION

The hardest thing about writing this book was finishing it. Closing it down. Because Elon Musk keeps making news every other day. By launching a SpaceX rocket to the International Space Station to pick up two stranded astronauts, or shipping Starlink terminals to parts of North Carolina ravaged by Hurricane Helene, or taking on some free-speech-muzzling despot overseas, or calling out the venal, the incompetent, and the stupid in our government here at home.

Elon makes waves and headlines just by saying something, unfettered by the restraints imposed by political correctness and needing someone else's favor. It must feel freeing. No wonder the X platform and its fealty to free speech are so important to him: there, he can say pretty much anything he wants to say. And the clincher is, so can most everyone else.

As I was turning in the manuscript for this book in July 2024, Musk's news-making intensified. After the first assassination attempt against President Trump, Elon went on X minutes later and declared: "I fully endorse President Trump and hope for his rapid recovery." Few CEOs of large, publicly held companies dare come out with explicit public support for a presidential candidate, even a likable one. It is all the more daring for Elon to embrace Trump—one of the most reviled and disparaged presidents ever.

This unlikely alliance joins two of the biggest egos on the planet, though Musk's net worth is seventy times Trump's ($270 billion versus $3.8 billion). Elon is undeniably brilliant and deeply versed in myriad fields and endeavors, while Trump is . . . less brilliant, and deeply versed in one business (real estate), and expert in the dark art of politics and persuasion.

Both men can be incredibly blunt, inelegantly and unkindly so.

Both give as good as they get, returning fire fiercely when criticized. This is because these two leaders are so very gossamer-thin-skinned, despite their larger-than-life personalities and the insulation of wealth and high status that they enjoy.

What these two leaders share most in common, though, is the hatred and derision felt for them by so many other people. Elon Musk feels Donald's pain. Both men are fighting for a better world and for a better America, yet they are despised and demonized by so many political leaders, government officials, media outlets, public-interest groups, and millions of regular folks.

This presents a puzzle: why?

The hatred for Musk and Trump may owe to something deeper than mere ideological bent, something psychological. We are taught to be modest and go along to get along; to bow to authority and abide by the rules; and, when in doubt, to keep our mouths shut.

It may be that many people abhor Musk and Trump because the two so unabashedly display the qualities we are supposed to suppress in ourselves: unbridled egotism, overconfidence, self-aggrandizement. Yet, secretly, they may wish they had the moxie and swagger of Musk and Trump, who fuel their success with same.

It is doubtful that a South African–born, naturalized U.S. citizen, who is the richest person in the world, has the pull to persuade millions of people to vote one way or another. Though Elon certainly tried.

"After sleeping on it," he posted on X on the morning of August 10, 2024, "my conclusion is that the United States is indeed lost if there is another four years of open borders, failure to prosecute crime, lawfare and increased censorship. It's not even about the candidate. Kamala is obviously just a docile puppet of the system."

On September 30, someone on X said that if Harris wins, Musk "will be targeted through lawfare and the Harris administration will show no restraint. There will be no guardrails to hold her back." Elon added to this at 2:48 a.m. Eastern on October 1: "To be precise, the machine that controls the Kamala puppet will come after me even more than it currently does."

Elon's bigger impact lies in the X platform itself and its staunch rejection of government efforts to ban certain content. As I reported on the issues for this bestseller (am manifesting), it became redolently clear that the most important lesson of all is Lesson 6: Free speech is everything. Stand up and be heard.

It should be everything to all of us. Elon is almost our only hope, like Obi-Wan, at a time when free speech is under attack not just in China, Russia, Iran, and North Korea, but even in France, Germany, the UK, Australia, Brazil, and elsewhere. And right here at home from Vice President Kamala Harris, former Secretary of State John Kerry, Congresswoman Alexandria Ocasio-Cortez, Governor Gavin Newsom, and Clinton cabinet member Robert Reich.

Even the media, once self-serving champions of the First Amendment, are all but applauding this. Headline on an article by a *New York Times* nonfiction book critic on August 31, 2024: "The Constitution is sacred. Is it also dangerous?" On September 24, the *New Yorker* published an article in a similar vein by Harvard professor Louis Menand: "Is It Time to Torch the Constitution?"

No, it isn't. Just so awful, all of it.

For me, Lesson 10 also was pivotal: It is better to launch and burn than never to launch at all. Our fear of failure stops us from living life in the richest and fullest ways possible. Seeing how Elon and his team at SpaceX thrive on so many setbacks, I vow to make bolder decisions and take on bigger risks in my life—and to refuse to be fearful of failure.

Because, after all, what have we got to lose? See Lesson 1: This all may be fake, so just go for it. In exploring the simulation theory, I came away utterly fascinated by this very real possibility—what if Elon is right?

This changed how I feel inside my own skin. It made me more philosophical about life's outcomes and how to view them. I even started looking for signs that the simulation is for real. Then, on X and Instagram, I started seeing real-life videos of "glitches in the matrix"; in one, a man at an airport in Israel walks through a metal detector and disappears, startling several bystanders. Surely this is fake, right?

Still, you have to wonder, and that is part of the fun. It is time to raise our game and start enjoying life a lot more. My hope is the Eleven Lessons of Elon will help you do exactly that.

ACKNOWLEDGMENTS

At this point I feel like Julia Roberts at the Academy Awards ceremony in 2001, when she won Best Actress (*Erin Brockovich*) and said she wanted to thank "anyone I've ever met in my whole life." Me too.

Lacking space for that, let us start by thanking Elon Musk himself for providing such great material; nobody does it better. After my many attempts to reach him, Elon finally responded to one email—"Cool"—and declined an interview, adding, "I've said pretty much everything I can think of publicly." After which he kept on saying a lot, everywhere.

Also, there are avowed Enemies of Elon who deserve no thanks at all: the Democrat Party, the White House, the Department of Justice, the Securities and Exchange Commission, the Federal Aviation Administration, the National Highway Traffic Safety Administration, and the Federal Trade Commission. Plus Joe Biden, Kamala Harris, Elizabeth Warren, AOC, Thierry Breton (former European Commission member), and Alexandre de Moraes, chief justice of the Supreme Court in Brazil. Among many more. Why can't they just leave Elon alone?

Any book is the work of a lifetime of experiences and insights, crammed into a year or two of assemblage. I am grateful for the guidance and incisive editing of Eric Nelson at HarperCollins's Broadside Books. Without him, this book might not exist: it was his idea. And my thanks to his team—James Neidhardt, Hannah Long, and legal eagle Trina Hunn, all of whom found more typos, factual errors, and redundancies than I ever will admit.

For inspiration and truth-telling, I owe a debt to Charles Payne of Fox Business and Joe Kernen of CNBC; and to Keith Ferrazzi for two decades of sage, sound, soulful advice. Chris Ruddy opened doors for me at Newsmax, where Jerry Burke, my friend and mentor, and Jason Rosen give me loads of airtime with anchors Sarah Williamson and Michael Grimm; and Lidia Curanaj, Bob Sellers, and the great wise guy John Taranto. My sincere thanks to all of them, and to Joanna Chow, Amanda Fortunato, and Nora Hogan at NewsNation, as well. And my former agent, Wayne Kaybak.

Steve Forbes and Tim Forbes gave me the best job of my career, and I still owe them for this. My gratitude also goes to Jonathan Wald for hiring me at CNBC, Larry Kudlow for taking me under wing there, and to the late Roger Ailes for bringing me to Fox. And to Neil Cavuto, Greta Van Susteren, and the late Lou Dobbs. At the *Wall Street Journal*, where all of this began, my thanks to James Taranto, Michael W. Miller, and Jeff Trachtenberg.

And in my second life as a media strategist and podcaster, I owe Michael Sitrick, Terry Fahn, and Seth Lubove at Sitrick and Company, and, at Ricochet, Charles C. W. Cooke, Rob Long, and Brian Johnson, who is a producer, magician, and alchemist.

The closest friends you have for the longest time contribute more to your life than they will ever know. Unless they attend their own funerals. Mark Robichaux (thirty-eight years of friendship) provided constant counsel and comic relief. Rob Cohen (forty-nine years) offered encouragement and sent me Elon videos that would have eluded me otherwise. His brother David (eighteen years) gave me valuable feedback, as did Johnnie L. Roberts (forty years). Felipe Prestamo (fifty-four years) has been my stalwart supporter from the start. All of them have my heartfelt appreciation. As does my brother, Rick.

Lastly, and most importantly, my everlasting devotion and love to my mom, Doreen, for giving me gumption and drive, and my sweetie, Sophia, who makes life worth living out loud, and my daughter, Jing Jing, for making all of this worth it. I am so blessed.

ABOUT THE AUTHOR

Dennis Kneale is an award-winning journalist, a media strategist, and the host of the podcast *What's Bugging Me* on the Ricochet network. He was an anchor at CNBC and at the Fox Business Network after serving as a senior editor at the *Wall Street Journal* and as the managing editor of *Forbes*. He helped the late, great Lou Dobbs write the bestselling book *The Trump Century: How Our President Changed the Course of History Forever*. Kneale lives Brooklyn, New York, and dreams of having dinner with Elon Musk someday.